PORTFOLIO
SPEAK WITH IMPACT

Meenakshi Sharma is an associate professor at IIM Ahmedabad. She earned her PhD and masters from University of Queensland. Her teaching and research areas are organizational communication, cultural studies, and postcolonial theory and literature. She has published books on postcolonial Indian writing and criticism, and management communication. She has also written for various international journals.

At IIMA, she coordinates and teaches an executive training programme on effective communication strategies for leaders. She also runs workshops on presentations skills, written communication, and persuasive communication in training programmes for executives of government services, PSUs, and MNCs.

INDIA'S BESTSELLING BUSINESS BOOKS SERIES

SPEAK
WITH IMPACT

MEENAKSHI SHARMA

An imprint of Penguin Random House

PORTFOLIO

USA | Canada | UK | Ireland | Australia
New Zealand | India | South Africa | China | Singapore

Portfolio is part of the Penguin Random House group of companies
whose addresses can be found at global.penguinrandomhouse.com

Published by Penguin Random House India Pvt. Ltd
4th Floor, Capital Tower 1, MG Road,
Gurugram 122 002, Haryana, India

Penguin
Random House
India

First published by Random House India in 2014
Published in Portfolio by Penguin Random House India 2018

10 9 8 7 6 5 4

ISBN 9788184004069

Typeset in Sabon by R. Ajith Kumar
Printed at Manipal Technologies Limited, India

www.penguin.co.in

MIX
Paper | Supporting
responsible forestry
FSC® C043100

To Shishir, Ruchir, and Ananya,
the wind beneath my wings

Contents

Contents

Foreword

Speak with Impact, Meenakshi Sharma's book in the IIMA Business Books series, published in collaboration with Random House, offers clear and straightforward guidance on a subject of importance on which little has been said thus far: how to be impactful in your spoken communication.

The book begins with a discussion of why speaking effectively is a key requirement for leadership. It emphasizes the importance of preparation through introspection and seeking feedback. Through a discussion of the pros and cons of spoken versus written communication, circumstances that might be particularly amenable to spoken communication are identified. In the second chapter, she details a 'recipe' for effective speaking. Successful speech is built on preparation, which requires: (a) having clarity on objective, listener, and context; (b) gathering materials that include facts, examples, and evidence; (c) planning the structure; (d) presenting with energy and sincerity; (e) employing body language well, including facial expression, eye contact, posture, and movements; and (f) using voice effectively, with attention to clarity, tone, pace, and pauses. I particularly enjoyed practising the tongue-twisters she listed, such as 'We surely shall see the sun shine soon' and 'Lesser leather never weathered wetter weather better.'

In subsequent chapters, Meenakshi focuses on the distinguishing characteristics of particular settings and offers concrete advice on how to be an effective speaker in those settings. She devotes a chapter to conversations and discussions, paying particular attention to phone conversations and teleconferences, and another chapter to how one might prepare for and be effective in a selection interview. She offers guidance on how to be good at extemporary speaking, including several settings such as introducing guests to an assembly, and offering a vote of thanks. She offers detailed advice on making presentations effective through focus on elements of content and delivery, offering specific dos and don'ts to make presentations succeed. The book concludes by emphasizing the importance of spoken communication for leadership success.

In a straightforward and practical manner, the book offers practitioners thorough and specific advice on how to be effective at spoken communication.

Speak with Impact is one of a series of books authored by IIMA professors who are not only academically proficient but also have rich experience in consulting and teaching executives. These books are intended to disseminate knowledge in relevant topics in management to practising executives. Written in conversational style with illustrations from the world of practice, the books are eminently readable and applicable in daily life.

I hope you will enjoy *Speak with Impact* and find it useful, as you will other books in the series. Please do let us know if there are particular topics that you would like covered in the books published in this series.

Ashish Nanda
Director
IIM Ahmedabad

Introduction

YOU CAN MAKE SPEAKING EFFECTIVE AND MEMORABLE

As we go through life, there are occasions when we encounter someone whose ideas ring in our minds for long and create a strong, positive impression of them. There are also times when some of us have wrung our hands in desperation, feeling that our ideas or deep knowledge is not being appreciated by others. On both occasions, it boils down to a skill that this book attempts to de-mystify. This is the skill of articulating ideas through the spoken word. We must remember that it is through communication that our ideas can leave the space of our own mind and impact another's. On countless occasions this is through the spoken mode. It is not just the act of speaking but the *quality* of speaking that often sets the successful individual apart. Speaking is a powerful way to impress others not only with our ideas but also with our personality. In all areas of life, our relationships with others go a long way in paving the path to success—whether in terms of providing support, receptivity to ideas, ease in persuasion, or openness to suggestions. And these relationships are largely based on the way we speak with others in our everyday interactions with them. People are constantly forming ideas about our intelligence, level of awareness, depth of knowledge, originality of ideas, integrity, level of involvement, and much else from what we speak and how we speak. Speaking not only serves particular objectives but is also an expression of one's personality. As Dorothy Carnegie writes in the introduction to Dale Carnegie's *Effective Speaking*, when one is 'unable to say clearly what he means, through either nervousness, timidity, or foggy thought-processes, his personality is blocked off, dimmed out, and misunderstood'. How true it is, not only in terms of what blocks the clear articulation of one's ideas but also in terms of the damage it does to fairly presenting one's knowledge, creativity, ideas—in short, one's entire personality.

We must remind ourselves that in order for our ideas to be appreciated and rewarded, we need to be able to convey them to others. The greatest harm and injustice we do by not presenting ourselves fairly and completely through our communication, are to oneself and if others are not able to recognize and reward us for what we are, the fault may really lie with us.

Not everyone is able to present their thoughts and ideas to others in the best possible manner. That means in the manner that most truly and most lucidly presents to others what we wish to convey. It involves everything—from finding the most suitable way to express our ideas without any loss of meaning, and presenting them in a structured manner that provides clear and coherent meaning to others. With the spoken mode, an important ingredient is a confident manner that may add credibility to the ideas and convey the feelings behind them.

No doubt it is a tall order, requiring a number of components to come together just right. Not only must we be clear about why we wish to communicate and make useful choices about what to say and how to say it in view of our objective and intended receiver, we must also ensure that our communication has clarity for the receiver both in terms of ideas and feelings. Of course, it is not easy to achieve all this, especially in the spoken mode that does not allow for editing and revising. Moreover, it is especially challenging because we, as a whole, rather than only our words, are subject to scrutiny by the receiver.

No wonder many of us find the task daunting! Many of us feel acute anxiety and self-consciousness when it comes to interacting with new people, seniors, or when the stakes are high as in a selection interview, or a presentation before potential investors or buyers. I am sure many of us would admit having avoided speaking, as in the case of confidently contributing our views at a discussion, countering a point, or raising a question; seeking an interview to present our ideas or clarify something; or engaging in small talk with someone we have just met. And when not avoidable, how many of us have agonized over a speaking occasion, suffered sleepless nights because of apprehension, and found ourselves breaking out in a sweat on the occasion? How many of us have tried to make the task of spoken communication more bearable for ourselves by increasing our reliance on the written word through over-reliance on notes and slides?

Let us stop and ask ourselves the following: By letting go of opportunities to speak or by not fully utilizing the opportunities for speaking, are we losing out? Are we doing justice to our abilities and our potential, through fair and impressive presentation of our knowledge, intelligence, and creativity, through our spoken communication? Are we able to use it as an opportunity to add the strength of our personality to our communication? When we speak, are we doing so with clarity about how the advantages of the mode can better help us meet our communication objective? Do our listeners take away clarity about the ideas we shared? Do they find it easy to follow our ideas? Do they feel that their time and effort was well spent? Asking such questions is very important. This introspection would lead us to recognize if there is room for improvement in the way we handle speaking opportunities.

Introspection would lead us to recognize if there is room for improvement in the way we handle speaking opportunities.

Introspection is a necessary starting point for any efforts to improve our ability in this area. At the same time we should take heart from the fact that one does not need to be a born wit or to have a suave, charismatic personality to be successful in spoken communication. The skill of connecting with people through our spoken words, and leaving an impact with our ideas and personality is one that can be polished through effort, just like any other.

This effort is worth making because most of us would like others to appreciate us for what we are in terms of sharpness of mind, knowledge and information base, as well as for our human qualities. It cannot be said that people whose communication does not reflect a sharp mind, critical capacity, brilliant and innovative ideas, and a repertoire of information and knowledge, truly lack these. They may possess these in the truckloads, but if it all remains locked up in their minds, it cannot contribute to creating a fair perception and assessment in the minds of others. We have to accept the fact that no one has access into our minds and hearts other than what we provide by our communication. Taking care over projecting both our knowledge and our attitude through our formal and informal communication is essential for impacting others, and in being fair to our own capabilities. In our performance- and success-oriented world, we are being constantly assessed and evaluated. We must not forget that while our track record may speak for itself, we can add many dimensions to the way we are perceived, by self-presentation. When it comes to our ideas and articulation of our views, our thinking, our perspective, and much more, it is we alone who can provide access to others through what we choose to communicate, and how effectively we do it.

No doubt there are some people we know who interact with others so effortlessly and seem to relish opportunities to speak that we are tempted to attribute it to an innate quality in them—something one is either blessed with or not. So, do we sit back and admire others who we think possess the 'gift of the gab' and can easily impress others with their ideas, break the ice with strangers, or have a large group of listeners listen in rapt attention, while we feel we were not 'born that way'? Or do we go through life complaining about the unfairness of it all when we see others make an impact with ideas or information that we ourselves possess but are not able to articulate as well as them? It doesn't have to be either of these. We can polish our own skills in order to reach that same level of ease and comfort, and reap the benefits in terms of better relationships, and greater impact on others.

The challenge lies in demystifying the skill, or art of effective speaking, and seeing it as something that can be mastered with understanding and practice. The motivation must come from within—from the realization of the immense benefit it can have in all areas of life, from the personal to the professional. From this realization one needs to move to others—that wherever we are, it is possible to polish it further, and that it is never too late to begin.

In John Maxwell's words, 'You are only an attitude away from success!' And that attitude is one of belief in oneself.

Having developed this attitude, it is only a matter of keeping one's desire to communicate clearly and effectively at the forefront, and clearly identifying whatever is preventing this from happening so as to address these shortcomings in the best possible manner.

There exists a huge need for demystifying the daunting task of spoken communication and for helping to unlock the potential within each of us. No doubt practical demonstration is very useful for doing so. However, it is also very useful to supplement fresh, face-to-face discussion, demonstration, practice, and feedback, with more detailed and comprehensive coverage of all aspects of the topics in a written format. Such a treatment also has the advantage of ready reference and self-learning for anyone motivated to polish this essential skill for professional and personal life.

Although there are a number of books on this subject, I have long been looking for one that treats the topic with sufficient depth and comprehensiveness, without becoming an academic tome. While the subject has had importance from time immemorial and for all walks of life, a contemporary treatment, from the perspective of professionals is required to appeal to today's professional who is keen to polish their comfort and confidence with the spoken word. This book offers practical guidelines in a readable, direct and unpretentious style, unburdened with jargon and theorizing. Eschewing a plodding textbook approach, it picks out the crucial contexts for spoken communication at the workplace. Although, spoken communication is ubiquitous, there are certain situations that are common but hardly ever become less daunting for most of us, and these need special attention. This is so because these often play a critical role in shaping the perception others have of us, the impact we leave on others, and in affecting the outcome in terms of effectively meeting the objectives of the communications. In a conversational style, the book lays out in simple and practical ways, a path to travel on your way to the position you aspire to be in and feel you deserve.

The following chapters deal with a variety of speaking situations in the professional context and show the importance of speaking with impact, as well as practical tips on how to polish one's skill in the area. Chapter 1 addresses the importance of speaking skills and why we must care about making the effort to introspect, identify our areas of strength and those needing more care, constantly review and invite feedback to polish our ability to communicate effectively through the spoken word. Chapter 2 provides an overview of what constitutes effective spoken communication, looking at the constituents that are common to all speaking contexts. The following chapters then take up the specific challenges of various contexts namely, conversations, meetings and discussions, interviews, extemporary speaking, and formal presentations. Each chapter is designed to provide deeper insight into our objectives as well as practical tips for speaking effectively in such situations. These speaking situations at the workplace give us the opportunities to make an impact and not only effectively meet the objective of the particular communication by conveying our ideas, information, and feelings to others, but also make us stand out for an ability that is not common and consequently, is much-prized!

CHAPTER 1

Speak with Impact to be Noticed and Get Ahead

If we want to be noticed, to differentiate ourselves, and to get results, we cannot neglect—nor be complacent about—our ability to get our ideas across to others through our spoken words. Getting ahead in our career and meeting our aspirations depends on our performance, potential, and determination. Given these, our ability to impact others through our spoken words may make all the difference. At the same time that we acquire knowledge in our functional area, widen our information base, and sharpen our technical skills, a crucial area to focus our energy should be our communication.

Scholars posit that spoken language evolved in human beings due to social reasons. It allowed social contracts and social stability, negotiated cooperation within groups, efficiency in cooperative tasks, and in monitoring resources.[1]

---

[1] Buckley, Carina and Steele, James. 'Evolutionary Ecology of Spoken Language: Co-Evolutionary Hypotheses Are Testable'. *World Archaeology* 34.1 (2002), Archaeology and Evolutionary Ecology, 26–46.

The significance of spoken language has not changed very much in the millennia since then! Humans remain social animals and the business sphere, as almost every other human sphere of activity, requires us to engage with others and we do this primarily through the spoken word. In fact, the uses of spoken communication and its importance have only grown since pre-historic times when it allowed our hunting and foraging ancestors to work together more efficiently in small groups.

We are still using spoken language in the twenty-first century to cooperatively work along with others, to negotiate, to monitor progress, and to share ideas and plans. Our speaking ability creates group cohesiveness, stability and allows us to reach out to others to share our ideas. It would be hard to imagine how we could ever address many of our objectives if we were to remove spoken communication from the equation. Think of problem solving situations where identifying and articulating the problem, specifying objectives, coming up with options, and evaluating the positive and negative features of the alternatives, may all be helped by discussions. Think of consensus building, motivation, persuasion, and argumentation. Also think of rapport building and networking. You will recognize the immense value of spoken communication in meeting these objectives regardless of the nature and size of the organization or business. In addition to meeting these important objectives, spoken communication provides an excellent opportunity for individuals to impress upon others many positive personal

11

characteristics and abilities such as clarity and originality of thought, breadth and depth of knowledge and awareness, critical faculty, articulateness, assertiveness, and self-confidence. What a wonderful tool at our disposal it is! At the same time that it helps us to work better with others to achieve larger goals, at the individual level, the way each one of us uses its potential in the professional context becomes, to a large extent, a measure of our success.

It is estimated that over 75 percent of the time of an executive goes into spoken communication. Human beings are distinguished by their ability to speak and in today's world we sure make a big deal of it. Meetings, conclaves, conferences, speeches, presentations, advising, discussing, conferring, interviews, counseling, phone calls . . . our professional lives revolve around speaking. Beginning with the interview for our first job, speaking and listening extend to orientation and training, instructions and explanations, exchange of information, conversations and discussions, descriptions and analysis, reviews, feedback, and much more. The list is endless. While the mode of communicating remains the spoken word for these and many other contexts, the objectives are different and the skilled speaker knows how to effectively serve these varied objectives.

While no one can really avoid speaking and everyone needs to engage in activities that require speaking and listening, not everyone makes the most of these opportunities. As your experience may have shown you, the average speaker fumbles, mumbles and creates confusion rather than lucidity, does not get the listeners interested or involved, and does not satisfactorily achieve the objective of the communication. Most speakers either seem to not care as much about communicating as about somehow getting through the ordeal, or seem too focused on their own objective without proper regard to relevance for the listeners and their engagement in what is being said. Only occasionally do we find a speaker who stands out from the crowd in terms of making the desired impact on others with their ideas and personality, and in meeting the objectives of the communication through their spoken communication.

If you are one of these few, you must congratulate yourself on a rare ability that you possess. If you introspect, you will find that it is the result of a happy combination of opportunities that you have utilized to become comfortable and confident in this kind of communication. You will also find that you are constantly working on finding even better ways of achieving your objectives through effective spoken communication in a variety of contexts. You may have realized that this is an unending journey of constant improvement and polishing rather than the achievement of perfection. Having enjoyed the satisfaction and pleasure (and, of course, the rewards) that come with excellence in this area, you are perhaps excited by this journey of discovering your full potential.

If you are among the many others, you tremble and break into a sweat at the thought of facing an audience, hesitate in offering an opinion or in presenting their viewpoint or in questioning someone in a discussion, feel drained rather than energized at the end of an interaction, and disappointed in not having really been able to present a fair account of your ideas or feelings. When this happens a few times, we begin to feel that spoken communication is not our forte and we begin to avoid it as far as possible, and when we cannot avoid it, we go through it anyhow, reconciled to not making much of an impact. We see a few others using these opportunities more effectively but tell ourselves that they are exceptionally gifted and that we are like most others and therefore, it isn't much of a problem.

It also happens to many of us that we attribute the ineffectiveness of our communication in serving the purpose, not to any problem with the way we presented our ideas but to the listeners' inability to focus, or to keep an open mind. When we feel that we presented our ideas fairly but the feedback from the receivers suggests otherwise, we feel upset at their inability or refusal to get what we wish to convey. We may tend to blame our intended receivers for not understanding us and attribute it to their inability to control their inner distractions and to listen actively, or to various other reasons such as jealousy, egocentrism, or disinterest. This tendency is quite natural but it does not help in getting a fair understanding of our limitations in the speaker's role. Of course, it would be ideal if our listeners were properly trained in effective listening. But since we cannot ensure that, we should look at what is in our hands—how we play our role as a speaker. Moreover, how we play our role determines, to a large extent, our audience's response. Focusing, therefore, on how we can improve our effectiveness as speakers would be much more useful than attributing the problems to various drawbacks in the listeners.

Perhaps some of us may also experience some envy at others no more qualified for greater responsibility and recognition, getting these and moving ahead of us. Perhaps you complain of the unfairness of it all and sometimes attribute the success of others to good fortune or some other factors. Even if you recognize that their communication gets them noticed and rewarded, you may regard it as only glibness of tongue or an outgoing personality rather than merit. However, this realization of the relationship between success and speaking effectively should highlight to us how it is not enough to possess the necessary attributes but also to communicate effectively. Speaking is a powerful way to impress others not only with our ideas but also with our personality. In all areas of life, our relationships with others go a long way in paving the path of our success—whether in terms of providing support, or receptivity to ideas, or ease in persuasion, or openness to suggestions. And these relationships are largely based on the way we speak with others in our everyday interactions with them.

Speaking is a powerful way to impress others with our ideas and personality. Our relationships with others pave the path of our success; these relationships are largely based on the way we speak with others in our everyday interactions with them.

People are constantly forming ideas about our intelligence, level of awareness, depth of knowledge, originality of ideas, integrity, level of involvement, and much else from what we speak and how we speak. The ability to speak effectively is not only for serving particular objectives but also as an expression of one's personality.

If others who we think are less deserving are able to get ahead with the help of their felicity with words, it should make us realize how this one area of lack may be standing between us and the success that we feel we deserve. Just pause and think: If you have what it takes—solid achievements under your belt, bright ideas, strong skills, and relevant knowledge for your field—imagine what a great impact you could make on people through your interactions if you could improve your comfort and confidence levels in speaking to others in an effective manner!

DON'T LEAVE IT TO IMAGINATION—HELP OTHERS UNDERSTAND YOUR IDEAS CLEARLY

We must keep in mind that if all that we are, and all that we know and think, is to be appreciated by others, we need to present it to them clearly. Just as we only know as much about others as they are able to get across to us, others cannot be expected to be aware of our brilliant ideas and insights, our great store of knowledge and experience, and our acumen, if we are not able to share these with them. What is in our mind remains only ours, getting us no recognition or reward. If we are happy with that, it's quite fine. But if we want others to be aware of our achievements or our ideas or our knowledge and insights, it should be our objective to convey these in the most effective manner. If we don't do this, we do ourselves an injustice and also make it impossible for others to value us for our ideas, our knowledge, or our personal qualities. We are doing a disservice to ourselves when we are not able to effectively impress upon others what we carry in our mind and heart. All that we possess, remains locked up within ourselves and we feel frustrated at the world's inability to appreciate and reward us. We must understand that we are not helping our case by expecting all our impressive abilities to get appreciated by others without making any efforts to communicate these. We cannot expect others to read our minds. And it is not simply by communicating, but by how effectively we do so. That is, how well we meet the objective and faithfully articulate the ideas and the underlying feelings of what we wish to get across.

We would all accept that recognition of our capabilities and appreciation of our achievements by others is important for a sense of satisfaction as well as essential for our career progression and success in our chosen fields. Take the example of a person seeking a promotion. If she is not able to speak up at an interview and present her views, her achievements, her distinction, and to back up her record on paper with details that demonstrate learning and ownership of ideas, is it any surprise if the reviewers are not impressed? This may not necessarily mean that the person is not worthy of the promotion. But it might mean that the person has erroneously

17

assumed that her ideas are transparent and others will automatically be aware of all that she knows, has achieved, and will be able to use that to gauge her potential.

Spoken communication is at work in creating an impression on others not only in such formal settings as presentations and interviews. Even in the course of our everyday interactions with people, we create impressions about our personality, our qualities, our knowledge, skills, and strengths. We network and forge relationships with our bosses, colleagues, juniors, with business associates, and with others we meet in the course of our work. All of this largely happens through our behaviour and spoken communication. Through these we share ourselves with others; we open up our minds and hearts and get close to people. We may have a heart of gold, a mind packed with wonderful ideas, all the dedication and sincerity to our organization one could imagine, but is anyone going to know and appreciate these unless we are able to translate these into messages that others can receive?

Our desire to get our ideas and feelings across to others is the starting point of the journey of communication. Without this desire, we can keep everything locked up in our minds and hearts, safe from the eyes and ears of others. We can do this if we do not care if our true worth is not recognized, we are passed over for advancement, and overlooked when it comes to appreciation and rewards being passed around. Since most of us really *do* care for recognition, appreciation and rewards, it is critical that we understand how we may be responsible if these are not coming our way.

Our desire to get our ideas and feelings across to others is the starting point of the journey of communication. This desire needs to be combined with that for being recognized and appreciated, so that we take responsibility for improving our communication skills.

Remember the words of Plato: 'Wise men speak because they have something to say; fools because they have to say something.' Do we have what it takes? In order to have something worth others' attention, we should have equipped ourselves with the knowledge and skills that are valued. Have we accumulated experience, learning, and have we got achievements under our belt? Do we have understanding, empathy, sincerity, acumen, and incisiveness? If we lack in these or any of the attributes that are prized in our field, we still have work to do in terms of equipping ourselves for appreciation and rewards. But if we possess the necessary attributes, another set of questions arise: Do we simply trust these to speak for themselves? Or are we doing all we can to facilitate the recognition of the worth of our ideas, experience, understanding, and our personal traits, through our communication with others?

If we look around ourselves we will find that those who move ahead, faster than others with the same abilities and knowledge, are helping their case by excellent communication of their qualities and not assuming that these shall themselves become manifest to others. Why do we fool ourselves into believing that in our case, our sterling qualities will be enough and we need not bother ourselves with communicating in such a manner that we make the best impact? Why, also do we feel somehow cheated and discriminated against when others like us or even below us in terms of technical skills, knowledge, or experience, get ahead of us? When we stop to reflect, do we accept that while they were able to impress others with their abilities, perhaps we did not succeed so well? And what is that one distinguishing quality that it boils down to? Communication!

DISTINGUISH YOURSELF THROUGH YOUR SPEECH

While all communication adds up to presenting a fair idea of ourselves to others, the value of making the best of our speaking opportunities simply cannot be over-emphasized. It is essential as much for being effective in our work, as for standing out from the average in terms of an ability that is very much part of the necessary skill-set for leadership positions. As Harry Simmons puts it, 'While a good executive speaker is not necessarily a good leader, it is an incontrovertible fact that a good leader must be a good speaker!'.[2] Although some professions may put speaking more noticeably centre-stage—sales, medicine, law, counseling, training, teaching, to take a few examples—no professional can ignore the value of speaking effectively in order to work well with people and to

---

[2] Simmons, Harry. *Executive Public Speaking Techniques*. Philadelphia: Chilton, 1959.

play one's role in meeting organizational goals. At the same time, our personal growth objectives are also tied up with our effective communication, in addition to our abilities, knowledge, and skills. We only stand to gain by doing our best to polish our ability to express ourselves effectively.

The importance of effective communication is significant at all levels but as one rises up the ladder of an organization's hierarchy, the importance of communicating, and doing so with a wide range of people, increases exponentially. Much of this communication is done orally and for a variety of important objectives that are crucial for the leader's role. From building strong interpersonal relationships, to sharing information, guiding, advising, motivating, and inspiring, speaking serves many objectives for the leader. Building and polishing one's ability in this particular form of communication can go a long way in serving the varied roles of the leader—whether establishing one's authority in a field, sharing vision and plans, getting people to rally around ideas or initiatives, or obtaining cooperation and building consensus. Thus, it is a very valuable skill to be honed for leaders and everyone aspiring to be one. In fact, it is this ability that caps all others, by literally giving voice to all that we know, or think, or feel.

Moreover, speaking effectively is not a common ability at all! Look around you—do you find most people excelling in articulating their ideas and feelings clearly, pertinently, and engagingly? Now ask yourself—do *you* feel satisfied with how well you are able to articulate your ideas, do you feel confident and comfortable when you try to convey your ideas and feelings through the spoken word? The person who can effectively convey what he wants to in a manner that connects with the receivers is so exceptional, that there is no way it cannot get him noticed. When we make the effort to refine the effectiveness of our speaking, we not only feel much more satisfied with doing justice to our ideas, we stand out from the crowd! Working constantly on improving our effectiveness through every spoken communication opportunity is the equivalent of laying the bricks on the pathway to success. The ability to speak effectively with ownership of ideas and confidence in putting them across, helps you in networking and making friends, in putting your weight behind your convictions and viewpoints, and being a person of influence. In fact, it boils down to what Dale Carnegie calls 'preparation for leadership'! If we do not have the necessary attributes for leadership, we should devote ourselves to acquiring those. But it would be sad if we possessed all that is needed and yet miss out on what we deserve simply because we could not impress others with our abilities, and all that qualifies us for the position.

SPEAKING EFFECTIVELY: AN ESSENTIAL REQUIREMENT FOR LEADERSHIP

In the course of executive training programmes on communication strategies for leaders, I have met a number of executives who have been earmarked for promotion to top management levels. These were people who had excelled in their performance and were found to be suitable for higher leadership roles with respect to the technical and professional track record, but it was felt that their comfort and confidence in communication—especially spoken communication—needed to be honed before they made the transition to more senior positions. This stems from the awareness that along with demonstrated technical competence, the higher positions would bring a lot of responsibilities that would need much more visibility and direct interactions where the effectiveness of spoken communication would be tested. **The more comfortable the person is in this, and the better he or she can achieve the various objectives for which such communication would be required, the better they would be able to do justice to their role.** These executives themselves admitted that on introspection they found that there were certain areas in their speaking repertoire that needed more attention. For example, some admitted that they are not quite comfortable with small talk or when dealing with new people or with a large number of listeners, while others accepted that occasions of extempore speaking were the stuff of nightmares for them. At the same time, they realized that the more senior positions would have a greater requirement for such interactions and these would have a significant impact on the way they were perceived by others and how well they were able to perform in that role.

Whether you are already in a leadership role and wish to improve your comfort level and impact in spoken situations, or are aspiring to get there and wish to start preparing yourself for the position you dream of, you should give attention to the effectiveness of your spoken communication. No doubt, this is not all that is needed. No amount of speaking skills can make up for real worth of the individuals as a person and as a professional. One cannot but agree with Ralph Waldo Emerson's words, 'What you do speak so loudly that I cannot hear what you say.' Our spoken communication cannot make up for deficiencies in our actions and behaviour, or change the impression people carry about us and what we stand for. It is a continuous lifetime's work to build credibility in ourselves through our actions and behaviour as well as through all our communication, and this needs all the attention in the world because without it, every other skill and ability may be irrelevant. Our smooth manner may mask our weaknesses in character for some time, for some people, but it is hardly possible to do so all the time and for all people. Assuming that we are aware of this and are continuously and concurrently giving positive messages through our actions and behaviour, we turn our attention in this book to how we present ourselves to others through the spoken word in different contexts so as to reach our potential.

THE HARD BUT WORTHWHILE WORK OF POLISHING OUR SPEECH

Polishing our ability to speak with impact involves demystifying it and looking at it as a set of practical steps that we can train ourselves to perform once we are convinced of its necessity for reaching our full potential and fulfilling our ambitions. It requires motivation and ambition, understanding, conviction, faith, and effort in unlearning and relearning. **We must keep these words of Ralph Waldo Emerson before us: 'Without ambition one starts nothing. Without work one finishes nothing. The prize will not be sent to you. You have to win it.'**

If you want to win, as I am sure you do, it is never too late to begin polishing your ability to impress others with all that you are through your speech. This would involve improving your ability to effectively identify your purpose in speaking in different occasions, analysing your audience and making modifications to content and style so as to make your ideas relevant and interesting to them, to deliver in a way that the listener understands your feelings for the subject as well as your authority on it, feels that you care about communicating with him, feels engaged and is able to get your ideas clearly, and with the intended meaning and emphases. A tall order indeed! No wonder that all of this does not happen effortlessly and automatically all the time! Even the few people we see speaking apparently effortlessly, have put in effort, thought and practice into it. In fact, paradoxically enough, the more the effort, the greater the appearance of effortlessness!

Therefore, we should be willing to put as much effort as we can into honing our ability to impact others around us through our spoken communication, knowing both that this requires effort even when it may look effortless, and that it is well worth it, not only for our current roles, but also as preparation for future roles. These roles, as we move up the hierarchy, will bring additional requirements of communication with larger sets of people. At the same time, our very suitability for these positions may turn out to be a function of our ability to impress others with our abilities, knowledge, and experience. This is an effort that pays so many dividends and is so much in our interest that it should be something we are constantly engaged in. It is really an unending quest for self-improvement as there is no perfection to be aimed at, but drawing out the best we are capable of. Why should we let our real capabilities and potential remain unrecognized and unfulfilled simply for want of being effectively communicated to others? One would agree that we would be quite unfair to ourselves if we allowed that to happen. And even more so, when it depends on something that can be learned, corrected and improved upon!

However, it is easier said than done! If speaking makes you stressed or takes a lot out of you in nervous energy, you may be declining responsibilities that may involve extensive spoken communication thus restricting your growth, you may not only be struggling to meet work objectives, but also be reducing your ability to open the doors of career opportunities, business deals, and overall of making a positive and memorable impact on people you deal with. Surely, people who are not very skilled with words and with their 'presence' in making an impact, are also able to achieve these goals through long association with the same set of people and the credibility they may build up through the quality of their work and personal qualities such as commitment, loyalty, and integrity. But imagine what a manifold boost it would give to such qualities if they could combine it with impressive speaking skills!

GETTING STARTED

Once we are clear about the importance of making the most of our spoken opportunities, and keen to hone our ability further, how do we go about it? After all, every one of us communicates. And no doubt, we have done so with some success, to be where we are today. We have given interviews for selection, made presentations, taken part in conversations and discussions. However, if we are honest with ourselves, we may recognize that while we were acceptable, perhaps we did not rise above the average. Our own experience would show us that while there is a certain, average level of proficiency in this area common to most professionals, there are some individuals who definitely make a much greater impact through their spoken communications. Not only are they much more effective in meeting the objectives of the communication but also in leaving a positive personal impact. More often than not, they are more successful in their careers than those who struggle to articulate their ideas and impact others.

Let us make this recognition our starting point. Is there someone you can think of who stands out in this respect? Not a remote historical figure or a public personality or celebrity speaker, but someone from your circle? Once we identify one or more such persons, let us go beyond attributing it to their personal charisma and innate ability. Let us ask ourselves the following questions to try to understand exactly how such speakers stand out and why listeners are more impressed by them than by most others.

- Are there certain things they are doing that make us feel that our objective in listening to them was well-served?
- What is it that makes us feel that listening to them is less tedious than to many others?
- What makes us better comprehend and retain what they said?
- Despite personal style variations, are there any common features of such speakers that are different from those who leave us cold?

If we can generate answers to these questions we may be in a much better position to realize that effective speakers stand out from the crowd and have a greater impact on their listeners because of specific things they do differently. The impact on the listeners is the key. **After all, we speak for the listeners, not for our own selves.** For the speaker, getting the intended message across and having the desired effect is important. But these are dependent on the listeners finding what is being said, useful, relevant, interesting, and meaningful. The response of the listeners is the acid test for determining the success of any spoken communication. Our personal impact on others is a function of how and what we demonstrate of ourselves through our communication—

what brilliance of mind in terms of original ideas or sharp analysis, what personal qualities such as empathy, compassion and dedication, what skills such as clarity of articulation, vividness of description, lucidity of expression, sense of humour, humility, and the like. Do our listeners get a sense that we own the ideas from our manner of presenting these and are they able to grasp the feelings underlying them? Do they see focus and sharpness in the presentation of the ideas that helps them to grasp the matter clearly?

The importance of such an impact on our listeners lies in the difference between success and failure in achieving the purpose for which the communication was meant. Merely speaking does not mean that the purpose for which it was meant has been achieved. In fact, it is important to be aware that not all purposes are best served by spoken communication, and our effectiveness as a communicator lies also in making the appropriate choice of mode according to the objective, the audience, and the situation. This is an important primary step in our communication strategy. Only when we are well aware of the importance of spoken communication, recognize its potential advantages and the appropriate contexts where these may be effectively applied, can we make the appropriate choice of mode for our communication.

From this, we move to another essential step in the journey to self-improvement—that of introspection into our own capabilities. Let us ask ourselves: Are we prepared to critically analyse our effectiveness in speaking situations? It is not easy, but it is something we need to do objectively to understand where we are and where we could be. If we are to candidly review our ability and comfort in spoken communication, we may find ourselves not quite where we would like to be. And this is no reason to be disheartened but an essential requirement for change. If we were perfect, why would we be ready to take the trouble to work more? It would also do us good to keep in mind something we tend to overlook when we allow ourselves to be self-critical—that this discovery does not reflect as much on any innate inability as on our learning right from education and socialization during the formative years, to that as adults, from experience at our workplace.

While writing is a much-reinforced skill at school, much less time is spent on speaking. Even in written work such as assignments and tests, we are evaluated and awarded grades that we may take as feedback on the correctness of the content and perhaps, indirectly, on the effectiveness of the communication; often the feedback is not specifically on the structuring of the ideas and clarity and coherence. During the course of our schooling, we get even less opportunity for spoken communication and hardly any specific academic courses on it. Only a few of us who are confident, assertive and perhaps have received encouragement for initial attempts at public speaking or debates, are able to build on these experiences and stand out. Today, forward-looking schools are recognizing the importance of developing students' confidence in expressing ideas through speaking in front of small groups. Those of us who did not have this experience during our early years of school, need to actively address this gap rather than assume that it is something we naturally lack or that it is too late to address it. At home too, some of us have had encouragement to articulating our thoughts and received constructive feedback on it, while others have largely been expected to be seen and not heard. Much of our comfort and pleasure, not to speak of confidence, in face-to-face spoken communication, may trace back to these early experiences.

Our experiences at the workplace may also have gone to reinforce our sense of lack in this area. Once we feel we do not shine in this area, we often tend to regard it as an unalterable fact and try to avoid such opportunities as best we can, and when unavoidable, grit our teeth and get on with it as a painful responsibility. Unfortunately, this is quite easily perceived by the audience who then takes no real interest nor shows any enthusiasm, further making us convinced that we lack the ability to make an impact. At the same time, we see many others who are more or less like us, and we take comfort in at least being no worse than the average in this area. And when we do encounter those who display a greater degree of ability in it, we are prone to regard it as a natural 'gift' or 'blessing'. 'How wonderful to be a born orator!' or 'How easy it is for an extrovert like him!' or 'I wish I was gifted with her way with words,' we say. Rather than regarding the performance of excellent speakers as 'amazing', we should analyse these to see the constituent parts that are eminently do-able and replicable. If you have assumed that the ability to speak effectively is really a matter of personality, with some people simply blessed with the gift of confidence, sociability, and charm, you need to read about the countless people who have transformed themselves by unlearning and re-learning traits, habits, and outlook that shape personality.

Exceptional speaking abilities are not innate but acquired and polished over time. Each one of us acquires one (or more) language slowly and learns to use it to communicate through speech and writing. Comfort and confidence in spoken communication is born out of and feeds on a number of factors—ability in the language one wants to or is expected to use, desire and motivation to excel in this area, opportunities to emulate and learn from others, to practice in diverse settings, and to be able to get feedback to help in further refinement. Some of us may be blessed by a fortuitous blend of circumstances leading to excellent opportunities for doing so and may acquire a greater level of skill, apparently effortlessly. To some extent, experience is a good teacher; as we do, so we learn. However, if all of us were equally able to polish the ability to speak effectively in a range of situations to become confident and sure of being able to handle these with flair, simply by more experience of speaking, we would be surrounded by excellent speakers. While it is true that to some extent, mere iteration teaches us much about the requirements of various contexts of speaking and increases our confidence in handling them, it may not be enough to take us beyond a certain level. What that requires is reflection, introspection, and active seeking of feedback. If we are ready to take these steps, have the patience, motivation, and determination, there is no reason for any of us to settle for an average level. Since those who do this are few and far between, our efforts will be amply rewarded by making us stand out from the crowd, for a valued and uncommon ability.

Although experience of speaking situations can give us more confidence in articulating our thoughts through iteration, it is not sufficient. In order to stand out and be noticed for exceptional ability, we need to build on experience through:
- Reflecting and introspecting
- Seeking feedback

A large part of who we are is the outcome of shaping influences and circumstances. We have two choices: we can remain stuck with where we are in terms of abilities and skills or we can put in time and effort to re-shape and polish these whenever we find it needed. Before we can choose the latter, we must first, become aware of the gap between where we are and where we would like to be. Next, we need to identify the skills necessary to reach our goal and assess ourselves on our existing level. If the target skills level seems formidable, we need to break it down to component parts that may be acquired one step at a time. If our skill with spoken communication turns out to be in need of improvement, we can set clear guidelines to direct our efforts. We can be assured that by putting in such thought and effort, each of us can speak effectively in the various speaking occasions that comprise a large part of professional life. And, of course, our motivation has to come from the experience we have all had of watching people get ahead and reach their potential by being able to impact others with their ideas through out-of-the-ordinary communication skills.

The good news is that we are never far from our training ground. If only we could recognize it as such! Every day, every workplace buzzes with communication activity—much of it, spoken. At every turn, people are engaged in instruction, feedback, information, explanation, persuasion, argument, debate, analysis, and the like. As we interact with others, we are constantly getting exposed to a wide range of speakers and as receivers of the communication, we are in the best position to evaluate their effectiveness in engaging us, in making their ideas clear, and in serving the objectives. However, most of us do not make the best use of these opportunities by analysing these interactions and using the insight thus gained, to equip ourselves with concrete ways in which our own effectiveness in speaking may be enhanced. Each of us is a critic of other speakers, but if we could make our criticism precise and structured rather than merely judgemental and sweeping, we could turn the critical insight thus gained into guidelines for polishing our own skill. Even when we find ourselves having to listen to speakers who are unclear, incoherent, and tedious, these experiences can be useful to serve as a live demonstration of what annoyed or frustrated us and therefore should be avoided if we wish to avoid such an evaluation by our own listeners when *we* speak. On the other hand, the strong points of those we found lucid, focused, engaging, and memorable, need to be critically evaluated, and put to good use so as to have a similarly positive impact on our listeners. This exercise gives us a fair and usable understanding of elements that constitute an impactful speech.

Of course, it is not that we should model ourselves on any one speaker or try to clone their speaking style. Rather, we should try to identify the common strengths of effective speakers, although these may be manifest in various ways, and to imbibe these in our own style. In practical terms, whenever our critical listening shows us that certain delivery elements used by a speaker work very well to serve the objective of the communication, we should file these away in our mind and try these out in our speaking. At the same time, we must remember that things that work for others may not work for us, and we need to try and see what we can pull off with some practice. Certain things that worked really well for another speaker may not do so for you. Our personal communication style has to take into account our personality and needs to include what works best for us because each of us has a unique style and personality. But the good news is that there is no one correct way and you may choose from or devise any number of ways to present your ideas and feelings in such a way that you can satisfy the objectives of your communication, the expectations of the listeners, and make an impact.

Just as we need to identify the attributes of speakers who

are effective, it is good to be critical when we encounter those who are not so effective. By doing this we learn to focus on the receivers' perspective in terms of effectiveness. Such an analysis will show that the first thing often overlooked by average speakers is the very choice of speaking to communicate their ideas. They seem to have overlooked the proper reasons that *should* lead to this choice. These reasons are the appropriateness of the mode for the objective to be served, and the ability of the speaker to make the best use of it. We must keep in mind that spoken communication makes considerable demands on both speaker and listener, and unless this choice contributes much more effectively to meeting the objective for the receivers, it is not advisable to do so. By equipping ourselves with skill and confidence in a number of communication methods we give ourselves a wider range of choice. That is to say that we do not select one method over others simply because of our lack of ability in those—rather, we choose it because out of the options, it is the one that best serves our objective in the given context. For example, if we are not confident about our written communication, we may be turning to spoken communication even in contexts where the advantages of the latter are not best suited to our objective. When a very detailed and thorough treatment of an issue is needed, speaking may not allow us to develop the ideas in a structured manner with cross-referencing. Our listeners may also not find it easy to focus for an extended period or be able to grasp and carry away all the details.

CHOOSE YOUR MODE OF COMMUNICATION WISELY

Making the correct choices in this regard is the starting point of an effective communication. Firstly, depending upon the nature of our ideas, we decide to use words or non-verbal cues. There is much that can be communicated very effectively through painting, dancing, photography, whistling, even a glance or a smile. However, most of such communication is dependent upon shared significance of the codes for both parties involved in the communication and the active role of the receiver in paying attention to the context and deriving meaning from the non-verbal cues. As experience tells us, quite often this results in divergent meanings being derived. In fact, in some contexts, such as art or sculpture or music, the value and beauty may lie in the possibility of different interpretations from various perspectives. The person choosing to communicate through such non-verbal modes often cares much more about expression for its own sake, and is not too concerned about the particular sense that must be derived from it by every receiver.

Communication through words, especially in the world of business, aims at conveying, as far as possible, exact meanings. Verbal communication is generally chosen where precision and clarity are felt to be necessary. Sometimes a combination of both verbal and non-verbal cues is necessary in order to provide clarity. For example, verbal commentary or explanatory notes are used to facilitate the intended meaning of a graphic representation of data or an image.

Having chosen to use words in order to communicate a clear and unambiguous meaning, there is still a choice to be made between speaking and writing. The more this choice is made on the basis of what advantages and disadvantages each mode entails, the better we can hope to utilize the advantages for serving our objective. Not all potential disadvantages of the mode may be relevant if we consider our objective for that particular communication. The box below lists the chief potential advantages spoken communication offers us:

Advantages of spoken communication

- Building rapport with receivers
- Adding the force of our personality to the verbal message
- Reinforcing our verbal messages with supplementary cues from body language
- Immediate clarification and other response to constant feedback
- Adaptability of expression depending upon reception
- Spontaneity
- Inclusion of feelings and emotions

However, before we conclude that it is the perfect way to communicate, we must keep in mind that there are some drawbacks to spoken communication. Some of these are listed in the box below:

Drawbacks to spoken communication

- There may be no reliable record keeping
- Emotions may blur the issues
- Distractions may cause greater problems
- Ideas may not come out in a structured manner; digressions may occur
- Words once uttered cannot be taken back
- Mutual convenience has to be ensured to get speaker and listeners together
- Listening is quite challenging
- More expense of time, effort, and resources
- Limits to the number of people that can be directly reached

---

Awareness of these advantages and disadvantages should help in making a careful choice between speaking and writing. It would mean that keeping the particular objective of our communication in mind, we would assess whether the disadvantages are sufficiently outweighed by the advantages offered by this mode. If the particular advantages of spoken communication are of no great significance, it would be pointless to call for both parties to spend valuable face-to-face time and to engage in the challenging tasks of speaking and listening.

In fact, written communication has many advantages such as saving on time, effort, and resources as well as having a record for reference. It is also easier for a writer to provide greater clarity and correctness, given that writing allows one to do any number of rounds of editing and revision until one is satisfied with the content as well as expression. From the receiver's perspective too, it is easier to engage with complex material, to obtain clarity, and coherent sense from the communication. Written communication allows greater freedom to the reader in terms of convenience and time to go through the document thoroughly, to go backwards and forwards or to pause during the reading, to make notes and comments, and to re-read, if necessary. This is especially useful when the material is very detailed and the ideas are complex or when it is serious enough to warrant multiple readings.

Written communication also has the advantage of serving as a reliable record, which is an important feature for matters that are very significant and need to be available in records for future reference. Written communication would, therefore, be a better choice in such contexts. In fact, it would be a better choice than spoken communication in any situation where none of the advantages of the latter was particularly significant in meeting the objective of the communication. This is so because spoken communication makes a lot of demands on both speaker and listener as well as expenditure of time and money. If one decides to speak, it must only be because these disadvantages are outweighed by the advantages offered by it. The onus, then, lies on the communicator to use these potential advantages to their fullest. One must know what one is aiming at and how well it can be served by speaking as compared to writing.

Looking at the unique advantages of spoken communication, it is best suited for occasions when the direct personal appeal is important, where the supporting non-verbal cues add significant weight to the total meaning communicated, where the speaker's adaptability to the constant feedback from receivers is more important than a carefully structured and edited expression of the ideas, where certain important clarifications sought by the listeners allow for instant clarification that is of great significance in meeting the objective. The kinds of objectives where we can put the potential benefits of speaking to effective use are building rapport, persuading, requesting, explaining for instant understanding and clarification, discussions and brain storming, problem solving and generating ideas, and the like. While these may be done through the written mode too, an effective communicator weighs the advantages of the modes in relation to the particular issue/subject and the intended receiver's needs, so as to choose what best serves the objective. For example, a presentation of selected findings of a study and its unique features, highlighting what the particular audience will find interesting and relevant, generating excitement and curiosity for the full report or paper, and allowing for immediate responses from audience to give them clarity about the matter, is an appropriate objective for speaking rather than writing. The strengths of the latter may be used for a complete and detailed account of the study, its genesis, the rationale, methodology, complete findings and their detailed analysis and interpretation. When we make a formal application or request, it may be a requirement to put it in writing for record and follow-up action. But when making a personal request or appeal or for backing up a written one, it may be better to choose a spoken interaction to convey your needs and emotions, and to use the rich mix of numerous sensory cues to give a stronger message and increase the effectiveness in serving the objective.

Once we have made our choice to speak on the basis of conscious consideration of these reasons, it is easier to make the most of these potential advantages of spoken mode for meeting that particular objective. On the contrary, when we decide on speaking or writing without any conscious consideration in view of our objective, we may jeopardize the effectiveness of our communication in serving the objective. When the reasons for our choice are clear to us, we are better able to utilizing all the advantages offered by it to make our communication effective and impactful.

What kind of speaking are we aiming at when we wish to speak effectively and with impact? The attributes of effective speaking are given in the box below:

The top five attributes of such speaking

- Attuned to the listener
- Clear and concrete
- Structured presentation of ideas
- Engaging delivery, involving the listeners
- Increased effectiveness of message through multiple sensory cues

---

In order to achieve these, we need to be aware of the importance of each one of these and, knowing that it is not possible to achieve these by mere good luck or chance, we need to have a structured approach to our speaking opportunities.

In the next chapter, we will turn our attention to these ingredients of effective speaking and how one may break down what appears to be a daunting challenge when looked at as a whole. In the chapters following that, we will take up the specific challenges of certain critical speaking situations and try to identify practical steps for improving our performance in terms of meeting the objectives as well as the impact we can have on others.

CHAPTER 2

Speaking Effectively: The Recipe

You are in a group of colleagues, discussing some groundbreaking news that has just come in, and you watch in awe as one of them has the listeners eating out of his hand. Switch to a conference hall where the chair of a meeting is struggling to bring order to the discussion that is being monopolized by one person. In another room, a speaker making a presentation has her audience fully involved in what she has to say. At an interview, you find the candidate not quite succeeding in impressing the panelists with her abilities or making the most of her experience. At a formal meeting, there are those who have a question regarding an idea put forward by someone or an observation to offer, but hesitate and try to gather courage to speak up, while someone else asks the same question and is applauded for their perceptiveness!

What is happening in all these situations? People want and attempt to connect with others through the spoken word but do it with varying degrees of success. By success we mean here the satisfactory achievement of the purpose for which that exchange was meant, whether it is to inform, persuade, argue, or pool ideas. The questions arising out of this very uneven level of skill are:

- What do the speakers who are able to successfully communicate actually do compared to those who struggle with effectively serving their objective of getting their ideas across or who hesitate about their ability to communicate effectively and shy away from such opportunities?

- What care must a speaker take in any of the hundreds of situations of spoken communication so as to stand out from the crowd of those who largely do an average job of communicating ideas, information, or arguments in an interesting, effective, and memorable manner?

Let us keep these questions in mind as we try to understand certain overarching considerations that remain common in all speaking contexts, before taking up the specific contexts in later chapters.

PUTTING THE LISTENER FIRST

To answer these questions let us use our own experience, not as speakers but as listeners. By doing so we can get into the mind of our listeners with whom we want to speak. We begin with the listeners because they are the most crucial component. After all, we would be considered quite crazy if we were to speak without a listener! But listening is not something that happens automatically. It is not easy and involves effort on the part of the listener. Overlooking the listener is a big mistake because we cannot simply assume that the listener will put in the effort required to complete the transfer of the message that we are planning to send. They may do it, but only if certain conditions are met. Let me begin by asking you this—do you enjoy listening to others and are happy to make the effort? Your answer would probably be that you don't particularly enjoy it *unless* the following conditions are met:

- The speaker has something to say that is interesting and useful to you in some way
- The speaker has a style that makes you feel involved in what they are saying
- The mannerisms and body language of the speaker are not jarring, but actually seem to complement what they are saying
- The speaker seems to believe in what they are saying
- The speaker seems to possess authority on the material they are talking about
- The speaker seems to care about getting their ideas through to you
- The speaker presents ideas in a structured manner that makes it easy to follow

---

When we are not drawn into the role of the listener, we can avail of many attractive alternatives available to us and go on mental hikes while being physically present in front of the speaker. We could be planning our own responses and rejoinders, we could be drafting our plans for our own work, we could be reliving the cricket match we watched last night, or we could be anticipating the weekend getaway with our family. Successful spoken communication must take care to involve the listener so that they are more likely to control such mental distractions and engage in their role as receivers. Receivers of spoken communication have a challenging task—they need to control distractions, attend to verbal as well as non-verbal cues, make contextual sense of what they receive, and evaluate it against their experience and existing knowledge. But as your own experience would have shown, we are not inclined to put in the effort do all this unless the speaker ensures that the above are met. The box below gives situations when putting in your best effort as a listener seems not worth it.

Why would you put in the effort to listen effectively, when:
- the subject does not appear relevant or useful to you?
- the speaker does not seem to really care about getting the ideas across to you?
- the speaker does not display any authority on the subject or conviction in the ideas?
- the mannerisms and body language of the speaker clash with the ideas and display the speaker's lack of confidence and conviction?

- the speaker does not seem to make the effort to relate the ideas to you as the receiver but seems to be focused on the ideas in isolation?
- the ideas are presented in a jumbled manner without sufficient regard to sifting and organizing?

USE YOUR OWN RESPONSES AS A LISTENER

Simple guidelines for our own speaking are easily available if only we put our experience in the listener's role to work when it is our turn to speak. This will help us avoid the errors that make it more likely to turn the listener off and to take care of all that will help them to receive our message in a less taxing manner. It is surprising that so many of us make the same mistakes that others make when we are listening, as if some different rules apply when the tables are turned!

We can expect that our listeners will respond the way we do when we are supposed to listen. And what do we do when we listen? We generally use the speaker's body language to judge their level of confidence and conviction in what they are saying and tune out when we feel it is low. We yield to all possible distractions when the speaker doesn't seem to be fully involved in getting their point across to us. We find it hard to sustain interest if the subject is not made relevant to our needs and is not presented in a manner that makes it easy to follow.

Our task as the speaker would be so much simpler if we took this analysis of our responses as listeners and ensured that we avoided all that turned us off, and included elements that could help reach a message to our listeners. While the specifics of the particular communication contexts change, the common expectations of listeners remain constant. They expect clarity, coherence, structured presentation of ideas, and an engaging delivery that serves the objective as well as makes the effort of the listener seem less onerous. These, then, should become essential parts of the recipe for effective speaking, and all care must be taken to ensure that we plan for these as well as we can.

PLAN TO SUCCEED

Compared to those who struggle with their desire to share their ideas or views with listeners, speakers who are able to communicate successfully, plan every element of their communication in the context of the receivers, and their objective. The success of the actual spoken communication in meeting its objective for the particular listeners really lies in careful reflection and consideration of choices, before actually speaking. By taking this care, we are much more likely to match our own expectations in terms of meeting the objectives of our communication with the expectations of the listener.

While our objectives may remain constant, a different set of audience may have different objectives as listeners, and overlooking this fact may lead to ineffectiveness of our communication. It is essential to try to put ourselves, as much as possible, in the shoes of the listeners, and figure out why they would care about what we have to say, how it could be of use to them, what can we assume them to already know about the topic/issue, what value addition would they appreciate, what details would be needed to back up assertions, what frame of reference would work best to bring clarity and focus for them? The more clarity we can bring upon these points while planning our communication, the better focus we can bring upon communicating with our listeners in an effective manner.

'**There are three things to aim at: first, to get into your subject, then to get your subject into yourself, and lastly, to get your subject into the heart of your audience,' says Alexander Gregg.** What a lovely and succinct formula for the most essential ingredients of an impactful spoken communication! Across the numerous situations for spoken communication, those who stand out from the crowd of average communicators ensure exactly this. The triple objective gets achieved by:

a) **Thorough knowledge of the material:** After all, if we have nothing more to share with the listeners than what they already know or what is easily available through alternate means, why should they listen to us? The thoroughness also means that we have the necessary details, evidence, examples, as the case may be, to support our material.

b) **Complete ownership of the material:** If we stand in front of people with some material to share, it behoves us to demonstrate that we own the ideas, the details, the conclusions, everything. There is no way we can get listeners to accept what we say if we don't seem to believe in it ourselves. It is easy, when we are in a senior position, to delegate the preparation of our material such as script or visual aids for an oral presentation to juniors. However, it is quite impossible to mouth words put together by others with the same feeling which we can put into our natural expressions. It is also easy to get confused about structure and layout of visual aids that we have not prepared ourselves. We must remember how easily we are able to spot this one-step distance of the speaker from their material when we are the listeners' position. We must remember that our listeners would also be easily able to make this out. Such a realization does not add to the impact of the speaker as it takes away significantly from their credibility.

c) **Connecting with the listeners:** We can hope to get our ideas into the heart of the listeners only by making them feel that we really want to communicate with them, that we care about getting our ideas across to them. They are hardly likely to get the ideas unless we put in the effort to ensure as far as possible that they follow the words, the logic, and the feelings behind the whole.

Effective speaking is a combination of many skills. One needs to be in excellent control of the material—data, analysis, ideas, solutions, as the case may be. One must have strong logic and rational support for assertions so as to satisfy the most critical of receivers. One must be able to exercise excellent focus and selection out of the jumble of ideas and information at one's disposal. One must be able to organize and structure the entire communication in an effective manner so as to have the greatest likelihood of satisfying the objective. One must have command over language so as to clothe the ideas into words without loss of meaning. One must be prepared to take painstaking efforts in preparation and practice. One must have a true desire to communicate with the listeners and to do everything to make sure that the message reaches them in a manner most conducive to its reception and understanding both in letter and spirit.

Does all this seem like a tall order? It sure does! But let's try looking at it in a practical step-by-step manner.

PREPARATION

Where does an interesting, effective, and successful communication begin? The answer is: way before the event, through a number of steps that may be put under the umbrella of 'preparation'. Whenever you have listened to someone speak in a memorable and effective manner, the essential ingredients would have been—belief in what they are saying, a real desire to communicate with the listeners, a confident, natural and spontaneous manner of presenting their ideas and feelings. However, every speech that appears natural and spontaneous is so because of strong preparation. Paradoxically enough, more preparation leads to greater impression of naturalness and spontaneity. Greater preparation reduces the pitfalls of spontaneity such as running out of ideas, not having supporting examples or cases, not having a structure that can present ideas in a logical manner for the ease of the listener. In speaking situations in the business context, these are of paramount importance. Listeners need to be able to find adequate value in spending their time in that role. Preparation allows for a better, and more satisfying, matching of speaker's intent with the listeners' perspective. **Done well, preparation also ensures that possible responses and questions in the minds of the listeners are anticipated. By having our ideas, structure and other details in place, it allows us to focus on the delivery aspect of the speech during the actual presentation.** Only persons who are confident in the knowledge that they will not struggle to recall information and to structure it well, can focus on delivering their ideas effectively and engaging with the receivers. Such confidence comes with preparation.

GAINING CLARITY ON OBJECTIVE, LISTENER, CONTEXT

It is amazing how often we overlook the most basic questions. And it is this common oversight that may be responsible for much of the spoken communication that fails to serve its purpose, to leave an impact, and to make a speaker stand out. These most basic and most crucial questions to guide our preparation are:

- Why am I speaking?

- Who am I speaking to? Who are they and what is my relation with them?
- What is the situation?

Of course, there are other questions that need to be addressed too, but clarity on these three is essential before we proceed.

Our objective: Why are we communicating?

Without exception, an ineffective speech can be traced back to lack of care in identifying the very purpose of doing it. Very often, I have asked a speaker to spell why they are speaking, only to get very general responses such as 'to convey', 'to share', even 'to speak'! These answers are no doubt correct but they don't take us very far. Of course, every communication is an act of sharing or conveying one's ideas or thoughts to others and if you are choosing to speak, it is obviously only the method and not the purpose.

So what does one mean by the purpose of speaking? And why is it so crucial for the success of that particular act of speaking? Purpose of speaking means the underlying objective to be served through that communication. The more clearly we can identify the purpose, the better we can focus on achieving it. For example, if I can identify that sharing information or facts is my purpose, then I can focus on how best to convey it. That is, I can go on to make appropriate choices for meeting the challenge of making information relevant, appropriate for listeners' needs, and for structuring it so as to help in providing clarity to the receiver. I may then ask myself about primary and secondary objectives—that is, is the information going to serve as the basis of an argument or persuasion that is the real objective of the communication or is sharing new information or updating of information status an end in itself? If I can identify that my purpose is to persuade I will be guided by this end in my selection of data, in my choice of details, examples as well as in the persuasive approach to adopt.

If you were to ask either party involved in a spoken communication about the highest priority, it is likely to be clarity. This includes clarity about focus, central idea, examples, and actual articulation. However, one must keep in mind that clarity for the listeners in these matters in the actual communication is only a reflection of the clarity in the speaker's mind. Before we speak, we need to spend time in gaining clarity about our objective and about our reasons for the choice of mode of communication in the first place. This is time well spent because it brings us closer to success in our communication. It does that by giving us a solid yardstick to measure our choices of content and style. The choice of every ingredient, whether inclusion and exclusion of certain details or examples, direct or indirect structure, plain or elaborate style, serious and formal or friendly and relaxed tone, may be best evaluated on the basis of how well it helps meet the purpose. We are less likely to provide a jumble of facts somehow related to a topic, when we are clear about the purpose for which we are communicating and the particular set of people with whom we are communicating. Through preparation, paying attention to our objective and audience, we are more likely to make choices about structure and content keeping the objective in mind rather than when we 'wing' it. That is when we are likely to make insufficiently considered choices that may endanger the objective. Not only can neglecting such preparation make all the effort of speaking pointless by jeopardizing the objective, it may also cause damage through the inadvertent inclusion of inappropriate content or style elements.

Why choose to speak?

Another very crucial way in which the question about why we are speaking needs to be addressed is in helping us make a conscious choice between communication modes of getting ideas across. If we allow our choice to be governed by the default setting, as it were, we do not consciously relate the requirements of the objective with the benefits offered by the particular mode. That is, we may speak or write simply because that's what occurs to us rather than choosing on the basis of the advantages offered by our choice in serving our particular objective. Whether it is writing or speaking, no mode is perfect for all purposes. While it has advantages, it also has certain drawbacks. When we consciously choose a particular method we weigh the advantages and disadvantages to see if the former outweighs the drawbacks in helping us serve the particular objective of that communication.

Let us look at the advantages of writing first. **Without question, writing allows one to develop ideas with much**

more attention to precision and concreteness, as well as to ensure a sound structure. This is especially valuable when dealing with complex ideas or matters deserving detailed treatment. The biggest advantage is that the writer has the opportunity to review and refine the message to better ensure that the idea has been articulated satisfactorily. This is in the interest of the writer as well as the receiver who gets a clearly articulated message. At the same time, the reader is at liberty to go through the document according to their own convenience and to reread parts of it or all of it in order to gain better clarity. For certain contexts, the fact that a written communication has value as reference, may become of crucial importance. With all these advantages, the written mode has certain disadvantages. Despite all the care taken by the sender, it is not in their control whether the receiver actually reads the document. If they do read it, their response is not immediately available to the sender to adapt to. The sender also does not have recourse to supplementary cues through body language that may enhance the meaning of the message.

Turning to speaking, we find that it has the advantage of immediate feedback from the receiver for the sender to adapt to and modify both the content and style of the message. It ensures that the receiver has immediately received the message. (Of course, we must remember that sometimes we only ensure hearing rather than listening.) We are also aided as speakers by a number of body language cues that can enhance the force of a message. The personal rapport that we are able to strike in spoken communication may build a receptivity that may be very difficult through written communication. At the same time, speaking is accompanied by a number of disadvantages. Very importantly, it is difficult to sustain the attention and engagement of listeners for sustained periods of time or for very complex ideas. It is easy for the speaker to get side-tracked and lose focus. Words once spoken, cannot be retrieved, reviewed, or modified unlike in written communication where any number of rounds of editing and revision may be done before the communication is sent to the receiver. Other drawbacks are that while spoken communication may have immediate impact, it does not serve as a reliable record or reference, and that spoken communication is generally more expensive in terms of resources of time and money, and the disruption to schedules caused by the requirement of speaker and listeners to be available concurrently.

Given these various ways in which both spoken and written communication have certain advantages and disadvantages; it is for the smart communicator to choose appropriately. Not every communication needs a record for reference, or requires people to match their schedules to be available at a given point of time and space (unless we're talking through teleconferencing), or need the extra dimensions of cues from body language. Depending on whether it is a sustained logical argument, a theoretical exposition, an impassioned appeal, a summary of key finding, or a comprehensive report, we need to consciously decide whether the advantages of a particular communication mode outweigh the disadvantages.

Generally speaking, unless there is value to be gained by the personal rapport, and adaptability to immediate responses, it is rather pointless to expect two sets of people to leave all other commitments, to match their schedules, and to engage in the challenging tasks of speaking, with its accompanying challenges of nerves, and of listening, with its challenges of ubiquitous distractions and poor listening skills. If certain objectives can be served without any loss in effectiveness, by written communication, it is far easier for both sender and receiver, and generally also cost effective in terms of time and other resources.

Speaking, therefore, is best reserved for objectives where the unique opportunities made available through this mode, can significantly contribute to the efficacy of the communication. Having chosen speaking in a conscious manner, we would definitely have a clearer idea of the potential advantages available to us through this choice rather than if it was a default option. We would have, while making the decision of choosing to speak, considered the requirements of the objective and of the receivers, and therefore would be more likely to try to fully utilize the advantages inherent in that choice. For example, while making a persuasive appeal, if we have chosen to speak, precisely because it offers us the opportunity to strike a rapport with the listener and to support our verbal points with supplementary cues from our body language, as well as to display the emotions that are appropriate to the topic and occasion, we are much more likely to try to use these to the best possible manner, than if we were speaking without really considering how the medium was more suited to the context than others, such as writing.

Our listeners: Who are we speaking to?

Clearly defining the purpose of the communication must also take into account the other party involved in the communication—the listeners. Why are they listening? What are their expectations? What do they hope to gain from the communication? What do they already know? A purpose decided only from the perspective of the speaker is likely to leave the listeners cold. Your purpose must address some need of the listeners or bring some value to them. For example, to continue with our example of information as the objective, our choice of objective for speaking is only going to be effective if we are going to provide information that is not already with the listener, cannot be obtained more comfortably and effortlessly by other means, is of use to them, and is presented in a manner that is easy for them to follow and absorb. To take another example, if we're narrating an event, we should take into account not only our own objective of sharing it, but also the perspective of the receivers—why would they be interested in this? What's in it for them? It could be entertainment. It could be education or increase in knowledge-base. It could be of use to them as precedent or example. But if it is only about the speaker, without consideration for the listeners, it is likely to fail in engaging them effectively.

While making choices about our content and approach, we will also benefit by being clear about our relationship with the listeners. Are they internal or external to the organization? If internal, are they at our level, senior, or junior to us? Are they from a similar vertical? If external, what is the relationship— are we pitching an idea to them, collaborating with them, or reporting to them?

The clearer we are about our audience, the better we can make choices about content and style. During the preparation stage, it is important to try to figure out questions such as: Why would they be interested in listening to us? What is their profile in terms of age, interests, or profession? What do they already know of the subject? Thinking of such questions will help us decide what will be relevant, useful, and interesting to the particular listener as compared to others. Effective content is not something that is good for all listeners and all contexts. Rather, it is particular to that listener or set of listeners. What will be effective in conveying the idea vividly and convincingly to one cannot be assumed to be the same for all. At the same time, context may change the perspective of listeners. Having a conversation with colleagues is quite different from speaking formally to them. Speaking at an interview presents different challenges from presenting one's ideas through a prepared presentation. There are challenges in all of these and these would be better met by spending some time in carefully understanding the listeners' perspective along these dimensions. Our decisions about content, structure, and even style benefit greatly by taking such care and help in strengthening the effectiveness of our communication.

Whenever we speak we expect that at the end, the listeners will be clear about what was communicated. However, clarity for the listener is inextricably tied up with clarity in the speaker's mind about the purpose and ideas being communicated. Whether we are speaking casually about a current topic of general interest, making a formal presentation on a technical subject, or trying to impress a panel of interviewers with our experience and achievements, we don't want our listeners to go away with fuzzy and disjointed ideas about some of the things we may have talked about. We want them to have complete clarity of what was spoken and an overall favourable impact of the ideas as well as the speaker. However, the only way to come close to ensuring this is by being as clear as possible about our purpose, our focus, our facts, our rationale and reasoning.

Here's a litmus test: from the briefest to the longest spoken communication you can think of, try answering, in not more than two sentences, the question—what is the purpose and central idea of your communication? If you cannot answer this crisply and clearly, there is more work to be done in refining your focus and in identifying your major purpose. Imagine what an impossibility it is for an audience to take away with them a clear sense of what they heard, if you, the speaker, cannot do so! The box below gives some examples of what answers to this question could look like.

- I wish to share the results of an experiment we have conducted in our department over the last three months with results showing significant reduction in stress levels by playing piped classical music through the work day. I show the projected increase in productivity if this was to be implemented across the organization.
- I argue that between the options of outsourcing our security needs and of keeping them in-house, the latter is stronger. For this I have used the primary criteria of stringent controls, and meeting our particular data security needs, and the secondary criterion of cutting cost.
- I will convince the listeners that shifting some of their advertising budget to local FM radio would bring them excellent value for money and not only increase the reach of their message to many demographic customers sets, it will also enhance the recall value of the visual messages. Among local FM radio stations, our station—PQR—will bring them the best customized deals and a loyal listener base that is the largest and most diverse as estimated by XYZ.

If, on the other hand, we approach the communication with a fuzzy idea that we are to speak about classical music and stress levels, or of our security needs, or of radio as a good medium for advertising, we are much less likely to leave our listeners with clarity about the central idea we conveyed.

GATHERING MATERIAL: FACTS, EXAMPLES, EVIDENCE

Let us now turn our attention to another crucial preparatory step. Remember the example at the beginning of the chapter of the speaker who had his listeners eating out of his hand? What is he likely to be doing right? He would know why he's contributing to the discussion. Speaking among colleagues, he would know their interests, their professional backgrounds, their linguistic abilities, and the like. He would use this understanding to decide what level of information and ideas would be appreciated by the listeners. He would also have solid material at his command. He would know more about the topic than the listeners and be able to make it obvious so that the listener sees the value in paying close attention to his words. He would also have given thought to material that would support his ideas and ensured that he had facts, and examples and evidence at his command in order to make his points lucid and convincing.

We must keep in mind that the usefulness of examples is only in relation to the receivers and choosing the right examples means thinking of what would make things clearer for the listeners. Referring to things from their experience base helps to make ideas more vivid and clear to them and this cannot be decided without considering who exactly we are speaking to. An example or analogy is meant to make something clear by giving a concrete instance that the person may be able to better relate to. If the receiver cannot quickly relate to the example and if it doesn't improve their comprehension of the idea, the point is lost. The same applies to references and allusions that one makes in conversations, speeches, discussions, and presentations. An allusion that works excellently with one set of listeners may fall flat with another. A reference that makes things clearer for a particular audience may completely fail to do so with another. Therefore, examples, references, and allusions all need to be selected with proper care to appropriateness and usefulness for the listeners. When listeners see from our references and examples that we have taken care to understand them and their background, it serves as a wonderful way to not only provide clarity but also to involve them in the interaction.

Returning to the presenter we visualized at the beginning of the chapter, who has the audience giving their full attention to everything she says and carefully following her exposition or argument, we can bet that she would not be talking in vague and generalized assertions but would have put in the effort to gather concrete facts to support her points and to pick out examples and evidence that the audience can easily relate to. She would have made sure to add value to the information she is providing to the listeners.

We must remember that we live in the age of information and how easy it is for almost everyone to access information. Consequently, we must understand that if people are to listen to us with interest and a sense of value addition, we must give them what they cannot get elsewhere. What is that one unique thing only we can offer? It is either information only available with us—that is information we have created through our own efforts—or information that has been processed in our mind to create our perspective, our analysis, and response. When we do this we bring to others what they cannot get elsewhere and if it is presented with a view to the listeners' interests and benefit, they will definitely find it valuable. Remember, that we cannot demand attention from the listener. Although face-to-face spoken communication may ensure hearing, nothing other than providing value to the receiver can ensure listening.

It would do well to keep in mind that the listener may be obliged, in a number of formal situations, to hear us, but no listener is ever obliged to actually listen. They will only do so if they find the talk engaging and valuable. After all, the listener also spends much in terms of time and effort of decoding and if they see no value in it for them, they do not see the worth of this expense and tune out.

PLANNING THE STRUCTURE

Another important element to prepare is the structure. There is a world of difference in terms of efficacy between something presented haphazardly and something presented in a structured manner. It is fallacious to assume that once we get speaking, things will naturally fall into place. I'm sure that all of us have had numerous instances as receivers when we have struggled to follow the drift of a speaker or have got lost in trying to keep pace with abrupt shifts of focus through backward and forward movements between ideas. I'm also sure that we do not recall such speakers with any great admiration. Why then would we similarly neglect to plan for this very useful element of spoken communication, especially those of longer duration and/or of complexity in ideas?

The disadvantage of speaking compared to writing is that there is no possibility of editing—of going backwards and re-doing any bits that did not come out as well as desired. Without this luxury, it is best to take as much care as possible through preparation, to structure ideas or information in a systematic manner so as to enhance others' receptivity to it. With sufficient care, a structured manner ensures that the listener receives the material with a proper opening that is interesting and engaging, an introduction that lays the basis, different parts that flow out of each other without odd and abrupt shifts, and a conclusion where all parts converge. This is a feature whose absence is more noticeable than its presence is appreciated. However, it contributes in a major way to the success of the ideas getting transferred from the speaker to the listeners.

Rather than depending on the stream-of-consciousness kind of flow of ideas occurring to us at the moment of speaking, it is much wiser and more useful to the success of communication, to spend time on planning the structure during preparation. Depending on the length of the communication and the complexity of the material, we may need to spend more or less time on this, but in all cases, preparing for it is definitely important and useful. For a long speech or presentation we need to break down our material into logically interdependent parts and plan the order that best provides clarity and coherence for the listener. We need to plan the transitions between these parts, as well as the opening, introduction, and the conclusion. **Our listeners can go along with our ideas much better if they are given a sense of purpose and direction through our introduction. The expectation built up here needs to be satisfied in the main part of the talk. And the entire coverage, underlining the main thrust and purpose needs to be brought out in the concluding part.**

All this does not happen by happy chance, and its lack often proves to be the undoing of the communication. Often the challenge we face is that of imposing structure on the sheer mass of material at our disposal. Even if we are clear about the need to do so, how do we decide the structure? We need to be guided by our objective and central idea in deciding the order and the arrangements of the parts. The question before us at all times needs to be: How do we proceed so that we give the listener the clearest way of making sense of the various points in a way that best serves the central thesis and overall objective of the communication? For example, when we are trying to sell the advantages of a proposed security service provided by us, every decision we make about what to include and in what order needs to be on the basis of helping the listener stay focused on the importance and benefits of our proposal. There would be many facts, figures, and points that are true but whether we include them and in what order and in support of what point we do so, are decisions best made in the coolness of the planning stage rather than during the actual interaction. Of course, some thinking on our feet would be needed as we modify what we say in response to the constant feedback we receive, but having a good sense of the structure of most of what we say will help us stay on track and not get diverted into issues that may be interesting and related, but not quite relevant to our objective or not helping the listener to make coherent sense of the parts.

Even in a brief talk or interaction, it is better to have thought about where to begin, where to take it, and where to close. Take the case of interviews. While we all know the importance of preparing ourselves by brushing up our information and awareness, we often neglect to prepare the structure of our responses. It would be profitable for us to have spent some time preparing responses to anticipated questions in a structured manner. There are some questions where we are tested on our factual knowledge and it is good to have thought of a correct answer. There are other questions where 'correctness' is more about appropriateness and having reflected on it in advance would help us give a more appropriate response than the first one that popped into our head. Remember, there are also questions where it is not really about a correct answer but about giving details, or making logical inferences, or about backing up an assertion. For responses to such questions it is best to plan, as far as possible, in terms of: Where should I begin? What example or evidence should I give to add concreteness and clarity? What implication should I draw out of the experience or incident? Even the apparently simple icebreaker 'tell us something about yourself', needs to be handled in a structured manner, rather than random rambling on the topic of 'myself'. Since the subject is so well-known, we may have trouble deciding where to begin, what to focus on, and where to conclude. This becomes a greater challenge if left to the actual interview rather than reflected on during preparation time.

Take another example, that of a presentation of recommendations based on our analysis. One of the decisions to be made during preparation is of structure. How do I present my material? a) Do I first define the problem and provide the recommendations and then give my reasoning and support for these? b) Do I proceed with laying out the problem and the available options as well as the qualitative and quantitative analysis from which the recommendations emerged? This decision on structure may affect the way the recommendations are received. It should be based on our analysis of the listeners and the expected response of the individuals, given the context. The first option is recommended for all contexts where the anticipated response of our listeners is positive or neutral. However, if we feel that our listeners may receive the recommendations with scepticism and negativity, this structure may colour their response by giving them the recommendations before we have been able to build a logically rigorous case for them. In this situation the more indirect structure b) would be advisable.

Focusing on the structure during the preparation stage also

helps indirectly in ensuring that we engage more closely with the logical connections between the parts, and the coherence and consistency of the overall message. Sometimes it is easy to overlook gaps in our own message because we often don't stop to examine ideas until we need to share them with others. If we work under the easy assumption that what is clear and coherent to us will naturally be so for others, we may find that our audience perceives gaps or lack of connection or inconsistencies in what we say. If we could try out our structure with a mock audience who can give us feedback, it would be a great help in seeing it from another's perspective and making suitable modifications. In the absence of this, we need to train ourselves for taking as objective a view as possible about our communication. Speakers who bowl us over with the force of their message, share this attentiveness to how they structure their information and ideas for us as listeners.

HOW MUCH PREPARATION IS ENOUGH?

Having looked at what to prepare, we may ask ourselves, how much should we prepare? The answer, of course, is 'it depends'. It depends on many aspects of the context, from the nature of the subject and the format, to the composition and expectations of the audience. However, what does not change is the need to over-prepare in terms of gathering information about the topic, reflecting on it to refine our understanding and to generate as clearly as possible our stance, response, analysis, or opinion, as the case may demand. There is no shortcut to this. And any attempt to cut corners in preparation only reduces the confidence with which we face others and also risks lowering the value and credibility of what we say. Under-preparation is an assured way to create anxiety for ourselves. If we know we are capable of making an impact if only we did not stint in our efforts, why not put in the required level of effort? Why settle for less than what we are capable of?

PREPARATION AND PRACTICE AS ANTIDOTES TO PRESENTATION ANXIETY

Hardly anyone in the world with anything worthwhile to say, can do so without preparation. Not only does preparation put us in control of what we are going to say, this very preparedness gives us confidence and works as an effective tool for combating anxiety. **The confident speaker is one who has spent time and thought in planning both the content and the style while keeping the purpose and the listeners in view.** The same speaker who is full of confidence on the occasion when he has done so, could very possibly be a nervous wreck on the occasion when he has overlooked this crucial step. The more practice we have of speaking in general, and the more positive those experiences have been, the less unnerved we would feel by the thought of speaking on a particular occasion. However, neither this experience not one's general confidence levels can help us much in countering anxiety if we are not sure that we have taken all necessary preparatory steps. The assured feeling that comes from knowing that one has prepared as thoroughly as it was possible, is the best antidote to anxiety. Even if anxiety begins to surface, it is easier to quell it by reminding ourselves of the preparation we have done, than by trying to bluff ourselves. I am sure you will agree that even if some of us may be good at bluffing others, bluffing oneself is quite impossible.

In the words of H. P. Lovecraft, 'The oldest and strongest emotion of mankind is fear, and the oldest and strongest kind of fear is fear of the unknown.' The more we keep away from speaking opportunities out of fear, the more unknown they become, and the greater the fear they generate. And we must remember that as Ralph Waldo Emerson said, 'Fear defeats more people than any other one thing in the world'. If we don't want to be defeated by the fear of speaking, we must defeat the fear! We can do so by removing the unknown element from it, by engaging with it, by testing ourselves, and by learning from these experiences. As we understand it better, our fear of it goes down.

There are so many elements to speaking effectively that if we sit and worry about these, we will get more and more convinced that it is not possible for us to do it all. But when we attempt to meet the fear head-on by doing what we fear, we have already won half the battle! And we do this from the understanding of all that we are missing out by not being able to get our ideas across to others in an impressive and effective manner. The other half of the battle is to be won by more and more practice, review, and reflection. This is true for building our confidence in speaking generally as well as for particular speaking occasions. **Preparation and practice are of immense help and they work by removing the unknown from the equation as far as possible, thus making the communication situation, familiar and comfortable.**

As Mark Twain said, 'Do the thing you fear most and the death of fear is certain.' When we face the fact that we find something fearful and daunting, we need to reflect on the root of the fear—is it the feeling that we may not have something relevant or significant to say and end up making ourselves the objects of ridicule? Is it our self-training of keeping quiet in front of seniors out of deference that is holding us back? Is it our mental playlist that shows us imagined scenes of our knocking knees, trembling hands, and wildly pitching voice, or worse, fainting or going blank? The more we stay in the arena of imagination, the more we are in the grip of these fears because they grow larger, the longer they stay untested.

It is a good idea to reflect upon the particular kinds of spoken interaction contexts that give us the greatest anxiety and to actively work out a way to combat that. We may begin with equipping ourselves with a good understanding of the requirements of the particular kind of speaking situation. We need to supplement this understanding with introspection into our own comfort with these requirements and to figure out exactly where we need to bolster ourselves. Is it in terms of stronger content? Is it a question of remembering what we have to say well enough? Is it about our body language that seems to get neglected in our focus on remembering our material? Whatever is our actual challenge, we need to pay particular focus to it during our preparation, to practice before the actual event, get feedback, and use the feedback to further refine our content and delivery. When we finally take the plunge after this, we have ensured that conscious effort has gone into making strategic choices about our speaking. Every occasion of speaking is practice for speaking in general and very valuable learning ground; we test ourselves and get our own sense of how our choices worked in meeting our objective. We must also make it a practice to not only welcome feedback about our communication, but also actively seek it from our listeners. Regardless of our actual performance, careful preparation prior to it and critical review after it, is invaluable for our learning and constant improvement. For those of us who shy away from speaking opportunities out of fear, it is the best way to get concrete evidence of the unrealistic nature of our fears and to shoot down the bogey of our mental images of disaster.

PRESENTING YOUR IDEAS

Capturing ideas in words

'The difference between the right word and the almost right word is the difference between lightning and the lightning bug'—Mark Twain

Our minds may be bustling with ideas, some so nascent that they are not yet articulated in language, others fully developed. However, for us, they are all very real and true. When we choose to communicate these ideas, the challenge arises of clothing and packaging them in the most suitable codes so as to present them to others as vividly as possible. While speaking, words are the primary codes at our disposal. Obviously, having a vast vocabulary at our command is essential so as to find the most appropriate correspondence between our ideas and words. The less well we are able to find this correspondence, the more the success of our verbal communication has been compromised from the start. The less our pool of words or the less of an effort made by us to search our mental repository for the most appropriate expression of our idea, the more the slippage between intended and communicated idea. A good speaker expresses ideas through words that are appropriate and clear and simple to comprehend for the given audience. An excellent speaker uses words with so much appropriateness that the listeners can not only follow the exact shade of meaning intended, but can vividly visualize scenes or feel the emotion or grasp the intricacies of an idea.

Building a rich and deep treasure of vocabulary at our command is a constant process and at any given point we reap the benefit of our accumulated mental treasure chest of words to capture our ideas into verbal form. However, it would be of immense help if we were to candidly admit to ourselves that there are occasions when what we meant to say is not quite captured by the words we selected. This could be due to a smaller pool of words at our disposal or from insufficient care in selecting between possible options to capture finer shades of meaning. We should make a conscious effort to match our thoughts and their expression in words and assess if we are satisfied with the conversion. This is very important because while speaking we do not have the luxury of stopping in order to search for the right word in a dictionary or a thesaurus or to refine our expression on review.

Most of us will find that there is still much room for expanding the pool of vocabulary readily available to us, especially for speaking. Without reference to other resources or time for review and revision, the words we can use in spoken interactions are those that are completely ours through deep familiarity and constant use. Therefore, at the same time that it is important to be constantly expanding our vocabulary, it is also very important to bring newly acquired words into usage as much as possible. Only by doing so can they become readily accessible to our minds during articulation of our thoughts. At the same time, it is also important to avoid the easiest and most common expressions or clichés that have lost freshness through overuse, and to take care over selecting words both for preciseness and freshness.

The vocabulary at our disposal is of primary importance. However, it is also essential to keep the listeners and the context in mind while making choices about expression and articulation of our ideas. By using our awareness of the background of the audience in terms such as their professional specialization, educational level, culture, interests and preferences, we can craft our message in ways that not only add clarity for our listeners but also involve them in the communication. A popular maxim says that we must keep our expression simple and short. However, it is important to recognize that simplicity is a relative term. We must definitely make our receivers' task easier by using words that are simple. But we must also be aware that what is simple for one listener may not be so for another. **Talking down to listeners by dumbing down our expression is as likely to turn off an audience as talking in a way that is too complex for them.** For example, technical jargon can be freely used when we know that our listener is from the same technical area and well-versed with this vocabulary. They will appreciate the use of short forms, acronyms, and technical terms rather than long-winded expressions. In fact, using general terms or going into explanations of terms may not only be redundant for such an audience, it may turn them off by making them feel that we are talking down to them, or not showing sufficient awareness of their area of expertise. On the other hand, of course, if we were to use technical jargon with an audience unfamiliar with that area, we will be creating more confusion than clarity. At the same time, we will be indicating to our audience that we have not taken care to modify our material keeping in mind their background. It is no surprise then, if this alienates our listeners.

The same applies to keeping it short. This again, cannot be an absolute principle because sometimes being brief may mean incompleteness or cryptic expression. We should surely prefer a crisp expression over a long-winded one. This means that the listener has fewer words to decode in order to get the idea. If we can say 'now', it is better than saying 'at the present moment in time'. It is better to choose 'because' rather than 'due to the fact that'. No doubt it is better if we can avoid redundancies in expression such as 'square in shape,' 'complete monopoly,' 'visible to the eye', or 'return back.' At the same time, brevity is in itself no virtue because it may be acquired at the expense of much-needed details and sufficient elaboration. Crispness and brevity are not to be confused. With communication at the workplace being objective-oriented, any loss of detail or concreteness in the name of brevity is neither likely to be appreciated, nor lead to clarity. Crispness, however, will be appreciated if it has been done with due regard to the existing level of the listeners and the issue in focus, and will show respect for the listeners' time as well as clarity in the presenter's mind.

Taking care with our choice of words is important for another reason—as a means to create a rapport with the listener. By being constantly aware of the particulars of the listeners in any given situation, we can use, as far as possible, personal pronouns 'we' and 'our' to connect ourselves and the listener. It is a good idea to find some way in which the listener is like you, and to use the shared pool of information, experience, expertise, and interests to increase both clarity and receptivity to the messages. For example, you could say, 'as we have seen on many an occasion,' 'as we can easily recall,' 'as you know, our experience of this has been mixed.' In different situations, despite your being the constant element, the shared ground with various listeners would obviously change. But you can always find some common ground. It is unlikely that you will be speaking to a listener or set of listeners with whom you cannot find anything in common. If not in terms of common technical background or shared interests, it could be a common industry, a common geographical or social background, a common age or gender profile. It is a matter of expanding the circles within which we locate ourselves and the listeners till we find ones that intersect. And despite all sorts of diversity, we may still relate to each other as fellow human beings living in this particular moment of time on the same planet!

At another level of language choice and expression is the question of formal vs informal words and expressions. In this, it is best to be guided by the culture and the nature of the interaction. While interacting with external people and those higher to us in hierarchy, and in a large gathering, it is generally advisable to use formal language. Formal language does not necessarily mean stilted or artificial language but it does imply avoiding slang and colloquialisms.

If we want our listeners to get our ideas and respond to them, we have to make the effort to get them to feel what we are talking about, to get them to see what we describe, to feel the emotion we talk of, to hear the sound we have in mind, to visualize the conclusion or result we hold out in promise. While details of argument and data are more appropriate for the written communication, details that bring ideas concretely to the mind's eyes are very important for spoken communication. For vividness and lucidity, it is advisable to prefer specific words rather than general, and simple expression of thoughts. While the written medium allows the reader time to process complex sentences by spending more time over it, or by re-reading it, the spoken medium is better suited to more natural cadences and succinct expression of thoughts. It is better to break ideas into short (not staccato) sentences rather than combine them into complex sentences.

Speaking being the perfect vehicle for conveying messages that primarily rely on connecting the subject more directly and personally with the listener, special care is needed to bring out the feelings behind what we speak. If we don't bring that dimension into our speech, we are giving an oral rendition of material more appropriate to written form. Whether it is enthusiasm, excitement, worry, concern, or frustration, it is the feeling for what we speak that makes it worth using a rich medium such as face-to-face communication. Having chosen it, if we do not, or cannot, convey the feelings or the palpable sense of our subject to our listeners simply because of our lack of care in clothing our ideas in words, we are wasting an immense advantage offered by the medium.

Taking the listener along: sharing your structure

Not only must ideas be structured for ease of the listener, we must remember that we need to take the listener along by sharing the structure. During our preparation of the structure, we have some logic for choosing to make it the way we have. At the time of actual presentation, this needs to be made explicit so that the reader can see the logic at work. It is useful to show the connection between points by using enumerative words such as firstly, secondly, thirdly; primarily, secondarily; further, in addition, in summation. Describing what we are doing is another good way to take readers along with your structure: for example, 'let me give you a brief background'; 'to give you an example'; 'let us compare'; 'let's quickly recap the main elements we have identified'; 'from these contrasting positions we can infer that'; 'to conclude from these facts'.

Structure becomes a way to share our logic with the listener. If we club ideas together and make this explicit through our structure, the listener will find it easier to follow the logic guiding our thinking. In contrast, a jumbled presentation of ideas may have an implicit logic for us but may prove challenging for the listeners to decipher. We may make the logic explicit by referring to blocks of our ideas with a label that we repeat, by drawing bridges with connective tissue, and by showing how ideas flow from one another and guiding our listener through the ideas we are sharing.

PRESENTING WITH THE SPOKEN WORD

Energy and sincerity

It is a common experience that people tend to regard formal communication as a stiff affair where one cannot be oneself and must adopt an artificial style of speaking. This is a myth that needs to be busted. The crucial importance of spoken communication lies in the direct appeal to the listener through the rapport that can be established between speaker and listener. And this rapport is possible to establish only when we can be ourselves and attempt to connect with the listener in all sincerity and to use our personality to support our message. None of this is likely if the listener senses that we are hiding our real self behind a fake pose.

Whether we speak to one person or many, it is important to be aware that we are conversing with the audience. We must remember that we are not talking to ourselves in the depth of a forest or in a desert, but to people in a certain context. If these people are to give us their undivided attention and actively engage in making meaning of the messages they receive from us, it is important that they get a sense of conversing with a real person, who truly wishes to get through to them. It is easy to forget that every such communication is a conversation even when one person does the major part or even all of the speaking. The role of the audience is absolutely crucial in the communication and our connecting with them and making them a part of the dialogue is essential in maximizing the potential advantages of spoken communication. Our purpose should be to let them feel that we are not reciting a memorized monologue but actually speaking to them, trying to connect with them and to convey something we are really keen to share with them.

While depth of knowledge and good preparation are, no doubt, valuable, they can be nullified if not accompanied by the speaker's energy and involvement in sharing their ideas with listeners. Rarely can one engage others by mechanical

---

Remember

The potential to connect with the audience is one of the biggest strengths of spoken communication. Make them part of a dialogue, let them feel your eagerness to speak to them, to connect with them, and to share your ideas with them.

---

recitation of facts, however well-researched and impressive these may be. Energy and enthusiasm are, to a great degree, contagious! If we want others to respond with these, we must be prepared to radiate these ourselves. We cannot get an audience to care unless we are prepared to show that we ourselves do so. Passion, conviction, and involvement in what we are speaking of, ensure that others cannot listen to us unresponsively. This applies as much to a conversation as to a formal presentation. There is no reason why formal presentations have to be dull as dishwater. Who wants to listen, except under duress, to a presenter who seems to be speaking under duress? Just as he or she seems to be fulfilling a workplace requirement and carrying out a duty, the audience sits as if trapped, and would be gone within seconds, if their responsibility, similarly, was not that of attending. But, we all know that only physical attendance can be regulated, not the mental and emotional engagement with the speaker's ideas. If the time and energy spent in presenting and listening to them are to have any worth, the communication must engage the listeners and convey more than what a mere written version potentially would.

That extra element in the case of speaking is brought in by the personal engagement of the speaker with the topic or issue. If the speaker does not bring in this extra element over and above the literal meaning of the words, the time and effort of both parties is rather futile. If the entire communication is to rely on the actual words alone it may be much more efficacious to put it in writing where both sender and receiver may have an easier task in framing as well as receiving it at their leisure. What makes the spoken communication more effective is that extra element of sincerity and personal conviction that can be conveyed through the speaker's presence. Of course, the content needs to be strong in terms of relevance, and credibility, and the style needs to be confident and assured, but an audience is likely to overlook small flaws in these areas, while any indication of less than perfect sincerity, completely dismantles the effectiveness of the communication in creating the desired impact. Time after time, at conferences and business presentations I have sat through talks and presentations where the speakers could not impress the listeners not because their material lacked rigour and depth, but because they did not seem to care about what they were speaking. Even listeners who came with the best intentions quite quickly turned off and left the room or took a little mental vacation. I have seen candidates in interviews present information about themselves or answer questions asking for their analysis or interpretation of something, in a manner that is either mechanical and apparently memorized, or dull, uninvolved, and consequently, unimpressive and unconvincing.

In business and even in social contexts, no one likes to be at the receiving end of a recitation. People may be willing to listen to us if we are able to bring something relevant to them and do so in an engaging and interactive manner. Whether in a casual conversation, formal discussion, speech or presentation, not only do they feel uninvolved unless they are treated as participative partners, they may also have real contributions to make through their insights, sharing their perspective, and responses, that may make all the difference to the success of the communication. Except in the rarest of circumstances, we do not speak of absolutely novel things of which no one, except us, has any knowledge. It is therefore fair to assume that a listener brings existing information, ideas, viewpoint, and experience to the situation and it would be at peril to the communication if we ignored this and went on speaking in a monologue. No doubt, some spoken communication such as conversations and discussions are meant to be interactive, while others such as speeches and presentations are less so. However, I am sure we have all seen some individuals who, once they get the opportunity to speak in a discussion, are quite unwilling to let it go. Rather than an interactive dialogue, they make mini speeches and brook no interruption! We would also have seen the rolling of eyes, or the seething exasperation of the poor listeners who seem trapped. A gracious speaker not only makes points relevant to the listeners, utilizing the preparation in terms of audience analysis to anticipate the listeners' needs and, does so in a manner that involves them through choice of pronouns, examples, and details, that it seems less of a 'talking at' or worse, 'talking down' and more of a conversation, even when the speaker occupies most of the talking time. Moreover, such speakers constantly scan the listeners for continuous feedback and have the flexibility and ability to respond by thinking on their feet. In contexts where active participation of others is possible, they easily share the talking time and take interest in their role as listener just as in that as speaker.

EFFECTIVE BODY LANGUAGE

Remember the example at the beginning of the chapter, of a candidate at an interview, not quite succeeding in impress the panelists with her abilities or making the most of her experience? Given that the candidate has qualifications, skills, and experience well-aligned to the requirements, and given that she has taken adequate care to prepare in terms of having concrete fact, details at her fingertips, as well as presence of mind to handle on-the-feet thinking, why would she be unable to impress at the interview? Why would she not be able to present herself as well-suited to the requirements?

The answer is that perhaps she is overlooking a host of other crucial elements of the communication that add up to give a meaning to the receiver. For that meaning, in this case, to be in accordance with all that the candidate possesses, it is essential that the words are supplemented by all other elements of the exchange. Without careful preparation along the way we discussed above, we would be on a very weak footing at the time of the actual spoken communication.

Given that preparation has been done adequately, some very crucial elements come into play at the moment of actual presentation of the idea through spoken words. The value and interpretation of a lot of what we say is determined by not the words in isolation but in combination with the way they are presented. This applies as much to speaking at an interview as to a formal presentation or a conversation with colleagues or other people in the work context. Not only may our spoken words be decoded in quite different ways depending upon the way they are said, even more importantly, the worth of our ideas is affected by many accompanying signals. This happens largely at the subconscious level and has a crucial impact on the way the communication is received. As most of us are not professional actors or terribly good liars, we are quite likely to reveal our real attitudes and accompanying feelings about the subject, about the occasion, or about the listeners, through cues we may send out without being aware of doing so.

The biggest advantage of spoken communication is lost when these cues begin to clash with our verbal messages, rather than support and supplement them. It is a fact that people are more likely to trust our non-verbal signals over our verbal ones when they perceive them to be at variance. It is generally believed—and perhaps rightly so—that although people may be able to plan, rehearse, and quite glibly mouth words they may not believe in, it is much harder to control the numerous features of accompanying non-verbal cues. Not only do we, therefore, need to be aware of the importance of ensuring that a coherent meaning emerges out of the sum of all verbal and non-verbal messages reaching the receiver from us, but also to be careful about all the messages that may be going from us to the receiver.

By being aware of these rather than only focusing on the verbal content of what we are saying we can be in a better position to prevent inadvertent messages reaching the listener and confusing or contradicting our main message. **The receiver is more likely to continue to trust the speaker— including their intentions and their material—if they see a connection between the words and the unconscious cues that accord higher credibility to these.** It is true that many of us worry about spoken communication precisely because of this. We fear that such situations lead to unavoidable nervousness and keeping our body language cues aligned with our message becomes very challenging. In fact, we fear that our heightened state of nervousness will be glaringly obvious to the audience. However, it helps to remember that the receiver has no way of knowing what we as the speaker are really feeling. All they can interpret is what they see and hear, and what they sense from that. I have pointed out to many a speaker who feared that their shaking legs gave away their nervousness, that the audience did not even notice it. In fact, if we display cues that are interpreted as confidence and comfort, we not only begin to be seen as confident and comfortable, but we also begin to feel truly confident and comfortable.

Body language cues have many possible interpretations, and the listener generally combines a number of these to reach a conclusion about the feelings underlying these. For example, if we are standing behind a podium or keeping too much distance between the listeners and ourselves without giving much thought to it, the receivers would have no way of knowing whether it is an oversight on our part or whether it indicates a lack of conviction in the material, lack of the desire to really reach out to the audience, defensiveness, or fear of the audience. They may want to match it with cues they get from the facial expression, voice, or gestures to interpret. It would be in our interest to try to ensure, as far as possible, that we mask our nervousness, anxiety and convey positive meanings through our body language. Once the listeners begin to respond positively, we may actually begin to feel more comfortable and confident. On the contrary, if we neglect this and give cues that may be interpreted as unfriendly, uninterested, or nervous, the audience may turn off, refuse to engage with the ideas, or actually respond in a hostile manner thus adding to our nervousness and defeating the objective of the communication.

The non-verbal part of our spoken communication can be used to project confidence, ownership of ideas, conviction in what we say, appropriate attitude such as enthusiasm, concern, and sympathy. 'All well and good!', one may say. 'But how does one project these?' We project these through everything at our command—from our choice of words and structure to every cue that may support and amplify the value of our words. Through appropriate vocabulary and diction we maximize our ability to faithfully capture our idea without any loss. At the same time we would wish to convey a number of other things—for example, our feeling of excitement, our conviction in the value of what we are espousing, our enthusiasm about an idea or proposal, a sense of concern or caution. In addition to, or alternately to reflecting these in words, we have at our command, a number of other cues. Let us look at the elements of body language that we may employ to supplement our verbal message and to utilize a powerful advantage of spoken communication available to us through the choice of this mode.

Facial expression

When presenting our ideas whether in a conversation, a formal discussion, presentation or speech, a wooden expression is likely to be taken by listeners as conveying extreme self-consciousness and nervousness. Such a meaning is attributed because that is not the expression that one normally associates with a relaxed state of mind. In normal life we express a lot through our facial expressions, whether it is through our eyes, mouth, or facial muscles in general. We express joy, excitement, keenness, surprise, concern, sympathy, fear, worry and a range of feelings by variations in our facial muscles. **By freezing our face and not expressing feelings as we normally do, we convey to others that we are**

feeling uncomfortable and self-conscious which may be quite contrary to the impression we are trying to make through our words. At the same time, we lose out on an effective way to support our words and to show full involvement in what we are saying and in communicating with the listeners. Worse, these contrary messages may be taken as conveying lack of confidence and conviction in the ideas we are sharing.

A very important part of facial expression is smiling. During practical training sessions, many a times I need to remind presenters to smile, unless there is a specific reason for not doing so. Let us think of our own experience as listeners. How do we regard a person who comes up to speak with a smile on the face as compared to one does not do so? With the exception of sombre occasions such as a condolence meeting or a crisis situation, we expect the speaker to approach us and the task of speaking to us with an eagerness and comfort, and a smile effectively conveys these positive messages. Of course, during the length of the talk or discussion, what is being said will vary and a smile may not be appropriate for all parts of the speech. As listeners we get a sense of the speaker's comfort when they appear to be speaking in a natural manner and that implies that their facial expression would vary according to the words and the underlying feeling they are trying to communicate in various parts of their interaction. In fact, a frozen expression—even if it is a smile—begins to jar after a while. Excessive and continuous smiling or smiling at inappropriate parts, may convey nervousness for a casual approach to the communication, and thus mar the impact we have on our listeners. Smiling at the beginning is a great way to show our friendliness to the audience and a comfort with the occasion as well as the pleasure we take in speaking to the listeners. Smiling when it suits the lightness of what is being said is also appropriate and indicates to the listener the sense in which the words are to be interpreted.

It would be useful to apply this insight into our responses as listeners to our own facial expressions when we take the speaking role.

Eye contact

Looking at the person or persons we are speaking to is the best way to connect with them. While cultural variations may determine the extent to which people across hierarchies of position or age, or across genders, may hold the gaze of others, it is generally true that avoiding the eyes of one's listeners is taken as a sign of nervousness, indifference, or hauteur. When we are trying to communicate face-to-face with someone through our spoken word, it is given that we are trying to gain their attention and to engage them with our ideas. **Eye contact is a powerful way to make that connection between speaker and listener. Even in a one-on-many speaking context, it is crucial to establish this connection with as many individuals as possible.**

How many times have we, in the position of listener, felt almost slighted by the speaker's apparent unawareness of our presence, as gathered from the fact that he or she never once glanced at us? If we put our mind to it we may not recall much of the communication or the speaker. It is easy to slip into the role of a passive audience member rather than an active listener when the connection with the speaker has not been made for us. Along with other things, the speaker's eye contact with all listeners creates that sense of involvement in the communication.

It is also important to keep in mind that the speaker who avoids eye contact by looking away at the wall or ceiling or notes or supplementary material, is also taken by the audience to be ill-at-ease and that, in turn, fails to convey a sense of ownership of the ideas being presented. By contrast, the speaker who makes good eye contact with listeners also, indirectly, establishes both ownership of ideas and the eagerness to convey these to us. Yet another way in which eye contact pays rich dividends is in helping us utilize one of the biggest advantages of spoken communication over the written one—namely, the opportunity to immediately respond to the way our ideas are being received by modifying our message in terms of further elaboration, clarification of unclear points, supporting with different examples or alternate approaches. The best way to gauge the listeners' responses is to keep our eyes on them rather than elsewhere, and to stay alert to what they display both verbally and non-verbally.

When we really care that out ideas get through clearly, we should be constantly connecting with our listeners by meeting their gaze, by observing and responding to what we can gauge about the reception of our ideas. One may ask if it is possible to do so when the audience exceeds twenty or thirty. Of course, it is not. However, our purpose may be served quite well by attempting to maintain eye contact with people across the room and doing so in a manner that is clearly not an above-the-heads sweep of the room but actually connects with the eyes of people in various sections of the audience. The audience knows the impossibility of actually making eye contact with each and every one of them and is usually satisfied by the positive implications they derive from seeing the speaker trying to connect with the audience in a direct manner.

Voice

Enunciation: The way we actually form words when speaking determines to a large extent, how well a listener gets them. Unless each sound is clear and distinct, the entire basis on which spoken communication works, breaks down. For listeners to be able to follow the spoken words of language, these need to reach their ears in a manner that they are recognizable as known words that convey a meaning. For sentences to have meaning for the listener, they need to be received as distinct grammatical units. When words are mumbled or parts of sentences are not distinct, the listener has to do extra work in guessing at the meaning. **When each word is not distinct from the other and sentences from each other, what the listener gets is a jumble of sounds rather than recognizable verbally coded bits of meaning that may be added up to give a coherent sense.** Most listeners would quickly get tired of this and yield to distractions to occupy their minds.

It is important that we do the best we can to ensure that we form our words carefully, paying special attention to vowel sounds and ending of words, making sure that the invisible punctuation of sentences is made audible through our expression. Imagine the confusion caused if the sentence, 'Come, let's eat, my dear friend' is not spoken with sufficient care in communicating the intended meaning as indicated by the punctuation. Further, without adequate care in enunciation we may end up causing confusion between words such as fifteen and fifty, ever and never, cost and cause, graze and gaze, employer and employee.

Once we realize that we tend to eat up the ends of our sentences, we can consciously take care to take sufficiently deep breaths so as to not run out of air when we reach the end of our sentences. If there are certain vowel sounds that we find that we typically get wrong, leading to confusion in meaning conveyed, we can practice these sufficiently so as to avoid the problem. To get our tongue loose and be able to say words that we find hard to pronounce in a clear and distinct way there is no way other than practice.

Slowing down and taking care over clear enunciation will always bear fruit in terms of our listeners' better comprehension of our speech. Remember the tongue twisters we used to challenge each other with as children? We gain a lot of confidence in our ability to get our tongues over tricky sounds when we can easily and distinctly say aloud such arrangements of challenging vowel and consonant sounds.

Why not try some of the following, keeping our aim not breakneck speed but clarity as we speak?

Try practising with these tongue twisters

- 'The sixth sick sheik's sixth sheep is sick.'
- 'We surely shall see the sun shine soon.'
- 'Lesser leather never weathered wetter weather better.'
- 'She was a thistle sifter and sifted thistles through a thistle sieve.'

And my particular favourite:

'Amidst the mists and coldest frosts,
With stoutest wrists and loudest boasts,
He thrusts his fist against the posts
And still insists he sees the ghosts.'

[I find that getting our tongue around –sts endings is particularly hard and many people mumble these or indistinctly articulate such words, leaving the listeners guessing at the words.]

Tone: I am sure we all know how easy it is to succumb to a lullaby, which has a soporific effect not because of its words but because of the tone. One can read out the editorial or a dense article on finance or law, or even the telephone directory, in a lullaby tone and a baby would still fall asleep! The same effect can be created in fully grown adults too by an unvaried, droning tone in presentations and speeches. This doesn't have to be so. In fact, tone is a very important tool in spoken communication. Used appropriately it can infuse extra shades of meaning into our words. Through variations in tone we can sound warm, friendly, sarcastic, strong, harsh, excited, disinterested, happy, worried, and much more. It would be a pity to throw away this potential and to present our listeners with a bland tone that adds nothing to the literal meaning of the words and in fact, turns them off.

Imagine how many meanings can be given to the following sentences by variations in tone:

'Are you ready for action?'
'When are you going to do something?'
'I'd rather be flying off to laze on the beach.'

If we find that there is room for improvement in our intonation and articulation, it means that there is a lot of potential that we are missing out on to make our speaking more effective. It would do us good to practise putting more feeling into our way of speaking through our tone by trying out variations on sentences spoken with different emphases, lift and fall of voice, to bring different meaning to the word. Take the following:

'Take a chair and sit down.'
'Why don't you close the door?'

You will discover that by little variations in tone these can turn into a simple request, a strict order, a gentle suggestion, an exasperated reprimand, or a sarcastic response. And here lies one of the beauties of spoken communication. When we choose to speak we should be utilizing the extra opportunities it brings to us; if we are to ignore or overlook these, we may as well not speak but use other modes of communication that have their own advantages.

Pace/pauses

It is often easy to overlook something as simple as the pace of speaking. When we are in the listener's position we may be annoyed or put off by speakers who go to one of the two extremes in this regard—either so slow that we feel insulted or begin to wonder about the person's command over the material, or at such breakneck speed that we give up trying to keep up with it after a while, and begin to suspect that the person is in a great hurry to finish this ordeal. When it comes to our turn to speak we may also be aware of how we may begin to race when we are uncomfortable or slow down terribly when we seem to not get a grip on our nerves. Any concern about the rapport with the listener or with ensuring their ease in following our words takes a complete backseat. When this happens, we have, once again compromised on maximizing the full potential offered by spoken communication.

In fact, if used well, the very pace of speaking may become an important tool for adding additional shades of meaning and engaging the listeners through variations and well-placed pauses. **On reflection we may recall that all outstanding and memorable speakers that we may have heard, used—among other things—pauses and variations in speaking pace to create and keep interest and to signal significant parts.** These also provide an aural sense of the punctuation in sentences. Variations in speaking pace may be effectively used to indicate excitement or to drive a significant point, while avoiding both a slow, plodding pace and a breathless, breakneck one. An unvarying pace may indicate negatives such as anxiety or disinterest.

Pace and volume of speaking are also important ways in which we may indicate our comfort and confidence as well as support our intended meaning. Either extreme of high or low pitch or an oddly fluctuating pitch is taken to indicate acute emotional stress. The receptivity of listeners to a speaker who displays this, goes down. Similarly, inappropriate volume of speaking given the size of the audience and the venue may be seen as an indicator of nerves. By bringing variations in our volume we may easily indicate excitement, create anticipation, humour, or suspense.

Thus, in addition to conveying the ideas to the listener through spoken words, the voice is crucial in adding layers of meaning through elements such as tone, pace and volume. As a speaker, therefore, it is important for us to keep in mind that our voice should add to the effectiveness of our communication and not provide cues that may have any negative connotations for our listeners. Energy, commitment, sincerity, irony, emphasis and many other messages are conveyed through our voice. The confident speaker has these elements of voice fully under control and makes the words come alive so as to involve the listeners and drive home their point. Even sleepy audiences nodding after a full meal wake up and take interest when a resonant and well-modulated voice reaches their ears! The trick to achieving the best results with voice is variation—don't allow your tone, pace, and volume to become set. Aim at having variety both for effect and to match the verbal content as well as to convey your sense of urgency, excitement, concern, or worry. Match your volume to the size of the audience. It seems obvious enough but in my experience, I have found many a candidate at an interview sitting a mere couple of feet away shouting at the volume to be heard across the walls in adjoining rooms and presenters speaking to around thirty people doing so softly as to be inaudible beyond the first row! Of course, you shouldn't worry about taking your normal volume and voice modulation a few shades up when addressing a large crowd in a big room. At the same time, you need to be aware of the amplification through a microphone, if you are using one. It is a good idea to check the volume before one begins, so that one is neither shouting at the audience, nor unduly soft.

While voice is the very medium through which we are primarily communicating, through speech, its best use is when listeners are facilitated to get a true and complete meaning of our words without shifting focus to the voice. When the latter happens, it is because of some incongruence with our words or because it fails to hold our attention or does not allow us to catch the words and their meanings. When the articulation, intonation, pitch, pace, and volume are just right for the intended meaning and suitably varied so as to keep in sync with the verbal content as well as for holding the attention of the listeners, we don't even notice these elements. But we immediately notice when any of them is inappropriate. We tend to make judgements about a person's confidence and sincerity from the way they use the voice in an interaction. A shaky or high pitch is taken to signal nervousness or extreme emotion, while inability to intonate is generally interpreted as lack of conviction, enthusiasm, and genuine interest in communicating. Inappropriately high or low volume and pace may again signal a lack of confidence.

OUR POSTURE AND MOVEMENTS

It helps our communication greatly if we use our awareness of the kinds of messages that may be inferred simply from how we sit or stand or move about during an interaction or a speech/presentation. By neglecting this element of our communication, we may allow it to indicate lack of comfort and confidence, thus undoing all the good impression we may have created through other elements. **Standing upright to indicate energy and confidence, or sitting in a manner indicating enthusiasm and interest in reaching out to our listeners, leaning forward, reducing the distance between our listeners and ourselves, standing still when coming to a crucial point, making sure to position ourselves in a manner that we** are in view of our audience, are all ways in which we may use our posture and movement to add to our effectiveness.

Gestures

Our hands need not become heavy and inconvenient appendages when we sit or stand before others to speak. Rather, we should use our hand movement to indicate our comfort and confidence in our speaking role and to supplement or emphasize the meanings we are conveying verbally. As in the case of all non-verbal elements of our communication, gestures should appear so natural to the speaker and the words being spoken that they should not draw any attention to themselves. If they do, it is because of incongruence with the verbal meaning or because they are perceived to be excessive or inappropriate. The best gestures are the ones that appear natural on us and we need to be guided by what we can use without getting distracted from our attention to the myriad other things we need to take into account. One must also be aware of cultural norms in the case of gestures as these are, like most non-verbals, very much shaped by culture. In a new setting, it may be best to observe and correctly understand the way gestures are used and interpreted so as to not make a gaffe.

Appearance

Shakespeare wrote, 'the apparel oft proclaims the man'. Our first impression about others seems to come largely from our appearance and our clothes are an important part of it. People read meanings or implications in how we are dressed on a particular occasion. This is, no doubt, a culturally determined dimension whereby we perceive certain ways of dressing as appropriate in terms of showing adequate courtesy and significance for the occasion and others as being inappropriate for the context. It may even be a matter of organizational culture as to the expectations and the divergences tolerated within it. It is generally advisable to dress conservatively for formal occasions unless you have certain knowledge of other expectations. When not possible to determine norms, it is better to err on the side of a conservative style rather than a flamboyant or adventurous one. Tidiness and good grooming are always appreciated and give a positive impression to others. Our care over our appearance gives a subtle message of our self-assurance, and in turn, makes the audience more ready to listen to us. It also shows that we respect the occasion and our audience enough to take care over our appearance and to not present a dishevelled and unkempt appearance.

What sets apart a speaker who is perceived to be engaging, confident and credible from one who seems to be unsure, insipid, and lacking ownership of what they are merely mouthing, boils down to 'Being in control of all elements of body language'. Speakers from the first category are able to use all these elements to work for them in conveying the messages in as coherent a manner as possible, while ineffective speakers not only lose out on the additional support to their message from these additional cues, but end up conveying contradictory messages. With body-language, the overall rule is—what blends seamlessly into the material and draws no attention to itself is best. Whatever body language allows our intended meanings to become clearer through emphasis or substitution or mirroring, without drawing attention to itself, will effectively contribute in a complementary role to the effectiveness of the communication. So, to every question about how much is right, the answer remains 'just enough'— sufficient to appear natural and uncontrived and to support the verbal content without drawing attention away from it. The primary cue should remain the spoken words, rather than the gesture or movement or eye contact becoming ends in themselves. When we talk of these elements as part of the body language accompanying spoken communication, it is different from how any of these elements may be used to communicate by themselves. Here their best use is as secondary, reinforcing cues, while the major attention remains on the meaning of the words.

PRACTICE TAKES US CLOSER TO PERFECTION

With so many elements to manage, it is no wonder that we are often unable to use speaking to its full potential. This is where the importance of practice comes in. Whether it is about varying our facial expressions or about maintaining eye contact, about our posture or movement, or our gestures, practising as part of the preparation can immensely add to our ability to use these more effectively.

Practising means trying out various things and figuring out what works best for us. It helps us to seek some feedback on how effectively these non-verbal cues are conveying what we intend to. Such feedback may be obtained from others by asking them to focus particularly on these and in telling us what sense they derived from them. Another source of feedback can be ourselves. We can record our voice and play it back to get a sense of our clarity of enunciation, and the additional shades of meaning that we were attempting to convey through our variations in speaking pace, intonation, pitch, and volume. We can also video record ourselves in various speaking situations. We may find that we are able to see ourselves to some extent as others do and be able to assess whether our body language is helping in better conveying our thoughts and feelings by supporting the verbal part of our communication. The more we speak and the more critical we are, the more we can learn about our weak spots and the better we can address these so as to improve our effectiveness.

The solution to furthering our existing effectiveness in our use of body language lies in awareness of such problems that may be hindering our ideas from reaching listeners in the best manner, and through practice to address the specific problems that we become aware of through more critical understanding, self-analysis, introspection, and feedback.

We have debunked the myth that speaking effectively is an innate ability or a matter of luck and shown how there are steps we may take to enhance our effectiveness as speakers.

Now let us turn, in the next chapter, to specific speaking contexts. We may grant that some element of luck will always be there but we should do all that we can to make luck work for us. As Thomas Jefferson said, 'I'm a great believer in luck, and I find the harder I work, the more I have of it.' With proper care in analysing our existing level of comfort and effectiveness, and by approaching the task of communicating through the spoken word in a systematic manner, we can arm ourselves with a tool that could transform the impact we leave on others.

CHAPTER 3

Conversations and Discussions

The ability to present a positive, self-assured image in all interactions is a valued one, whether in formal meetings or in unstructured interactions such as conversations and discussions. While we may give a lot of attention to our preparation for a formal meeting, we need to remind ourselves that we need not wait only for such formal occasions but may avail of the numerous opportunities for informal interactions to leave a good impression through our spoken skills. As one rises up to senior positions, such interactions become more useful and more noticeable as one is in a more central place, critically observed by many. Suaveness and ease on such occasions is very helpful in rapport building and increasing one's network and sphere of influence. Such interactions also open up the possibility of learning something new, whether on a topic of interest or in a new area, and about the people we interact with. It also gives us an opportunity to make others comfortable by letting them know us better in terms of our own personality, outlook, and views about various things. Of course, we need only offer as much disclosure as we ourselves feel comfortable with and the other shows interest in receiving. When our messages and the impression we give of our attitudes and views comes across as consistent in formal and informal channels, it adds to our credibility.

Developing this skill is important for all those aspiring for senior positions not only because it is something that will be called for in such positions but also because it is a sure way to stand out and get noticed. Whether it is getting noticed through engaging, pleasant, and intelligent conversation or through excellent input in a meeting or discussion, this ability makes you stand out from others and be remembered for positive reasons. Sitting like a wallflower during such occasions is a waste of our presence there in terms of value addition to the discussion and also provides no way for people to know our ideas, views, or information and to thus form a positive impression of our personality, sharpness of mind, critical ability, or knowledge base.

So, whether you are a leader or aspiring to be one, you would definitely benefit from gaining greater awareness of the requirements for communication in small groups for purposes such as conversations or small talk with new acquaintances or colleagues, and discussions/meetings for reporting, information sharing, brainstorming, problem solving and decision making.

CONVERSATIONS/ SMALL TALK

This is an important, but often overlooked kind of communication that works as the glue binding the social links or as the lubricant that smoothens the interactions between people. One cannot hope to work among people and be productive and happy if one's engagement with others is limited to formal purposes. **Being able to have general conversations or small talk is essential to bond with colleagues and team members, and to build a sense of camaraderie.** And these are essential building blocks for productive and happy working conditions in a workplace. When it is a case of people outside our circle or those we may have newly met, breaking the ice and making conversation may seem quite daunting for many of us. But when we shy away from such interactions, we forego a number of opportunities: to make a good impression; to ease into the more formal part of the interaction; to discover common interests; and to make a connection, perhaps even a friend.

Small talk allows us to win people over by showing positive personal qualities such as openness, warmth and self-assurance. It is an assertive person, secure in their own self, who can make the first move in terms of breaking the ice with someone. It thus creates a strong first impression and when backed up by content that is relevant and interesting to the listener, goes a long way in making a personal impact while laying the foundations for a cordial working relationship. Naturally, this is much more crucial, as well as visible, when it comes to inter-organizational interactions that are required more and more at the top levels of management. No wonder that this ability is seen as not merely desirable but as essential for growth on the path to top rungs of the hierarchy. Within our own work place, the relationships that one builds through talking and listening to each other are immensely valuable in our growth and satisfaction. Our credibility and reputation in an organization build as much from our experience and competence as from our communications—both formal and informal.

We cannot make a very positive impression on people if we make no attempt at conversation and restrict ourselves to only formal, serious discussions. While we may think it shows us in a positive light as someone focused and serious, we may inadvertently be giving a signal of being haughty or unconcerned about others, or limited in our range of interests and knowledge. Naturally, we would want to establish our seriousness in approach when it comes to our area of expertise, but that is not necessarily in contradiction to our pleasantness as a person. When we speak in contexts where doing so may not be a requirement but a choice, we indicate that we are comfortable and self-assured enough to make that choice. In fact, it is a common experience that on most such occasions, people often choose to be quiet, waiting for the other person to make the first move or questioning the need for speaking or wondering what to say. This is exactly why we stand out from the crowd when we do make the choice to speak and go on to engage in interesting conversation or discussion. Our silence may be masked with appearing busy in something or even in our thoughts and we may think that the other person will not notice. Or even that they will think kindly of us as suffering from diffidence or shyness. But there is a danger that our silence or reluctance to go beyond the minimum polite but empty and clichéd remarks, may be seen not as diffidence or reticence but as unfriendliness.

While we may think that we will save ourselves for the big presentation or the formal part of the meeting for which we have prepared ourselves with due care, we must also keep in mind that being tongue-tied, shy, and awkward in the informal contexts of business does not serve us well at all. Our not making the most of such opportunities to reach out to people—whether internal or external—may harm further interactions and business with that person as well as create a negative personal impression about us as disinterested, self-absorbed, or snobbish.

Our network is often built primarily on the strength of the impression we create through our informal interactions. **When we speak to people in a comfortable and easy manner there are many positive messages about ourselves that we give out. We show that we are willing to step out of our preoccupations and extend ourselves. We show friendliness and an easy, relaxed attitude, and that we don't feel threatened or vulnerable so as to retreat in defense.** Further, by the content and manner of our conversation, we show the breadth of our knowledge and interests. We may also be pleasantly surprised by finding common interests that help to build a rapport with people.

There is no doubt that the ability to break the ice and carry on conversations or indulge in some small talk in the workplace, in the lulls between formal situations is a valuable one for all professionals. One can create a positive impression about one's ability, knowledge, and personality, and create an atmosphere of comfort for the formal communication. This can be of immense importance in interactions with external people, but it also has immense value even in everyday, internal communication. After all, making a good impression on people with whom you have to work and on those whose opinion of you matters for career growth and fulfilment of your aspirations, is of great value. My discussions with a large number of senior managers have revealed to me how this ability can become an important consideration when it comes to making the transition from middle to higher management. A number of senior mid-level managers that I have spoken to in workshops on communication strategies for leadership roles, have confided that it was felt in the company's higher circles that although they were eminently qualified for the next move in terms of requisite domain knowledge, technical skills, and experience, they were found wanting in this area. All things being equal, the weakest link in the communication skill-set often emerges as that of the ability to be at ease in interactions with a wide range of people. For polishing the content of formal communications we have time, and may also take recourse to assistance from others, although for delivering the content in an effective manner we definitely need to develop our own skills. But when it comes to unplanned, impromptu, informal communication occasions, we are really on our own, both in terms of what to say and how to say it. Polishing this skill gives us the confidence to step forward and project ourselves as open, outgoing, warm, congenial, self-assured individuals in interactions that may not be apparently crucial, but that, nevertheless, play a big role in others' perceptions of us.

The more we practise this skill, the more we polish it. 'Where do we practise it?', you may ask? There are many occasions: Imagine you are in a room with people you don't know. It could be while waiting for others to arrive for a meeting, or during a tea-break during a talk where you did not get to interact with all the audience members, or you are visiting another organization and are in the lounge with others who are also waiting. What do you do? Well, if you are not comfortable breaking the ice, or see no value in the effort, I am sure you can come up with a variety of interesting things to do that make you seem very busy and preoccupied. But what *should* you do? It would be best to speak to those around you. If you cannot get started on 'business talk' straight away, it should not mean that you sit or stand quietly, putting the onus on others to strike up a conversation and to keep it going. An assertive person does not shy away from making the first move and does not hesitate about striking up a conversation. Thinking negatively about the other person or oneself and imagining bad scenarios if one speaks up, is the sign of an unsure, apprehensive, diffident, self-absorbed, or haughty person. If you are—or even wish to appear as—someone who is comfortable and self-assured, you need to reach out in a pleasant manner and try to make conversation with people rather than keep to yourself. Remember, the other person or persons have nothing much to go on to make an assessment of you if you don't speak. And assess they will, because it is human nature to do so! Why not speak and let them assess you on your views, your knowledge, and your personality? Why not make an acquaintance who may remember you at some point in the future in a situation where it would help to be a known entity, and moreover, as someone who made a good first impression?

There are other occasions when we are with colleagues at work but in a relaxed and informal context. Water-cooler moments, conversations over a coffee break, and brief chats during a lull in the work day provide opportunities for face-to-face interactions to make a positive impression and to strike a rapport with people that will ease our work environment. The key questions to reflect upon are: Are we able to hold an interesting conversation on topics other than our work role with our colleagues? When we run into people at the water cooler, the coffee corner, on any such social space at work, do we contribute to the conversation or smile weakly, avoid direct contact and escape? Can we and do we participate in conversations without agony and come away feeling good about both ourselves and our colleagues? Or do we feel inhibited, tongue-tied, and awkward? Is it because we are not sure of being able to have anything interesting and relevant to say or is it that we are unsure of the effectiveness of our impromptu articulation of ideas? Or is it the perception that we need to only engage in 'meaningful' discussions on significant issues, especially those where we have particular knowledge and authority? Whatever the reason, we are throwing away opportunities to create an impression, build connections, and learn something.

First of all, we need to dispel the thought that only 'meaningful' discussions on significant issues are important for our impact on others. We need to understand that the impression we create is a cumulative effect of all interactions and the more we are able to interact with others in various ways, the more we increase our total impression. In fact, when people interact with you on general topics and outside of formal contexts, they may feel that they are getting to see the 'real' you and favourable impressions cast here may then carry off into those made in the formal contexts. Of course, we have to keep in mind that the most favourable impressions are created when we do it well! However, even a willing – albeit halting and awkward – interaction is better in comparison to not participating in such interactions at all. Not interacting at all may give off unfavourable impressions such as standoffishness, snobbery, or hauteur. Such attempts are also to our advantage as they give us practice that helps us to break out of our diffidence and gradually reduces our discomfort.

Once we are aware of these wasted opportunities and the value of changing our approach, we may analyse what is holding us back. By doing so we will be in a better position to fill in the gaps and equip ourselves to benefit from such interactions in terms of building stronger relationships with colleagues and leaving a favourable impression on them about our personal qualities. We can then take care with required preparation and practice, necessary to give us the confidence to use this form of spoken communication to our advantage.

The occasions for small talk are many and on all occasions a memorable impact may be left in the minds of people we interact with. Slowly, by a process of accretion, the perception of you as a smart, well-informed, balanced, confident, caring person takes root. People know how to regard you, when to turn to you (or not!), what to look up to you for, and the like. Such an assessment is hardly ever formulated in words and people may be hard-pressed to say how the perceptions have been formed—except, perhaps, for some very striking or spectacular occasions—but they are very strongly etched in people's minds. It is an unpardonable disservice to ourselves if, simply by oversight, we do not maximize the impact we make on others through our everyday interactions and informal communications. It is easy to fall into the trap of seeing others having a great impact on those they interact with, and to credit it to personal magnetism or to allege craftiness, rather than to deconstruct the process and to see it as an ability that we too may master. All you need is awareness of its great value, observation, and willingness to unlearn and learn.

The need for unlearning may come in because sometimes it is our perceptions of 'proper' and 'improper', 'acceptable' and 'unacceptable' that may need to be re-examined and

117

re-framed. I have had occasions when some perceptive, mid-level executive has accepted that their ineptness in small talk and social graces goes back to socialization, usually by parents and other senior family members, that reinforced the idea that one must keep to oneself, not speak in front of elders or outsiders, and not talk for the sake of talking. When such individuals see a person who is comfortable taking the lead in informal as well as formal communication situations, they tend to attribute it to inborn ability rather than to a similar process, only in the opposite direction. The person's formative years may have been spent in an environment where articulation of ideas, confidence in expressing one's thoughts, comfort in speaking to new people, and the like, were praised and rewarded. Thus, it is useful to recognize that it is an acquired ability and one that is polished by practice. And of course, we make the effort to polish and practise only that which is valued. When we begin to see that such ability gets people noticed, increases their network, and creates a positive impression, we feel motivated to make the effort to enhance our comfort level in this kind of communication. We must make the effort with the knowledge that it will take some conscious effort, but it *can* be done—slowly but quite surely! So, how do we go about it?

VOCABULARY

The first step is to identify the ingredients of this form of communication. Words are the essential building blocks of conversations as of all spoken communication. **Building up** a rich and deep reservoir of vocabulary through listening, reading and making it ours by absorbing it into our own communications is the most basic preparation for translating our ideas and thoughts into messages to be conveyed to others. We must all have encountered people who can frame ideas very vividly and clearly. Such people stand out from average speakers who often leave much to be desired. One of the ways to enhance our clarity of expression is by increasing the range of words at our disposal so that we can make good choices with a view to appropriateness and correctness. Our sensitivity to the context is often displayed through our choice of words and if we are hampered by a limited vocabulary, we may leave a bad impression with the receiver perceiving it as insensitivity or uncouthness rather than the fact that we did not have other words at our disposal.

At the same time, we should avoid pedestrian and clichéd expressions so as to make what we say interesting and memorable through our style of expression of ideas and turn of phrases. While doing so, our awareness of context should enable us to assess the level of the receiver so that we don't alienate them or create an impression of talking down at them. With the inbuilt disadvantage of spoken communication that words have to be instantly recognized and decoded, the use of simpler language becomes a necessary requirement. We must, therefore, keep in mind that although building a deep vocabulary base is always in our interest, it is not necessary that we use all the words at our disposal regardless of our receivers. Speaking merely to impress with the sound of our voice and the bombastic words at our disposal is quite unlikely to create a very positive impression on our listeners. We must aim at a level where our words are simple to follow, while being appropriate to the topic and its treatment. We must remember that 'simple' is a relative term, and it is important to keep our listeners' level as the yardstick rather than ourselves. It is also important to use words, phrases, and sentence structure that will roll off our tongues easily, rather than using the latest buzzwords, which we may not be able to use comfortably. This is also true of idiomatic usage that we may not be able to carry off with ease. One also has to be careful to avoid words that could be seen as offensive to our listeners or politically inappropriate. We may need to remind ourselves that informal conversations with people in the work context, or even in a social setting with colleagues, do not warrant a casual, let-your-hair-down approach. While we may speak in a much freer manner with those inside our close circle, it is best to be careful with the appropriateness of the choice of words in conversations with those outside it.

BUILDING A WIDE INFORMATION BASE

Often we do not try to make small talk or converse with people outside of structured interactions, because we are not sure of these two questions: What do we talk about? What do we avoid? Let us begin with the first.

Naturally, no amount of self-assurance will get us very far

if we have nothing to talk about. Knowledge in our technical area may not be the best subject to bring up in small talk as it may be seen as talking shop. We have many other contexts in which to establish our expertise and depth of knowledge. It would be better to display some other facets of our personality in these less formal interactions. **People generally find those interesting who have a unique and interesting area of interest or even better, interesting ideas or information or perspective on issues pertaining to mutual areas of interest.** However, if the uniqueness borders on eccentricity or oddity, it is unlikely to be seen as attractive. Nor does a rabid belief in the rightness of our ideas or obsession with our perspective make us appear interesting and worth engaging with. We should aim at presenting ourselves as balanced and open-minded, with something interesting to share, but not exclusively focused on our views or perspective. A wide knowledge base and information about issues in the world around us and the world at large, and balanced views on these are not to be gained overnight. It is a storehouse we build up, in the manner of a recurring deposit, over a long period of time. But even if he have not consciously done so yet, it is better to start now than never.

In order to prepare ourselves for engaging in conversations on general topics and issues outside of our specialized knowledge or authority, both as interesting speakers and interested listeners, we need to adopt a general habit of wider reading than only our particular technical field. Developing a critical mind that processes information rather than storing only trivia would stand us in good stead when it comes to making an impact with our ideas in conversations. Rather than attempting to memorize facts and details and rattle these off like a well-rehearsed parrot, it is better to combine openness of mind with a critical approach so as to have well-founded opinions with depth as well as breadth. Curiosity about the past and current state, as well as projections for the future, on a range of subjects, helps us in coming across as an interesting person to talk to. Every bit of information that we accumulate through our reading and other sources, every reflection, and analysis, is preparation for conversations. The more varied and deep our interests and knowledge, the greater the range of people you can participate in conversations with. And the ability and comfort in speaking with a wide range of people is useful to gain as its importance does not get less however high we may climb. However, it is not a question of ability and comfort alone, but also of attitude. In order to make the effort to prepare ourselves for conversations with people regardless of their position, we should genuinely take interest in, and be willing to open ourselves to others, and value the benefits of doing so in terms of good relationships, a strong and wide information base, and wide perspective on issues.

We must also give thought to what we must avoid in our conversations. It is good to keep in mind that small talk is not the occasion for delving deep into intricate issues and trying to settle them or to score a victory by establishing the superiority of our viewpoint over those of others. In Oscar Wilde's words, 'conversation should touch everything, but should concentrate itself on nothing'. Pleasant and non-controversial topics are best, rather than those where we may demonstrate our incisive mind or profound thinking. Criticizing one's seniors and colleagues is to be avoided; it may help to get some feelings off one's chest but does not show us in a positive light. In fact, all negative talk is best avoided. A good way to develop the conversation is by showing interest in the other person. At the same time, while asking questions to appear interested in the other person and in what they have to say, it is best to limit such questions to impersonal issues and about topics the other person is comfortable with. We should avoid anything that gives an impression of prying or encroaching on personal territory, especially in someone we do not know very well. Although we wish to appear self-assured as well as interested in the other person's views, we should take care that we don't appear to be prying. Not only should we refrain from making personal comments such as complimenting someone we have just been introduced to on their attire or their cologne, we should also keep away from asking for personal information. What we can do is to offer personal bits of information and see if the other person reciprocates, and leave it if they are not willing to delve into that area.

HOW DO WE TALK?

Hugh Fellows in his 1964 book, *The Art and Skill of Talking with People*, uses a striking metaphor for conversations as a tennis match where the same ball is volleyed between the players, rather than a game of golf where one player hits one ball repeatedly while the other hits another one. This is as relevant now as it was half a century ago. Turn-taking is an essential element of conversation as opposed to monologues. This cannot be divided equally, or set according to a formula which would make it very artificial. Even though turn-taking may not be as equal in proportion as in the case of a game of tennis, we must nevertheless keep in mind that our role is to take the ideas of the other person forward by appropriate responses rather than snatching the ball and proceeding to juggle it cleverly. For some parts of a dialogue, we may talk for a longer while but we must always engage with the points of others and keep the flow going, rather than break it to launch into something entirely unconnected, and perhaps of interest only to ourselves. **We must also be alert to the responses of the listener and be willing to ungrudgingly yield to them if and when they show keenness to respond.**

I am sure you have met a few people you remember as great conversationalists. It is a good idea to try to analyse their style. I suggest that you are likely to come up with something along these lines: a lively style—both verbal and non-verbal—involving a witty way with words, vivid descriptions, and complete involvement in the communication. We may also find that often such conversationalists tap into the almost universal interest in listening to stories with a human angle rather than pure facts or emphatic assertions. Such speakers have a way of recounting events and anecdotes that makes people and events come alive before the mind's eye of the listeners. If we recall such conversationalists as the ones that stand out for us, these attributes then, are what we must keep before us as the target in terms of polishing our own conversational style. The effort to build the ability of storytelling through practising it in conversations will serve us well by helping us engage with audiences in various speaking contexts. As we assume leadership positions, this ability will serve us well not only in breaking the ice with a greater number of people, but also in motivating and inspiring people, and in enthusing them with a sense of ownership and involvement.

For conversations, we should aim at an agreeable and amicable manner of speaking. **If we gauge by our own responses, we would agree that an aggressive, blunt, and rough style is a big turn-off and is interpreted as showing little respect for the listener.** Just as we dislike such a style in others, we must watch out for ourselves lapsing into it. Rather than help us win friends, such a manner is likely to make people dislike us and avoid us in future for casual conversations as well as perhaps prejudice them for formal interactions. Although we may feel that we must stand by our expressed views, a belligerent approach to protecting these should be avoided in conversations; it makes the environment non-conducive to amicability, which is the main note to be struck on such occasions. Instead, we should try to bring an easy and pleasant eagerness into the conversation to engage the other person in a discussion where good manners and respect for the other's point of view are of utmost importance. During conversations, our objective should not be to enter into debates or be set on converting people to our viewpoint or to 'win' over others. It is better to engage in a non-competitive and friendly give-and-take of ideas than to prove that we are right.

One may stand by one's point during small talk but not in an aggressive manner. We also need to be alert to the other person's responses. If we see them beginning to get agitated or angry, it is better to back off with a mild statement such as 'that is an interesting point of view' or 'I hadn't thought of it in that light' or even 'let us agree to disagree on that'. Said in a pleasant tone and accompanied by positive body language that does not reveal anger or resentment, this can work fine.

MEETINGS AND DISCUSSIONS

Deborah Barrett cites a study conducted by University of California, Los Angeles and the University of Minnesota that found that, 'executives on average to 40%–50% of their working hours in meetings'.[1] Given that so much time goes into this communication medium, it provides a great platform for us to sharpen our effectiveness through spoken communication and to make an impact on people we interact with. This is a great platform to impress. It is true that meetings

---

[1] Barrett, Deborah, *Leadership Communication*, New York: McGraw-Hill/Irwin, 2011.

are group communication occasions with common objectives rather than personal ones. This being true, another way to look at these occasions is as opportunities for making an impression on peers as well as seniors with one's sharpness of mind, diligence in preparation; crisp, lucid, and persuasive articulation of ideas that add value to the objective.

While we wait for opportunities for presentations and speeches as occasions to shine through our spoken skills, these may not be very frequent for some of us. However, meetings and discussions give us frequent opportunities to practise our spoken communication and to gain the confidence in our speaking ability that will serve us well in other occasions later. The features of effective speaking here are no different from those in formal presentations or speeches. We need to be clear and coherent, while staying focused and relevant. At the same time, we need to be alert to feedback on our input as well as to the direction of the discussion, so as to keep the communication dynamic. We also need to practise the consistency of our communication, given that in such face-to-face media, messages are received as much from verbal as from non-verbal cues. If we do not consciously ensure that we send out consistent and supportive messages through the non-verbal cues we provide, we are likely to send out messages we are not aware of, and these may result in contradicting or seriously compromising the value of our verbal messages. When we gain confidence in our ability to communicate effectively on such occasions of communicating in small groups, we can quite easily adapt ourselves to the requirements of one-to-many communication such as presentations and public speaking

OBJECTIVES OF MEETINGS AND DISCUSSIONS

Let us look at the common objectives of meetings and discussions and how, as individuals, we need to help in best serving these through our value-adding contribution. Such interactions are generally aimed at reporting and sharing information, generating ideas or brainstorming, planning, problem solving and decision making. While reporting and information sharing by definition involve more than one person, not all planning, decision making, or even idea generation need to be group processes and on many occasions we may do these activities in our individual capacity. But there are other occasions when it is either required or desirable that we process ideas through multiple minds in order to reach a decision or to plan something. The hope is that having more minds involved would enhance the quality of the resulting ideas and decisions. Very often meetings are meant to facilitate this pooling together, critiquing, and cross-fertilization of ideas. We may be included in the group because of the particular pool of knowledge, experience, and expertise we possess and the unique perspective we may bring to examine the ideas being discussed. Therefore, our aim should be to help meet this expectation by doing as much as we can to make our presence translate into value addition for the quality of the discussion and thus, for enhancing the quality of the outcome. **Our input in terms of ideas, facts, analyses, creative suggestions and solutions must help in meeting the objectives of the discussion.** The quality of this content is a function of our level of knowledge and preparation. As in other kinds of spoken communication, the basic strength of our information, knowledge, and ideas, is a prerequisite for impactful communication. If this base is weak, the effectiveness of our communication is doomed.

PREPARATION

We should be ready to put in adequate preparation so as to be equipped to contribute effectively to meeting the objectives of a discussion as well as to leave a positive impact of our contribution. Adequate preparation will show us in a favourable light by equipping us in terms of required data and information, analysis, or ideas and suggestions, as well as in terms of structured and clear articulation of our ideas.

Thorough preparation and practice, combined with reflection on our performance are the keys to improving our effectiveness in this very important kind of communication. If we wish to make an impact with the quality of our input as well as of our articulation and expression on such occasions, we cannot expect it to happen without preparation and practice. Of course, we must first inform ourselves of the importance of various elements of this particular form of communication, of its potential advantages, and of the objectives it is used to serve. We must also reflect on our existing level of comfort and effectiveness as a participant in discussions. Our preparation and practice should be informed by our awareness of the importance of such communication and by our reflection.

One worry may be that preparation will take away the spontaneity and dynamism out of your communication at a discussion. Of course, we do need to retain spontaneity and dynamism as these are the features of direct, face-to-face communication that make it valuable for generating ideas and building on each other's input concurrently. Here, it is important to keep in mind that preparation does not mean working out an exact draft that we may deliver word-by-word on the occasion, regardless of where the discussion goes. Rather, it involves, first of all, gathering information and readying all material on which we may base our contributions to the discussion. We are included in a discussion for our expertise in a particular area or a particular perspective that we bring on board. We need to be thoroughly prepared to really add value to the discussion by being ready with whatever will be expected from us in terms of our input. Secondly, having gathered our material, we need to work out where our focus should lie and identify parts relevant to the objectives of the discussion and the objective of our contribution. It is best to sort out our key points and marshal the necessary supporting material beforehand rather than being caught unawares during the discussion.

On the basis of our experience with the particular individuals involved or of the general dynamics of the group, we should analyse the group in terms of professional and technical background as well as personality, if possible. This will help us greatly in anticipating the kinds of questions or responses likely to be evoked by what we plan to say. **The better we can analyse the group composition and the objectives of the discussion, the closer we can come to an approximation of the likely trajectory of the discussion.** Although we may not be able to anticipate all likely directions that the discussion may take, spending some effort in anticipating this may help us in preparing how best we may contribute so as to make our presence in the group relevant to the objectives of the discussion. In fact, we may specifically be expected to contribute on certain points that lie within our specific area or role. Further, we may be asked to elaborate or support or explain points made by us. Being able to understand such expectations and anticipate the likely directions of the discussion, may prove very helpful at the preparation stage as we still have the opportunity to gather material or to work out certain points in more detail or along lines that may be expected. Expectations would depend not only on the issue at hand, agenda, and the objective of the discussion, but also on the participants in terms of their background and personalities. The better we can analyse these, the more we can understand their perspectives and use this to prepare accordingly. Even though there may still be certain points where we may have to think on our feet or even promise to get back later, if we don't have the necessary details, our thorough preparation will help us make a good impact by equipping us with better content to handle most parts of the discussion.

Good preparation, therefore, amounts to the marshalling of ideas rather than to working out the exact words we would speak. While expression and articulation should have the freshness of impromptu speaking, the ideas should be best marshalled in advance. Thinking about the points we will make and the kind of support we will need to have at our disposal to back these up will not only add to the effectiveness of our communication, but can also help to calm the nervousness we quite naturally experience in such situations. While wit and presence of mind are always our allies, they work their magic best when we spare no effort in terms of readying our material.

The next step is practising so as to get a smooth and effective style of presenting our ideas. Along with strong and relevant content, it is a winning combination. The more we practise speaking at all opportunities we get and are ready to reflect on our performance and to get feedback, the better we can hone our ability to articulate ideas in a clear and interesting manner while engaging with others in all kinds of situations. Every bit of successful experience adds to our confidence and comfort in speaking and the less daunting it appears.

MAKING OUR VERBAL MESSAGES STRONG

Once we have taken care of preparing our material, we come to the presentation of the ideas through our facility with speech. The best ideas may get lost in a jumble of ill-chosen words or fail to have an impact when presented without lucidity, crispness, and completeness. Every time one speaks, the hope is that the ideas will be clear to the other person. However, it is not a given that what is clear to us will get clearly conveyed to others.

Our common experience of confusion or ambiguity as a receiver of messages should help to remind us that very often there is a mismatch between the intended meaning and that conveyed. While there may be some role of the receiver in incorrectly interpreting the verbal message, there is a possibility that the message itself did not adequately and completely capture the idea to be presented. **To a large extent, the listeners' role is not in our control when we speak; the only way we can control the listeners' response is by making our messages clear, focused, and useful to them.** It is for us to ensure to our best ability that we express our idea in the most clear and complete manner. This involves choosing the most appropriate words and capturing the idea fully, and in a manner designed to get it across to other minds. This needs care because sometimes we assume that what is clear to us would also be so for others. This may lead us to not express it with adequate clarity and completeness. In a dynamic communication such as a discussion, no doubt people may ask for clarifications, giving us the opportunity to fill in details or to elaborate on certain points. However, it is best if we take care in finding the best and most complete fit for our ideas through choice of words and concreteness. We also know from our experience as listeners that lack of focus in a speaker is seen as rambling and gets annoying. The ability to organize our thoughts coherently around a clear focus comes in very handy in discussions as in all spoken communication. Not only do the listeners appreciate our focus and clarity, it also allows us to get more points across, and with greater sharpness than if we create a woolly effect that turns people off as well as blurs the significant and insignificant into an undifferentiated mass.

Much of the boredom generated by meetings is due to the highly structured nature of the proceedings and the fact that often they suffer from a lack of leadership by the chair to keep the discussion from straying or being dominated by a few participants. Not only this, at the individual level, many people lack the ability to structure their ideas in a succinct and precise manner and to stay focused on a definite and clear subject. When you display the ability to offer relevant input in a well-structured, concise and clear manner, you display an ability that is generally in short supply and you are bound to stand out. As in all spoken communication, we must keep in mind that the attention of listeners is limited and we should aim at expressing our ideas crisply and succinctly. Of course, if we sacrifice clarity and completeness to conciseness, we may only succeed in being cryptic, and defeat the purpose!

BODY LANGUAGE FOR CONVERSATIONS AND DISCUSSIONS

You are to meet a group of prospective clients for a formal meeting. As they arrive and are being ushered into the conference room, a quick sizing up of the other party is being done by both sides. **Facial expressions, postures and gestures are all silently adding to the impact before the formal communication has even started. People assess each other for comfort and confidence, eagerness to communicate, and pleasure in the interaction, through body language signals.** Awareness of this can help us in ensuring that we convey positive messages and those congruent with our verbal messages as well as the context. When we are not aware of the messages we are sending out, we are in danger of inadvertently displaying messages that do not help our case.

We must all have met people who are well-read and knowledgeable but conversing with them is simply a drag. They either dominate the dialogue or discussion, not allowing anyone to get a word in, or they give off a brooding and drab or even hostile vibe so that one is discouraged from engaging with them. We must make sure that we do not come off as sour-faced or surly, thus putting off others from speaking with us. In fact, we demonstrate our pleasantness and openness when we participate in conversations and discussions in a friendly and amicable manner. An image built indirectly by such interactions is a good asset to possess and is valuable at whatever stage of our career we are in.

Like any other face-to-face spoken communication, a conversation or discussion places a very rich medium at our disposal. Our aim should be to use its potential to the fullest in conveying our ideas and information to others. Not only should we aim at making an impact by adding significantly to the quality of the discussion through our insights and idea generation, depending on the objective, but also show our enthusiasm and involvement through our body language. It is not enough to be engaged but also to show that we are engaged. We do so through our posture, animation in our gestures and facial expressions, and vocal elements. This is true as much of our speaking time as of our listening time. If we only become animated when it is our turn to speak and then seem to doze off, or to become uninterested and vacant-eyed, it gives a message of self-focus that is contradictory to the group-focus of such communication. It also makes people feel less awkward about giving us the same treatment when we speak, thus contributing to an environment unlikely to get the best out of participants. The value of listening in creating an environment of collaboration, trust, and mutual respect cannot be overemphasized. **Our listening is evident as much by our verbal responses in terms of responding to and building on others' inputs, as by our non-verbal responses in terms of eye contact, posture, nodding, appropriate facial gestures, noting down of points, and the like.**

Moreover, the value of our verbal messages is enhanced manifold when our non-verbal cues support these and aid in our total impact. Whenever we converse with people or participate in discussions we send messages through not only our words but also through our entire presence. Our eyes, posture, gestures, tone, pitch, volume, and pace of speaking, all add to the cues received by the other person. If all these are consistent and in sync, the receiver gets a strong sense of the message and the meaning gets reinforced. However, if they are not so, there is a mixed medley of messages received by the other person and it becomes quite unpredictable which one they may see as more true or relevant. In fact, the messages received may be contradictory, and this may undo the entire purpose of the communication.

We need to be aware that like any face-to-face communication we should use the opportunity provided to impact the listener with cues from body language. We should show that we are happy to converse with the other person not only explicitly through our words but also through our body language. In fact, cues about our eagerness to connect with others and engagement in the interaction are best communicated through subtle means rather than spelt out in words. A posture that shows eagerness and interest, facial expressions that are pleasant and mirror our interest in conversing with the other person, gestures that show energy, and enthusiasm, and voice elements that convey our feelings as well as show energy and enthusiasm are a wonderful combination to the words that carry the main weight of meaning. Paying attention to any one at the expense of others means that we are not making the best use of the potential of this richest of communication media. It may also lead to overlooking the inconsistent messages that we may inadvertently be sending out, resulting in unintended meanings being conveyed to the other person. Only by being aware of all parts of our communication during a meeting or discussion, can we hope to ensure that it is all in sync and mutually supportive. If the participants of a discussion neglect this advantage of spoken communication over the written word, it amounts to throwing away the key reason for choosing the former. In such a situation, a discussion over email may be much better. In fact, it would be wisest to reserve the rich medium of face-to-face interactions for objectives where the extra dimensions of rapport building and personal impact brought in by attitude and personality as reflected in body language are of special value. This would particularly be the case in contexts of persuasion and of taking others along in the process of idea generation and consensus building. If we are organizing meetings it would be useful to keep this in mind. However, if we are a participant, without control over deciding the need for the medium, it is up to us to utilize the powerful potential of communicating through the combined force of our verbal and non-verbal messages to the best of our ability.

Given today's flatter organizational structures, it is no longer possible to lead on the strength of the power and position. However, as we go up the hierarchy, it is too easy to neglect displaying our open-mindedness and respect for others, regardless of rank. We must keep in mind that it is often through brief interactions and behavioural cues rather than our overt assertions that people judge our attitude. We can subtly indicate through our willingness to engage in general conversations and discussions that we are approachable and amenable to communication beyond rigid channels of communication. We are more likely, in this manner, to network well and increase our rapport across the levels of the hierarchy. We are also likely to be better in touch with the general tenor of ideas and feelings rather than if we depend only on the formal channels to bring these to our attention. In formal discussions too, it soon becomes apparent if our claims of inclusive and participatory decision-making are genuine or not. In fact, we fail to draw out the best from people if we demonstrate that we only pay lip service to participation, by monopolizing discussions and treating input with scant respect if it comes from those below us in the hierarchy. The damage done to rapport building and our sphere of influence is also considerable. As in the case of our genuineness about truly valuing everyone in our team and every one we speak with, we give non-verbal validation of our attitude in every interaction.

TELEPHONE CONVERSATIONS

With the dramatic development and spread of telephony, the phone has become a ubiquitous tool of communication used in both formal and informal contexts. At the same time, its technical prowess has been growing to an extent unimaginable only a couple of generations back. However, what concerns us here is its use for spoken communication.

From quick conversations to seek or provide information, to passing instructions, we now think nothing of picking up the phone to communicate. But are we making the most of our phone conversations? We would be making the most of it if we kept in mind both its advantages and limitations as a close second to face-to-face spoken interaction. It enjoys the same potential advantages of conversations in terms of rapport building and the personal touch, as well as the immediacy of feedback. It also has the virtue of being dynamic and spontaneous. However, its greatest difference lies in the absence of non-verbal cues through body language, other than voice. The low attention span of people due to distractions and the ease of multitasking when on the phone are additional challenges. Unless both parties actively avoid it, they may be tempted to concurrently carry on other tasks due to which the attention available to the conversation may be only partial.

To make the most of our phone interactions and to resist the distractions, it may be useful to think of our choice of this particular mode of communicating. Once again, we must think of it in comparison to other modes of communicating with the intended receiver and objective of the communication as the central consideration.

When deciding whether to pick up the phone or to send an email, for example, it would be advisable to compare the impact of the spoken word over the written, given the objective. While a quick exchange of information or clarification may be easily done over the phone, an attempt to use it for an extended argument or logical persuasion may not be most effective.

While a piece of written communication may have the advantage of strong structure and sufficient elaboration of complex or detailed material, a telephonic communication has the advantage of immediate responses and quick resolution of needs. A quick enquiry, an update about some work, checking on someone's availability for a face-to-face meeting, are matters where a phone call can really be useful. It may also be great for catching up with colleagues or business acquaintances but it would be generally considered courteous to fix a time through a text message or an email for the phone call.

In our busy work schedules, it would be impossible to try to have face-to-face communication for every purpose and the phone is often a good substitute for it. Moreover, distances across which organizations are spread today makes face-to-face communication very expensive and not practical for most needs. Where speed is necessary for a brief exchange to help gain clarity or some specific piece of information, a phone call may be sufficient, and in fact, preferable to writing as well as to a face-to-face exchange. However, if we need to persuade someone it may be advisable to prefer the latter two over a phone conversation. We need to be cautious about using the medium of voice alone for requests and persuasion. Williams[2] cites a number of studies that show that audio-only conversations were more depersonalized, argumentative, and narrow in focus, compared with face-to-face conversations. According to him 'it is easier over the phone, to ignore that

---

[2] Williams, E, "Experimental comparisons of face-to-face and mediated communication: A review," *Psychological Bulletin*. 84 (1977): 963–976.

people are real social beings, with individual personalities, wishes, feelings, and aspiration . . . [and to] treat others more like semi-mechanical objects, which can be ignored, insulted, exploited, or hurt with relative impunity.' You may have experienced that not being a face-to-face medium, the telephone also allows people to get away with certain responses and behaviour that would be less likely when facing someone.

If our persuasive appeal is largely logical and needs sustained explanation and support, it is best to do it in writing. But when we wish to use an emotional appeal or that of our relationship and personal credibility, the richer medium of face-to-face communication may have more probability of success. People may find it harder to turn down a special request made by a person in the flesh than only over the voice. However, it may not always be possible to reach the person for a direct interaction, due to distance or other problems and a phone call may be a substitute. In my experience, if a request for a favour rather than a routine matter has to be made over the phone, it is best to be direct about it rather than taking a circuitous approach and leading up to it after hollow small talk. The tone of voice need not be apologetic but we can certainly convey the emotions that lie behind the urgency or significance of the request. If we, in turn, are asked for a favour, and cannot help out, it is best to convey this face-to-face but if that is not practically possible, it is better to pick up the phone than to write a note or email. I have received emails turning down a request that sound quite curt and unhelpful, but when the same person gives the same message on the phone or face-to-face, there are additional elements that give the refusal a softer touch. While this may also be due to the insufficient care some of us take in crafting our written messages, it does reflect the importance of speaking, even if it is over the phone, so as to bring in the personal touch and to have an interaction rather than a one-way communication that simply states our inability to help.

Due to the lack of non-verbal cues other than voice to support and reinforce our ideas, telephone conversations are a considerably less rich medium of communication. However, it is still useful when face-to-face communication is not possible or the matter is not of sufficient importance to warrant the practical aspects of arranging a face-to-face interaction. Even though other non-verbals are lacking, our voice can make up for the other cues that make face-to-face conversations so much more effective for personal impact. Through voice elements of pace, tone, pitch, and volume, we may convey a personal touch and try to bring in emotional overtones in situations where these are likely to contribute to effective meeting of our objective. On the other hand, the absence of other body language cues may sometimes be an advantage in terms of allowing us to control what is communicated without the worry that non-verbal cues may give away more than we want to.

Technology also allows us today to have virtual meetings through teleconferencing or videoconferencing. When a number of people need to be involved in the objective such as information sharing, briefing or brainstorming, and it is not practical to get them all together for a physical meeting, a teleconference or a videoconference is useful. However, the availability of the technology does not mean it should be used indiscriminately. The choice should depend on the objective of communication. If, for the purpose of the proposed communication, gestures, facial expressions, and other visual cues are unlikely to significantly add value, a teleconference may be best. In fact, it may help focus exclusively on the verbal content without the additional visual cues that may add nervousness and self-consciousness without really adding any relevance or value to the communication. For example, in the case of checking the status of various sub-teams' work, where the focus is on concrete details, a teleconference backed by exchange of background material over email, may be sufficient and also keep the focus on the content. The additional expense or hassle of videoconferencing may not really be worth it for the objective. However, if the objective is to brainstorm, creatively propose and elaborate ideas and responses, it may be quite useful to use videoconferencing that would bring in more cues helping the participants to get greater sensory input that would be relevant in making sense of the communication more fully.

Only when the medium is chosen keeping in mind the objective of the communication, and not as the default, can it really contribute to the success of the communication. When we are clear that the objectives of the communication between two or more people really need the entire gamut of cues possible through face-to-face communication, and distance or dispersed location makes that not practical, should we use the option of videoconferencing. Casual use of the medium for objectives that could as easily have been served by other media, only reduces the care participants take over making the most of it. We need not use technology simply because it is available, but because a certain medium offers opportunities that would help serve the objective better.

Answering the Phone

We may have encountered various ways in which people answer the phone. This apparently simple response may indicate something about us even before the conversation. We may give an indication of irritation or guardedness or warmth and openness in the way we answer the phone. **It is best to answer the phone with one's name so that the caller immediately knows if they've got the right person or not.** On the mobile phone or other phones with caller identification, if we know the caller, we can begin straight away with greeting him/her appropriately and if not, then in the usual way of giving one's name or even saying 'Hello', and waiting for the other person to introduce himself and his reason for calling.

It is important, in the opening words, as in the rest of our phone conversation, to be very careful of the tone of voice as that is the only sensory vehicle for any supplementary cue to our words. We must make sure that we speak distinctly and with a lilt in the voice, showing enthusiasm and positive energy. We find a dull, bored, couldn't-care-less tone quite putting off; why, then, should our caller have to encounter such a tone as soon as the call is answered? Smiling when we answer the phone lifts our tone and gives our voice warmth. Hearing a pleasant tone, hinting at a welcoming smile is an assurance to the caller that we are happy to talk with them and keen to respond. It is also important to keep our phone conversations focused and to have all necessary information at hand before the call. These small things go a great way in demonstrating a professional approach and respect for the other person's time.

Keeping the Focus Sharp

When making a phone call it is a good idea to be clear of our purpose and focus. It is best to plan what we will focus on and how we are going to say it. For doing this we need to be clear about the person we are calling, our relationship with them, and the objective of our call. If we are calling to provide information, it is best to have all the details at hand before making the call. When asking for information or making a special request, it is best to begin directly, after a courteous greeting, rather than beating about the bush, hoping for the other person to pick up hints about our needs. It is again, a good idea to note down the specifics of our request so that we don't end up being vague or imprecise about our requirement or leaving out essential elements. The bottom line is to be efficient about time in terms of sharing and asking for information. **Unlike casual phone conversations, a business-like phone conversation needs to get to the point quickly, and stay focused on it, rather than to waffle or meander into irrelevancies.**

146

Voice: Special Care on the Phone

As our entire communication depends on voice, its importance for phone conversations cannot be overstated. Our skills of giving and picking up visual non-verbal cues are inhibited over the phone and we need to depend entirely on the aural elements. First of all, the communication of our verbal content depends on the clarity of articulation of our speech. If we don't take sufficient care to avoid missing out some syllables of our words, and of clipping off the ends of sentences, we may end up causing confusion. Our pronunciation also needs to be intelligible so as to avoid miscommunication. Using too many fillers and unduly long pauses also makes it hard for others to gather our meaning. This may be prevented by giving thought to what we wish to say and how we should structure it. We must keep in mind that unlike face-to-face conversations where a person has the advantage of seeing many other cues to stay interested in our ideas and to gather if we are searching for a word or phrase or mean to indicate a break, over the phone only our voice carries these cues and odd pauses or fillers may confuse the receiver.

We also need to take more care of our pace of speaking in the case of phone conversations. **A slightly slower pace of speaking helps the listener catch our words better, leading to more clarity of communication.** Our volume needs to be appropriate too, as we do not wish to come across either as shouting or whispering. If we use these at all, we should do so with the awareness that these would indicate additional meanings about us and our intent, and it is best if we consciously chose what we wish to convey through this subtle cue. The pitch and tone of our voice may also be modified so as to add shades of meaning to our words. As we know, the tone may change the way a word is interpreted, and inattention to this aspect of our speech, takes away, as it were, a powerful tool from our communication kit, making our speech flat and dull. With the visual cues of appearance, facial expressions, eye contact, gestures, and posture removed from the communication, our pitch of voice and the pace and volume of our speech may provide cues about our emotional state to the listener, and it would be good for us to use these consciously so that we may control what we are conveying.

With far fewer non-verbals to worry about keeping in sync, phone conversations give us more control over our total communication and may seem more manageable. However, it requires us to put in extra effort to compensate for the missing sensory cues at our disposal and to use our voice very effectively to carry all shades of meaning essential for the full communication of our intent.

Remember that our facial expressions and gesticulations are not visible to our listener. We may use these if we feel we can speak more naturally by doing so, but if we only smile or nod our head in agreement in response to the person at the other end of the line, he or she cannot know that we are doing so and may interpret it with the myriad meanings silence can have. No doubt smiling, frowning, or clenching of teeth translate into tone variations, but we may also need to translate these visual expressions into aural ones if they are parts of the message we want to get through to our listener.

At times, we may use the opacity of the mode to hide our emotional reactions or state of mind. We can do this by making sure that our voice stays even and does not reflect the feelings we want to avoid conveying. We need to use our voice to reflect our eagerness to communicate, warmth, confidence, authority. We may use it to convey our feelings or, if these may mar the objective, we may make sure that our voice does not give us away. In fact, phone conversations are perhaps advantageous in such contexts as we only have to control our voice whereas in face-to-face situations, many more cues need to be controlled if incongruences are not to give the game away. In a way, the focus only on the voice allows the opportunity to even a diffident speaker to be more effective, as there is one, rather than an entire range of body language elements, to be taken care of. Practice in improving the clarity of our articulation, of tonal inflections to add additional dimensions to the meaning, and of a controlled pace, can do wonders to the impact we are able to make in our phone conversations.

TELECONFERENCING

In 1977, Williams[3] projected that teleconferencing would have a considerable future for relatively routine meetings,

---

[3] Williams, E, "Experimental comparisons of face-to-face and mediated communication: A review," *Psychological Bulletin*. 84 (1977): 963–976.

involving people who know each other and tasks such as information exchange and problem solving. I am sure you would agree that our experience in today's world has borne this prediction out. Very often, our need to involve a number of people dispersed in various locations, in a concurrent discussion, is served by teleconferencing.

As in the case of phone dialogues, a discussion over the telephone with a group of people requires us to pay attention to the specifics in terms of objective, focus, and participants. Given our understanding of these, we need to be prepared with our material before the conference call. Doing so, helps us contribute effectively to the discussion and gives a positive impression of our diligence and sincerity.

We must also keep in mind that we need to pay special attention to our voice elements for effectively conveying our ideas to others. With a number of participants in the discussion, we need to keep to the structure set by the person leading the call, in terms of turn-taking, so as to prevent cross-talking. As the communication relies only on aural messages, it is vital to be distinct and clear in articulation and to keep our pace in check. If we speak without pause, we may risk becoming indistinct and also give an impression of nervousness or heightened emotions. **Tonal inflections need special care as these are essential to add to our meaning, to give shades of meaning, and to add energy and vitality to our speech.** If our pauses become too long, the other person has no way of knowing if we have completed what we had to say or there is more. Many awkward interjections and confusion about turn taking could be avoided by greater care in verbalizing some of the meanings that would be easily apparent in a face-to-face communication through the other senses.

VIDEOCONFERENCING

Today, technology allows us to involve a group comprising members located almost anywhere in the world, in virtual meetings and discussions through videoconferencing. Although this is potentially a very valuable medium, care in deciding when to use it is essential if we are to make the best use of it. As discussed earlier, we need to pay attention to its particular benefits and weigh these against the objective of the intended communication. The medium offers a close simulation of face-to-face interactions and it is best chosen when there is particular benefit from the kind of richness that it provides.

If we are a participant in such a conference we should be aware of the potential advantages of the medium and aim at utilizing these effectively in the service of the objective of the communication. The advantage of videoconferencing over teleconferencing is obviously the richness of the medium in terms of the visual as well as aural sensory cues that may be used. **In order for this richness and its potential for effective communication to translate into actual benefit, every participant must use these cues to supplement and enhance the verbal content of the communication.** As in the case of teleconferencing voice elements of pitch, tone, pace, and volume are important to convey our message. At the same time, with visual cues being available, we need to take care that our body language conveys appropriate and congruent messages. Our appearance must show that we take the occasion seriously rather than casually. We should treat it just as we would any formal interaction such as a meeting in the official context, in terms of appropriateness of attire and appearance. Our eye contact, facial expression, posture, and gestures are powerful ways to add to the impact of our verbal message and we should use these consciously to support our words, as well as to convey additional messages of enthusiasm, interest, positive energy, and appropriate emotions.

As in the case of a face-to-face meeting or discussion, we need to prepare our input beforehand in terms of collecting information and processing it in the way it would be expected of us. By anticipating questions or concerns of others, we may ensure that we have supporting details for our points handy. Deep familiarity with our material is also important to give us confidence to face questions and to contribute in an appropriate manner depending on the direction taken by the discussion.

Listen Well to Speak Well

We must keep in mind at all points that while our speaking skills are in focus, for a productive conversation, discussion, or meeting—whether face-to-face or over, the phone or through videoconferencing—it is as essential to speak effectively as it is to listen. Without effective listening, such communication lapses into a monologue or a series of monologues by a number of speakers rather than dialogues or discussions where one builds further on the points of others by engaging with ideas presented rather than presenting ideas unaffected by the dynamics of the conversation. This cannot happen without effective listening. Such listening has to be respectful, empathic, or critical, as the context demands. It is very important to understand the context correctly, and alertness to all available cues allows us to do this.

The objectives of putting together a group of people to discuss an issue are not served by merely listening with a focus on absorbing the content, but by critically engaging with the ideas, examining them against other information, checking for logical rigour and for credible support for assertions. Questioning the robustness of ideas by testing them out in a discussion may be the very purpose of discussing it with others, but if as listeners we close our minds to anything but agreement or admiration, or with refutation and disagreement to all that does not suit our position, this objective is unlikely to be served. The purpose is also defeated if people listen only out of courtesy and do not engage critically with the ideas. **Listening to others' input attentively does not mean agreeing with every point.** In fact, the value of the multiple perspectives in reaching higher quality decisions or generating more robust ideas and plans lies in the possibility of critical questioning and refuting by others. At the same time, we must take care that our disagreement or critical questioning remains pleasant. While challenging or arguing or criticizing another participant's points we must make sure that we phrase our response in a manner that is objective rather than directed at the person. We must make sure that even when we wish to refute or criticize, we refrain from using harsh language. At the same time we must take care that our body language, especially our posture, gestures, tone, and facial expression don't convey negative and hostile messages.

Not only should we adopt such an attitude of critical and respectful listening, we must also show our eagerness to listen through both our verbal and non-verbal responses, and through the congruence between them. Listening is a mental activity and unless we show through our non-verbal cues that we are listening, it may be assumed that we are not. This indication is important to convey that we are listening and taking interest in the other person's views, input and involving ourselves fully in the conversation. Doing so keeps the other person engaged and gives a message of respect for both the person and their ideas.

At all times, positive and supportive body language cues while listening help to show that we are participating in the conversation even when we are not speaking. We may indicate involvement with the communication by nodding and eye contact and appropriate facial expressions. While we do not snatch away the speaking role before the other person has completed what they had to say, it is not necessary to remain completely silent. Silence has very many possible interpretations—sometimes quite contradictory—and therefore, remaining silent while listening to someone may give a message we may not have intended. When we are silent we may indicate as extreme a range of meanings as agreement and disagreement, respect and disrespect, shyness and hauteur. We must aid the other person in interpreting our silence through other body language cues such as facial expressions, head movement, and posture. We may also make sounds such as hmmm, or brief exclamations of 'Oh!' 'Really?' 'Wonderful!' as appropriate. We may even ask brief questions that show our interest and invite the person to elaborate further.

The congruence of non-verbal messages with our words is important in conveying our eagerness to participate, and our keenness to listen with due respect to others in the interest of the overall objective of the discussion or conversation rather than one-way communication aimed at displaying our depth of knowledge and understanding, or proving the superiority of our views. While we may disagree with the ideas of others, we should take care that our body language does not show us as a disagreeable listener. And while people are generally prepared to handle the former as it brings out the best ideas by testing the opposite points of view, no one likes the latter. Display of churlishness or of disrespect for others' viewpoints is an easy recipe for inviting the antagonism of others in a discussion. We need to make sure that our body language during listening stays positive, displaying pleasantness, through posture, gestures, and facial expressions.

Although it is good to reflect our feelings on our face

and in our voice, we must be careful to avoid giving out negative signals or indications of negative emotions. While we are in the listener's role it is important to be careful of non-verbal signals that are generally interpreted negatively. Such signals are: arms crossed across the chest, angry frown, looking away, silence, curtness and sharpness of tone, and excessively forceful gestures. These and all other signs that are seen as indicating disinterest or anger or impatience make the environment less conducive to a fruitful and amicable discussion and to meeting the communication objectives.

There are people who feel, in the words of the famous artist, James McNeill Whistler[4], that, 'If other people are going to talk, conversation becomes impossible!' Our aim should be to avoid giving the impression of being such a person through our behaviour as listeners, if not our words. It would do us good to remember that if we were to talk to ourselves, we would be considered crazy; it is the participation of two or more people that makes it into a meaningful communication. While conversing seems to be all about talking, it would be a monologue rather than a conversation if we only saw it as an opportunity to speak. In a discussion or conversation, we need to take our role as a listener equally seriously. Listening with respect and interest to others is as important as the sparkling and witty or insightful input that we ourselves provide. At any point in our conversation or discussion we may need to switch between the roles of

---

[4] I am sure you have heard of the painting *Whistler's Mother*.

speaker and listener and we should do so readily, regarding both roles as significant.

Listening to others is a courtesy we extend and by doing so, are likely to be paid back in equal measure. When we show a reluctance to let go of our speaking role, we may either turn off the other person completely from the conversation, or we may start a competition of snatching the speaking role and not letting go. **Willingness to listen to others which is an important component of conversations and dialogue, is a quality that we need to develop in ourselves as much as possible by taking genuine interest in others views and feelings, in respecting others as individuals, and in controlling our self-focus and impatience that prevent us from listening to others.** While conversing, if every moment that we are not speaking is spent in planning what we will say next and in engaging with our thoughts rather than with what the other person is saying, we are not really participating in the conversation. Many of us may admit to ourselves that it is a strong temptation. But it is one that we need to control through self-discipline and by training ourselves to take genuine interest in others. If we are able to do so we will possess the rare ability of good conversational listening.

Not only is listening always important as a gesture of respect to the other person and their input, it has a crucial role to play in keeping the discussion focused and coherent. In such a situation no coherence is possible if people do not listen critically and engage with each other's points and build further on these. If rather than listening, we spend the free time between our speaking parts in planning what we have to contribute independent of others' input, we are not only likely to turn people off through our inattention and lack of involvement, but also end up making irrelevant contributions to the discussion. While we took a mental hike to plan our next input or allowed ourselves to be sidetracked by a distraction, the discussion may have gone along some other line. When we return with our pre-planned idea it may no longer be in congruence with the point being discussed. We may also have missed some input by others and our point may only be a repetition, thus exposing our lack of attention and full involvement.

It is easy to get distracted as a listener. As a participant in a discussion or conversation it is important to prevent distractions. It is easy to become impatient as a listener. It is as important to resist the urge to interrupt others and take back control of the conversation, as to resist the tendency to spend the gaps in our speaking time to frame our further input. While we may think that we can indulge in this silent activity without any perceptible signs, it is not so imperceptible. Most of us can quite quickly make out when our conversation partner has tuned out. It is very clear for us (and, equally for others) to read signs such as fidgeting and fiddling, repeatedly looking away, complete silence, as impatience, disinterest, or distraction. When we neglect to control our responses indicating impatience, disinterest, or distraction during small talk and general conversations we may think it is no big deal. But by doing so we may lose the opportunity to make a positive impression and to build a rapport with another person and this may later impact the success of the formal communications we may have with them. By our responses we may have subtly indicated lack of interest in a colleague or external person or in their ideas, or have insulted them by not listening with respect and this may prove disastrous for formal communication contexts and further relationship with them later.

However, we must also remember that merely listening with rapt attention is not likely to leave a very positive impression of our personal qualities or our knowledge or views. We must participate both by attentively listening and by extending the conversation through our role as a speaker. Although for some of us listening comes more easily, and seems to be a low-energy investment, we should be willing to break out of our shyness or self-focus and to make the effort to expend energy in such interactions. As we practise conversations with openness, respect, and pleasantness, we are likely to begin to enjoy such interactions, and would probably seek more such opportunities wherein the skill may be further practised and refined.

TO CONCLUDE

All in all, we would profit by treating conversations and discussions as opportunities to hone our speaking abilities and to leave positive impressions on others about our knowledge, sharpness, and personality. Much of the skill-set needed for these interactions is the same as that for formal presentations and public speaking; and we may use these opportunities to practise and gain confidence for those more infrequent, but very important, speaking occasions. No speaking occasion in the work context is immaterial or insignificant; everything adds up to represent what we are in others' perception. We never know what sticks in the minds of those around us and is used to evaluate us. We would not want all the positive impact made through dazzling presentations and impressive speeches to be undone by the impression left through our less formal interactions. These are opportunities for us to leave a good impression through the quality of our contribution, and the effectiveness of our articulation. At the same time, important objectives such as rapport-building, information sharing, problem solving, and decision making, to mention just a few, are served by these interactions and with proper care and attention to our contribution to serving these, we may again, leave a good impression.

I am sure that your experience will tell you that these interactions are often taken less seriously and not everyone is adept at communicating effectively on these occasions. Here lies our opportunity—when we make the effort to work on it, we will definitely stand out and leave a good impression.

CHAPTER 4

Selection Interviews

We have all faced interview situations where we are to be critically evaluated to determine a fit with the requirements of a position and all that we offer in terms of experience, ability, knowledge, and personality.

Let us begin with some questions:

* Do you get butterflies in the stomach before a selection interview?
* Does your mouth go dry and all rational thoughts desert you when facing grim interrogators across an Interview table?
* Do you kick yourself when all the details you wanted to share, only return to your conscious memory when the interview is over?
* Do you wish you could make a better impact on interview panels and impress them with your personality, competence, intelligence, and knowledge?

If you answer yes, you may take comfort from the fact that you are not alone! There are many in the same boat and this chapter is meant for all those whose answer to the above questions is a resounding YES!

The good news is that there is no need to despair. You have already taken the first step to improvement if you acknowledge that you need to improve. The next step is to believe that you *can* improve—that no one has to resign to a performance at an interview that does disservice to their achievements and capabilities. Whatever are your achievements and potential, your ability and your personality—and one obviously works on these long before reaching an interview—it is about being fair to yourself by presenting these in the best possible manner so that an assessment in line with your true worth may be possible to make. 'Sure,' you say, 'but how does one get to that stage?' This is a fair enough question for, obviously, the ability to present oneself in the best possible manner at an interview is not inborn nor one that can be mastered overnight. But we can slowly strengthen it by approaching it in a systematic manner and breaking down the formidable process into manageable steps.

WHY INTERVIEW?

First of all, we must analyse interviews in terms of communication objectives of the two parties involved. It is essential to understand why this form of spoken face-to-face communication is used. Generally, a shortlist is prepared from all the eligible candidates, and not only would everyone on this list meet the minimum criteria, their CVs would have included significant points to make them stand out from the larger pool of aspirants. If this was sufficient to determine suitability there would be no need for any further communication. But obviously, this is not so. Let us think of what the communication up to this point would have conveyed to those involved in the selection process and what remains to be assessed or validated through the interview. Ideally, the CV or résumé aims at providing a crisp account of the relevant information about the person in a manner that makes it easy for the reader to grasp quickly by ensuring that especially significant bits leap off the page. This is not a medium for providing supplementary explanations and elaboration on the facts and information provided. It is also not a place where one may persuade the reader except indirectly through the relevance of the information in itself. In situations where the résumé is accompanied by an application or cover letter, the factual details provided in the former could be used to build a persuasive case about one's suitability for the position and to help take us to the shortlist of potentially strong candidates. From the selectors' perspective, there remains much to be assessed to determine the best fit between the profile and organizational expectations and the candidates that seem to have potential based on these primary factual details. The depth of the learning from the qualifications and experience remains to be tested, along with sharpness of mind and other qualities essential for the particular position. At the same time, the personality of the candidates may need to be assessed in terms of interpersonal skills. Assessment of such aspects of each candidate on essential criteria determined by the selectors may be done through psychometric tests and other instruments. However, an interview (or a series of interviews) remains an essential tool for this.

While the interviewers aim at a more stringent assessment and selection from among a set of strong contenders, for the candidate it is an opportunity to take them closer to the objective of being selected. Having made it to the interview stage on the basis of their strong credentials, their objective for this interaction is to persuade the interviewers of the perfect match between the requirements of the position and the abilities, knowledge, and personal qualities that they possess. They would also want to demonstrate their potential for further growth and contribution, through the new role, to the employer's larger objectives. An interview allows a candidate to supply additional support to information already provided, to derive relevant learning from their background in terms of experience, knowledge, skills, and to show ownership of ideas so as to build a strong persuasive case for their candidature. The interaction also allows them to demonstrate certain crucial skills as well as reveal their personal qualities. Through the combined force of the verbal content of the communication as well as the personality elements demonstrated at the interaction, they hope to be able to impress the interview panel of their suitability in all respects.

Now let us turn to the mode of communication itself. What is it that face-to-face interaction allows effectively, and how could this help both parties in their respective objectives? From the interviewers' perspective, it provides an opportunity to further understand the candidate's professional achievements and skills. At the same time, it allows them to interact with the person behind the written communication, to observe and assess relevant personality attributes. From the candidate's perspective, the communication at the interview is not only the means to impress the interviewers with their ideas and knowledge, it is also a live demonstration of their communication and interpersonal skills.

Equipped with this awareness of our objectives and those of the interviewers, and the understanding of the potential of this medium of communication, we should take adequate care at the preparation stage as well as the actual interview to leave the best impact through our communication. Preparation and practice are also the solutions for tackling nervousness and anxiety that endanger our performance and may completely destroy all likelihood of impressing the interviewers. It may not be a magic pill, but it is the best solution to nerves, and one completely in our control.

The greater the effort we put into gaining self-awareness, awareness of expectations, and in using these to guide our preparation and practice, the more we feel in control. If we want to do well, we need to put in our best effort at presenting ourselves in the best possible manner. And we would be taking a big chance if rather than taking preparation and practice seriously, we left something so crucial, to take care of itself.

Prepare to Impress

In the words of tennis legend Arthur Ashe, 'One important key to success is self-confidence. An important key to self-confidence is preparation.' As for all crucial communications, preparation is an essential requirement for interviews. No doubt we wish to approach an interview with lots of self-confidence. That implies that we should be willing to put in the required effort in adequately preparing for it. But it is easy to fall into the trap of confusion by looking at it in a general haze. The key to confidence at the interview lies in *adequate* and *focused* preparation. For this, we need to understand the kind of information that is likely to be expected of us at the interview. If we are seeking to move to a new company or organization, we begin by gathering all nuggets of information about the industry, the company, and the specific position from publicly available but credible information sources. When it is for a promotion or a lateral shift to another position within our own organization, it may still be valuable to seek out as much information as one can get about the role in terms of responsibilities and expectations. In either case we may gain from discussions with well-informed people. In certain cases, one may have one's own experience base to draw upon. The first step would be to collect all this information and try to get a good understanding of what the expectations from a person at that position or in that profile are likely to be and therefore what the interviewers are likely to be interested in finding out in the course of the interview, over and above the information already available with them, in order to determine one's suitability for it.

a) Think like the interviewer

Determining the required direction for our preparation can be really helped by focusing not on what we want to say, but on what the other party wants to find out. You may ask: 'How is one to predict what the interviewers will want to know?' But, wait a minute! Is it really so hard to anticipate what the interviewers will be interested in? It is only fallacious thinking that locks us in the position of the interviewee, leaving us uneasy and nervous. Instead, why not try looking at the interview from the perspective of the interviewer? Proceeding in a clear-headed manner, anticipating what the interviewers would look for, not only helps in gaining clarity about areas requiring preparation, but should also help us structure our thoughts so as to be prepared to give clear, coherent, consistent, and concrete responses at the interview. We may not get all questions absolutely right, but even if we can get a good number worked out, we have fewer questions that take us completely by surprise and to which we respond by on-the-spot answers that may be lacking in details, concrete substantiation, or may be inconsistent with other responses, or be badly structured, leading to lack of clarity. No doubt there would be questions that we could not have anticipated and to which we will respond by thinking on our feet. But the more questions we can anticipate through good preparation and consequently, to which we can respond in a manner that does justice to our true worth and strengthens our persuasive case, the better position we are in.

In order to anticipate what the interviewer would be interested in, try to imagine you are the interviewer. As an interviewer, you would already have details of the candidates and sufficient information about their qualifications, experience, and track record. If you were to go by information on a CV or the persuasiveness of an application alone, you would not need to interview people. Why are you interviewing them? What is the objective of this particular form of communication for the larger objective of finding a good match between the person and the job? With a minimum qualification and experience base already used to create a shortlist and thus common to all appearing at the interview, what would be needed for a candidate to stand apart from all who satisfy the basic requirement? What, in terms of knowledge and specific experience, would be especially interesting and relevant for you? What personal qualities would you want, given all things being the same? How would you determine these from the face-to-face spoken communication at the interview? Once we have tried answering these, we are really in a better position to start preparing ourselves for the interview in a focused manner that addresses the specifics of the expectations from a person to be evaluated for a particular position.

b) What do we prepare?

So, where does one begin and what does one prepare?

Although the specifics will change, the information to be prepared will generally fall into five broad categories:

Self-awareness

The first step is to try to get a good understanding of our own self. Self-understanding is crucial, because without it there is no possibility of adequately projecting ourselves to others. To be unaware of our own strengths and weaknesses is a bad place to be in. Keep in mind that it was a curse that made Lord Hanuman unable to remember his own powers and strength until he was reminded of it by others! Don't wait for the actual interview to figure out what you want to do in life or career and why. Try to answer the following questions while preparing: Why am I keen on this position? What makes me truly suited for it? What do I stand for? What are my strengths? What is the unique package of qualifications, experience, track record, achievements, and personality that I represent?

It is important to try to honestly answer these questions as it gives us the opportunity to gain clarity about ourselves and conviction about our suitability for the position. In doing so, we have to aim at being objective about ourselves and seeing ourselves from an external perspective. When we do this we are forced to find concrete grounds for qualities and attributes rather than impressions and implicit beliefs. Finding reasonable grounds to support the image of ourselves that we wish to project to others would help us in our attempt at persuasiveness with interviewers. It would also give us clarity and conviction that would be very important in giving us a sense of confidence at the interview.

We should understand that interviewers would be looking for certain personal qualities in addition to knowledge and technical skills and that all else being equal, these qualities could lead to a candidate being assessed as more suitable than others. Your aim should be to show the interviewer the kind of person you are. No doubt it takes a while for people to get to know someone through everyday interactions at the workplace. At an interview, we have to make a special effort to project our personality through a very brief interaction. For example, we cannot assume that the interviewers can somehow recognize our enthusiastic nature, our friendliness, and our interpersonal skills or that once we get the position, these will be demonstrated in good time. Rather, we need to use our self-understanding to figure out our attributes as fairly as we can, and to make a conscious effort to project these qualities during the interview. This is not to suggest that one must fake an appearance of the kind of personality that one actually does not possess. Although it may be possible to do so, it would be not only a deception on our part but also something we would not be able to sustain. What it does mean is that we have given conscious thought during preparation to figuring out what we are, what parts of our personality are relevant to the requirements of the position and would be important to convey to the interviewers. We also need to plan out how we can ensure that these qualities get conveyed during the brief interaction.

It is for you to project your personality rather than to expect direct questions on it or others to make the effort to figure you out. **Remember, that your aim is to stand out and be memorable for the interviewers.** Your uniqueness in terms of track record, abilities, and above all, personality, should ensure that you are not just another one of the people they meet that day, but someone they will remember, and for the right reasons. This uniqueness needs to be conveyed to them through all that you say and do at the interaction. Are you great at networking? If so, you should not just claim it; your manner of communication should provide sufficient demonstration of it! Are you someone who can think on his feet? You should actually lead them to conclude this rather than assert this. Can you handle stress? Show them through the way you handle tough questions and by the account you give of such experiences. Do you have strong analytical skills? Back your claim with incidents from your professional and technical track record, as well as through demonstration of these skills through this particular interaction itself. Do you have an interesting hobby or do you have a side to your personality or an achievement that shows your versatility and creativity or some other positive attribute? Don't expect that mentioning it in the résumé is sufficient. What matters is the passion with which you can speak of it during the interview and in what way you can use it to make yourself stand out in a positive manner and be memorable. Can you present it as a story with narrative interest, to make it—and you—stand out?

Thinking of such questions in the calmness of

pre-interview preparation and reflection, polishing the comfort and ease with which we can talk of our interests, and activities in an engaging manner can be very valuable. After due preparation, we should give ourselves adequate practice in such conversations and work on the feedback that we may get from others to improve the effectiveness of our communication in terms of vividness of details, clarity of ideas, credibility, coherence, consistency of body language and verbal cues, to name a few.

Details of experience and achievements

Although we may think there is no need to prepare for answering questions on our experience and achievements, this information may not get conveyed with sufficient clarity and concreteness if we neglect to prepare well. While in the résumé it may be presented as information, this needs to be used for adding to your persuasiveness in the interview. It is useful to pull out the job description, your résumé, and application letter that you may have drafted some weeks (if not months) in the past when you expressed interest in the position. **A well-written application would mean you had already anticipated some key things a reviewer would be looking for; it would be good to refresh that understanding before facing the interviewers.**

Our own experience is well-known to us, but some of it may have become somewhat hazy. We may also remember things generally and in a subjective manner which may not convey the precise details and significance to another person.

It is important to collect facts and examples that would serve as concrete support to substantiate our claims. It is also important to keep in mind what our experience means from the interviewer's perspective. They are interested not in the experience or the achievements as ends in themselves but for what these mean in terms of our learning that is relevant to their needs and general enough to be transportable to different contexts and thus of interest and usefulness to them.

This is the stage at which to prepare ourselves to demonstrate complete ownership of the assertions made in the application and be prepared to back them up with solid support. Sometimes we mistakenly assume that the information in our résumé and application letter is sufficient to make us stand out from others. We must realize that these were sufficient to get us to the interview stage. The value of this particular interaction lies in the opportunity it provides for going beyond the facts and assertions in these documents whether in terms of gaining an understanding of the person behind these, or of trying to obtain more clarity on the information provided here. If we are to merely repeat the information on the résumé, the interview is redundant. We need to take that information further by turning it into stories with which we may leave a greater impact. Turning raw information into narrative form is quite difficult to do on the spot. Rather than depending on inspiration to strike us during the actual interaction, it is much wiser to give prior thought to this and plan how we could make the information more vivid and engaging, yet succinct and focused.

Domain knowledge specific to our area

Of course, our domain knowledge will be an important focus of the interviewer's probing. It would be wrong to assume that the details of our qualifications and experience provided in our résumé or dossier will lead to clear inferences about our knowledge level. It is best to avoid treating the domain knowledge actually acquired by us as obvious to others. Two or more persons with very similar sets of qualifications and experience may possess quite different levels of knowledge and expertise through these. **The interview is our opportunity to show the knowledge and exposure that our qualifications and experience really signify.**

When you are starting out straight after completing your qualifications, you should be aware that the interviewer is not interested in the qualifications in themselves or in your academic performance as much as in what you have really acquired and mastered from it. It is advisable to brush up your discipline-specific knowledge, so as to be able to demonstrate that you truly own what you show on paper. Even at all other stages of your career, it is best to keep in mind that while for you it may be a matter of pride to have the qualifications and experience under your belt, the interviewer cannot be interested in these as ends in themselves. Obviously, from their perspective, it is important to determine what you have made of these. Again, the learning and domain knowledge acquired from these may be clear as day to you, but we must understand that these would need to be spelt out for another person. An important reason why you should really put your mind to making the knowledge owned by you apparent to the interviewer is that this is how you can hope to stand out from amongst those competing against you for the position. A certain minimum requirement in terms of qualifications and experience defined for the position would mean that every single one of your competitors will be quite similar to you in terms of these. The interviewer, obviously, would wish to see in what way you are superior to others and this awareness should guide you in preparing to impress your depth of knowledge in the concerned domain on the interviewers.

You should consider questions such as:

- How can I meaningfully interpret the factual information regarding my qualifications and experience into a persuasive and convincing demonstration of learning and domain knowledge specific to my area that I have derived from these and would bring to this position?
- How can I present my belief about this in a way that is credible to another person?
- What support can I gather to demonstrate and substantiate my case?

Trying to answer these questions with specific and concrete details helps us to prepare in a focused manner so as to persuasively present ourselves in this crucial area of interest to the interviewer.

Desired generic skills

While domain knowledge and relevant skills are obviously of prime importance from the interviewers' perspective, there are certain generic skills and attributes desired at all levels that the interviewers would certainly be interested in assessing. Communication and interpersonal skills are the most ubiquitous amongst the desired skills for almost any profile across professions and industries. In addition, skills and attributes to be tested would include initiative taking, ability to handle change and uncertainty, ability to work in a group, innovativeness, problem solving and analytical skills, and willingness to take up challenges. For those of us who are starting out on our careers, we may expect the interviewer to be keen to also determine quick learning ability, intelligence, general awareness, ability to work on one's own initiative, to work independently with limited supervision, as well as ability to work well in a group. For those who are some way up the hierarchy, the interviewer is likely to be interested in ascertaining the ability to work under pressure, the ability to take up challenges, the ability to display leadership, problem solving and analytical skills, and the willingness to constantly upgrade knowledge and skills. Specifics of the context will, no doubt, shape the exact expectations.

Awareness of these general expectations as well as those specific to the context in terms of our level and the requirements of the position should guide our preparation for the interview so that we may be ready to respond to questions with an awareness of what the interviewer may be interested in ascertaining. We should plan how we may talk convincingly of our qualities and abilities. We may, accordingly, be prepared to provide concrete examples from our track record to support our assertions about our skills and the relevant learning from experience that we would be able to bring with us. We should also plan how best we can make the example or our elaboration vivid and memorable. We should be able to talk about it with enthusiasm, in detail, with an eagerness and conviction that make it more than an item in the résumé by putting our personality into it and weaving a story around it that has human interest and vividness of description.

All this needs planning and preparation, rather than the belief that it will all turn out perfectly at the interview simply because it concerns not theoretical stuff but our own experience. For example, without adequate preparation we may flounder about if asked to talk about the biggest challenge taken up and how we faced it, and offer the first thing that comes to mind, in an unstructured manner, perhaps without being able to recall all relevant details or to clearly articulate its significance. We will be in a position to provide a much better response by having given thought to this during preparation and having already identified the most relevant and illustrative examples or incidents or other support for our assertions, having recalled all relevant details, and having planned how to present our ideas with conviction and persuasiveness.

General awareness

For most positions, interviewers would be interested in ascertaining that the person is well-informed about general matters along with having a sharp intellect and an analytical mind. For junior positions, this may be seen as a positive attribute because it reflects well-roundedness, and an intelligent curiosity and willingness to learn about the world in general. For senior positions, again, it may be regarded positively, reflecting a broader perspective and a deeper and wider base of information. Keeping these expectations of the interviewers in mind, we should take adequate care to prepare in this area as well. **Preparing with a focus on our specific area may help to show our depth of knowledge in that area, but we should also be ready to show breadth of awareness and understanding if the interviewers should turn the discussion to such topics in order to assess us.**

We must also prepare ourselves to expect questions aimed at testing our analytical skills. This may be tested either by asking you to give critical instances of analytical tasks carried out or by asking you for analysis of information and data—either related to your area or general issues—rather than merely for information. Knowing this expectation can help us prepare and practise so as to be able to show our strengths in this skill with strong, well-structured responses with concrete details and presented with adequate energy and conviction.

c) Appearance

Our preparation should also take into account our appearance. We must take care of what we are conveying not only by our body language but also through our appearance. While in some contexts, attire will be more critical than in others, because of the greater need for direct interactions with customers or other external people, it is generally expected that one comes for an interview dressed formally. Although you may find out a bit about the work culture of the particular place, please keep in mind that that standard may not apply to this first interaction. It is better to err on the side of caution by dressing formally and conservatively. Dark, sober colours, well-ironed clothes, a conservative pattern in ties and shirts/blouses, formal footwear, well-groomed hair, and minimal make-up, jewellery, and perfume/cologne all give an indirect message that you are taking this formal interaction seriously rather than casually. **By taking care of our appearance we show respect for the other party and that we are mature enough to know the requirements of a formal business interaction.** While appearance and attire should be such as to quickly register as appropriate, they should not draw attention to themselves. You want the interviewers to remember you, not your clothing or accessories. If these draw attention to themselves, it may be at the cost of attention to you, and would indicate an error in judgement on your part.

Our appearance would also include our bag and/or folder for documents. A too-large bag or badly organized documents give a bad impression. If we are carrying a large bag, it would be best to leave it outside. A small handbag or document bag or folder is adequate. These should be left on the floor next to your chair and not take up too much room. It should be easy to access the documents from the bag or folder rather than fishing in it and pulling them out haphazardly. Arranging the documents meticulously and in an order that makes it easy to find what we need to, not only creates a positive impression but also prevents us from getting flustered.

Practice Makes Perfect

The more thorough our preparation, the more in control we would feel before facing the interview. However, our level of confidence can be further enhanced by practice. Gaining as much practice as possible of speaking, of putting our ideas into words, is a good starting point. **The more we are used to speaking out, the more comfort we have acquired in putting words to ideas, to articulating our thoughts, the better position we are already in.** Earlier experience of interviews can help by giving us a general sense of our performance that may help us in boosting our confidence or in identifying how we may improve our performance. By concretely breaking down our performance and reflecting upon it in terms of areas that we were satisfied with and those we could improve upon, we may get valuable clarity about improving ourselves. If we have received feedback on our earlier performance from others, it would be valuable to use that too. While speaking of our own self should be the easiest thing to do as no subject can be better known, our experience of interviews may help us realize how challenging it is to get others to appreciate all that we stand for through a brief interaction. Reflecting on the experience would also help us to prepare better and to practise what emerged as particularly challenging parts of the task for us in the past. Overall, such experiences would have provided us some measure of comfort and confidence through familiarity with the process and experience of speaking of ourselves.

In addition, practice for the particular interview is very helpful. What would such practice involve? First of all, we all know that even though we may have gathered information and planned what to say, sometimes the articulation of the ideas is unclear and a bit hazy on details. We wish to avoid this happening in an interview where our choice of words, the construction of the sentences, the weaving together of relevant details, and the recollection of facts, as well as clarity and coherence of our communication are what we are evaluated on. With the explicit focus on evaluation, interviews are generally high-pressure occasions and it is usually quite daunting to put our ideas and information across. Practice before the actual event helps by giving us the opportunity to try putting the ideas we wish to convey in words, trying out various options of conveying something, deciding the kinds of phrasing that would be clear and effective, and the like. Without practice, we may be in danger of being unable to recall the best examples to clarify our idea or pull out the strongest supporting details to substantiate a claim or to back up a point. When we have practised such articulation, we are better able to cope with the stress of the interview situation not only by having reviewed and polished our expression, but also because sentences may roll off our tongue better, since we have already done it during practice in a less daunting environment.

It is not being suggested that you prepare and practise every word you would say at the interview. Not only is that impossible given the dynamic way such an interaction takes shape, no one can know in advance how exactly it will go. Practice may involve a few things:

a) It may amount to simply thinking aloud, framing responses to anticipated questions, getting a comfortable feel of the ideas we wish to convey and trying variations in the articulation. It may give us the opportunity to try and see if we are able to recall our collected data and use these in the appropriate places to our satisfaction. We may review our attempts and try a few times more. By doing so, we are not aiming at working out the exact words and then memorizing them, but having practised in the manner makes it much more likely that these constructions will roll off our tongue more easily even if we get somewhat stressed on the actual occasion. This is very useful not only for the phrasing of our ideas but also for the most appropriate examples and other kinds of support for our assertions.

182

b) Our practice may also take the shape of a mock interview. For this we will need a friend, colleague, or family member who is willing to take the role of the interviewer and is also able to provide constructive feedback on our communication. It may be difficult to get someone who can get into the role of the interviewer and closely simulate the approach of the actual interview panel and completely adopt their perspective. However, all we may need at this point is someone willing to help us in practising our responses to the questions we have anticipated. Of course, how well we are able to do that depends on the understanding we are able to get of the interviewers' perspective in our preparation stage. What we would like at this point, is to try out the responses in terms of content and style that we have worked out in our head, and to check both for ourselves, and by feedback from the receiver, how they come out. This may be especially useful in practising how we will respond to difficult questions, rather than simply hoping they will not come up.

c) As in the case of any spoken communication, we need to be careful of the non-verbal messages we may be inadvertently sending out through our body language. The importance of non-verbal communication for a selection interview is even greater because the objective here is to assess the interviewee and non-verbal cues provide as important insight into the person as the verbal content. We must remember that all things being equal, the interviewer would always prefer a person who is agreeable, likely to get along with people, and hold his or her views without being disagreeable. Much of this assessment is made from our body language at the interview. We need to take sufficient care with our tone, facial expression, and posture, so that we are aware of and in control of, what we are conveying about our personality. We should not leave this to satisfactorily work itself out in the actual event, but practise doing so.

Getting a sense of how we are communicating in totality can prove very helpful in improving our comfort and confidence. By paying attention to this during practice we should aim at having our non-verbal messages completely under control. We should check that we are in control of what we are communicating and thus avoid sending unintended messages that may not be consistent with our verbal messages. At the same time, we should be checking if we are able to use the non-verbal cues to support and strengthen our intended meanings. In case of any gaps perceived at this stage, we can focus on this and strengthen our confidence in handling this aspect of our communication. Some useful ways to do this are practising before a mirror, videotaping, or seeking feedback specifically on this aspect from a helpful friend who plays the interviewer's role in a mock interview.

Thorough preparation and practice provide immense benefit by giving us a greater sense of confidence than if we were to arrive at an interview simply expecting to make an impact on the strength of the details on our résumé, however impressive it may be. An interaction as important as a selection interview should not be left to only impromptu presentation of ideas. Although we would wish to retain the freshness of impromptu phrasing and also be ready for new directions that the communication may take, we must draw our content from strong preparation and practice. We strengthen both our ability to convey our ideas and confidence in handling the interaction if we have given sufficient thought to what we wish to present and how we plan to do so, have reflected on the objectives of the communication from our own as well as the interviewers' perspective, and have practiced well.

At the Interview

Norman Vincent Peale urges, 'Believe in yourself! Have faith in your abilities! Without a humble but reasonable confidence in your own powers you cannot be successful or happy.'

All our preparation and practice, guided by our understanding of the general requirements of interviews as a communication tool and by the specifics of the context, lead finally to the interview itself. Having adequately prepared, we must make sure that we keep our conviction of our suitability for the position, and our substantial and objective support for this conviction, in clear focus. While waiting to be called in for the interview, it is important to help ourselves feel upbeat through positive self-talk. It is best not to dissipate our energy in fidgeting or in small talk at this point. **Focus and** calmness should be our aim at this point. Breathing deeply and letting our body go loose and limp and emptying our mind are helpful ways of making us feel calm and relaxed.

a) Using body language effectively

It would be an error to think that the assessment begins with the first question; it begins as soon as we walk into the room. It is important to use our body language to make a good first impression and to help support our communication throughout the interview. **Right from the moment we walk into the interview room, we need to be aware of what we are projecting, whether through words or through non-verbal cues.** At all times, we should be sending out cues that are consistent with the overall message we wish to convey to the interviewers. Our gait should be confident but not swaggering. A little diffidence, given that it is normal in the circumstances and shows that you are not acting blasé, is better than appearing nonchalant or displaying an inappropriate hauteur in one's bearing. As we greet the panellists and take a seat when asked to, our tone and posture should show respect for the occasion and for the interviewers.

Assessments about our personality would be drawn from not only our verbal responses to direct questions about it, but also indirectly from the way we listen and respond. Perhaps difficult or stress-inducing questions may be asked to see how we respond, whether we can keep our cool, and if we can disagree without being disagreeable. We have to be very careful to respond appropriately both in terms of what we say and the accompanying body language. In case of any inconsistency between the messages received from the two, it is more likely that the body language will be seen as more credible and showing our true feelings while words may be seen as more likely to be consciously modified to be in line with expectations. If we are able to give consistent messages it is a great boost to the credibility of our entire communication, and especially so in case of difficult or baiting questions.

Being aware of our facial expressions, eye contact, gestures, and posture would help us be in control of what these may convey. It is important to use our body language to show ourselves as keen, enthusiastic, and sincerely engaged in the communication. We should remain completely involved in the interaction, ignoring all physical and mental distractions. Our eyes should show that we are paying attention and when we respond to a question asked by one interviewer in a panel, we should make sure that we make eye contact with all panelists so as show that the response is directed at the panel as a whole.

Our voice is of the greatest importance in carrying our verbal message and we should ensure that we articulate our words carefully, taking care to not mumble or chew off parts of words or to trail off at the ends of sentences. Our volume should be sufficient to be easily audible given the distance separating us from our listeners. A volume too low or too high would clearly indicate nervousness or a sense of discomfort with the situation and would not go to make a positive impression. The pace of speaking should appear natural, with sufficient pauses as appropriate for conversations and impromptu speaking. **Even if we are answering something we have prepared well, it is best to speak in a manner that does not betray the fact that is something we have prepared and worse, memorized.** We should also take sufficient pauses to allow for registering the responses of the interviewers so as to be able to adapt and respond accordingly. Our intent should be to speak in a conversational style with good intonation and voice modulation. This helps both in adding additional, supportive undertones to our verbal meaning and in showing us as comfortable and confident.

b) Listening well

In our focus on making a good impression through our spoken words, we must not overlook the important role of good listening at the interview. It is important to remember that the communication skills demonstrated at the interview comprise not only speaking, but also listening. How we listen is as much a part of our communication ability as how we speak. If we demonstrate the latter, but show scant regard for listening effectively, we may still not make a strong impression. Our focus should be as much on listening effectively as on effectively articulating our ideas; both demonstrate our communication skills better than any testimonial.

Effective listening is crucial to our speaking as it shapes how we respond to questions and to any feedback that we may receive. Without taking due care with listening, we cannot hope to respond adequately, appropriately, or correctly. If not sure of a question, it is best to double check by repeating or to ask for clarification rather than risk giving a tangential or inappropriate response. We listen to both the words and the body language of the interviewer. Sometimes a glint in the eye, the tone, or the facial expression gives quite a different meaning to the question and needs to be responded to appropriately. If we are not listening carefully we are likely to miss these non-verbal cues of the speaker and consequently respond inappropriately. Any demonstration of poor listening skills goes against us not only through preventing us from giving the most apt responses, but also because it is shows that we are lacking an important element in our communication skills.

Listening is an invisible activity that happens in the mind; not only must we make sure to listen well, but also to *show*, through our body language, that we are listening. By showing that we are listening well, we demonstrate our alertness and focus—and these are attributes that add to the positive impression we wish to leave. Very importantly, we show that we are respectful of the occasion and of the interviewers and that we value the communication.

c) Our verbal communication at the interview

When we come to the verbal part of our communication, we need to be guided in every choice we make about what we say and how we say it by awareness that our objective is persuasion. We are, in effect, in a sales pitch where we are trying to convince the other person of ourselves as the solution to their needs, and as offering the best fit between what we have to offer and what they require. Our own sense of being convinced about our suitability is essential to give us the conviction that can shine through our communication. But obviously, this subjective assessment will not be sufficient for others. This is where the value of our analysis, planning, preparation, and practice comes in. We use the objective support we have gathered to back up our assertions and conviction. Our preparation and practice should help us easily put words to our ideas and bring in what we feel is essential to strengthening our persuasive case.

We should not aim at reproducing the exact phrasing of our prepared or rehearsed responses as this would give a stilted appearance to our responses and take away the freshness of the interaction. It may also throw doubts over our ownership of the ideas by giving the appearance of being prepared rather than a fresh response. **Our aim should be to provide the best presentation of our ideas through selecting our words carefully so as to adequately express what we wish to convey.** Having come up with good examples and critical incidents to illustrate our ideas and experience through our thorough preparation and practice, we would now be in a good position to provide persuasive substantiation and elaboration of the much crisper statements of facts and information on our résumé, if required. Having given thought to the most illustrative incident, and recollected all relevant details during preparation, as well as having practised how to add vividness to it in narration, we will be ready with a strong response rather than having to rack our brains and trying to come up with all this at the interview itself.

Thorough preparation would also give us the confidence to handle unanticipated questions without getting flustered. We may spend some time thinking about a response so as to collect our thoughts and to recall details or support. This does not show us in a negative light at all. Rather, it may be the appropriate way to respond to questions that require reflection rather than ready information. In fact, there may be some questions for which we may not have an answer. If this is a question seeking some information that we do not have handy, we may respond by explicitly admitting that we do not have it, rather than bluffing or beating about the bush. No one can be expected to know everything, recall every bit of information, and answer every question. As long as we can provide good responses to most of the questions, an occasional blank would not demolish our performance.

It is also important to recognize what a particular question is attempting to determine by listening well and by keeping the context in mind. Only a few questions are likely to require the recollection of random facts and information. Whatever can fairly be expected of us should have been anticipated and adequately prepared. The larger this set is, we can take a chance with the others. We may be able to respond well to unexpected questions on the basis of our general preparation. Even if we miss out on an odd one, no great harm may be caused. Moreover, most questions are likely to be focused on finding out our views or analyses of issues we are expected to be familiar with and here it is not so much about a right or wrong response as of its quality in terms of what it demonstrates of us.

Being in control of what we say, knowing in what light it shows us, is very important. Although our manner should be spontaneous and lively, there is no place for inadvertent or accidental responses. Thorough preparation is the best way to avoid this. I have seen candidates get trapped in their own words after mentioning things that revealed something negative about them or their attitudes or an empty claim that they could not support when probed further. Such inadvertent responses are likely to cause much more harm than simply the inability to recall some fact or information. Integrity of responses is likely to show us in a positive light to the interviewer as someone who is not merely faking a persona or mouthing expected answers. Emerging as someone who is seen as honest and truthful is a very big positive. In my interactions with interviewers and my own experience on interview panels, I have found dishonesty in self-presentation and inconsistency of responses that reveals some ill-intention, more certainly a disqualifier than a few incorrect responses.

Keeping this in mind, we must try our best to show ourselves through our responses, as honest and straightforward rather than cause doubts through dubious claims and inconsistencies. Remember, therefore, it does not take something as extreme as a forged certificate or plain falsehood to raise doubts in the panel's mind; a suspicion of one not being completely reliable in the genuineness of their responses may be enough.

This is something more to watch out for than what most interviewees generally worry about—not being able to answer a question or showing nervousness. It is not a disaster if some nerves are apparent or if one cannot answer every question. Generally speaking, interviewers understand that this is a stressful occasion for the candidates, and tend to overlook a few minor glitches, especially in the opening.

To some extent, what precisely may be excused is a subjective judgement and would depend on the panellists, but as candidates it is important to keep up our confidence by knowing that it is the overall impression we provide that is the measure rather than an expectation of perfection in every single response. Many times when I have discussed an interviewee's performance with a panel, it has emerged that the interviewers did not notice certain minor flaws in the body language or in the responses or were willing to overlook these when considering the total picture. We should prepare and practise well, but at the interview itself, we should not allow ourselves to get rattled by any small error we may make. Doing so saps our confidence, resulting in further mistakes that may then cumulatively add up to give a negative impression.

Although it may seem that as the interviewee we can only respond to the questions asked of us and that we have no control over the direction that the interaction takes, this is not necessarily true. Although interviewers do come prepared with their own set of questions, much of these are likely to be derived from our own case as presented through our application and résumé (or internal dossier, in case of our own organization). Generally speaking, the interview takes the shape of a conversation that flows out of the questions and responses. As respondents, it is clearly possible for us to influence the direction of the flow by what we say and how we say it—the information we divulge, the elaboration we are ready to provide, the enthusiasm with which we show that we are comfortable and confident in interacting with the interviewers. If we provide brief answers in a staccato tone, the conversation becomes stilted and uncomfortable for both parties. As we are the one being assessed, our being uncomfortable, uneasy, or unwilling to provide sufficient information would not go in our favour. We should recognize that further questions may be asked about any topic we provide and we should be prepared to respond. It is a mistake to assume that anything said in an interview will be disregarded and treated as casual or inadvertent. Any remark or information may provide an opening to a line of questioning and we should be ready to take it further, if required. We do not present a very good picture of ourselves when we fail to show sufficient depth on something that comes up in our own responses and is taken further by the interviewer. This is where the value of thorough preparation and practice comes in. Preparation gives us the depth and practice prevents the casual and inadvertent mentioning of points or of issues that we have not thought through. Practice of conversations in general also ensures that we are already comfortable with framing and conveying, in sufficient detail and in interesting manner, some of the things we talk of in the interview.

In the dynamics of a conversational style, we may also ask some questions. However, we should be careful to not appropriate the role of the interviewer and to restrict our questions to brief ones to show interest in the role and functions or to seek clarification about some information proffered by the interview. In case there is a set protocol for the interview, you may be told before you begin if questions will be taken from you and when. Usually it is at the end of the interaction that the candidate may be asked if they have any questions. It is wise to refrain from asking questions about remuneration, perks, and benefits at this point. It is also smart to have acquired sufficient information about the organization (unless it is another role in our own organization) from easily accessible and credible public sources. This would mean that our questions about it can reflect this knowledge and we can build further on it to show that we take an intelligent interest in it.

In my experience, there have been a number of instances where a candidate at an interview tries to plead their case for a position by trying to establish what the position will mean to them in terms of learning, future career prospects, and fulfillment of personal goals. While there may be nothing wrong in these and they may be good ends in themselves for you, please keep in mind that the interviewer is really not going through this entire exercise to help the candidate in reaching these goals. When we make a sales pitch about ourselves we must make sure that we are talking of *their* needs and our ability to satisfy it, *their* requirements and our skill-set, *their* goals and how we can help meet them. **Of course, a job or career advancement means much in personal terms for you too, but it is best to keep that as incidental rather than at the centre of the focus at the interview.** This is not to say that you brush aside the question of personal motivation or aspirations if directly asked, but only to say that your complete rationale for seeking the position should not emerge as self-fulfillment, advancement, and learning for yourself. Of course, we may be able to demonstrate our motivation by linking our personal aspirations with those of the organization and our skill-set with the requirements of the particular position. We should remember that just as the objective of the interviewers is to determine the best match between aspirants and the requirements of the organization and the position, our objective, in turn, should be to present the most persuasive case we can, of our own suitability.

Sometimes, it is erroneously suggested that we should present ourselves at an interview the way we would like to be seen, even if it has little relationship with the reality. Although it may appear easy to present a fake version of ourselves—especially in terms of personal qualities, aspirations, and particulars of work and life experiences—one must remember that many of these can be verified, if required. It would do us great harm it were to emerge that we had not been completely honest in any of the details provided or deliberately misled the interviewers. Moreover, unless we are accomplished actors, it is very likely that we may not be able to present a credible and consistent image through all our verbal and non-verbal cues. Even more importantly, we have to understand that even if we are able to pull it off at the interview, we are only creating a fake persona that we will have to maintain for a long time. Not only would that be very difficult, the most important problem is that there would really be no match with our real self and the requirements of the organization and position, and this is a recipe for discontentment and failure. **This is where the importance of self-understanding as the first and foremost step in our preparation, comes in. There will be no need for effort in presenting a fake persona if we have already taken care to understand ourselves well and to make a convincing case for ourselves of the match between us and the position.** Not only will this give us conviction and confidence for the interview, it will also mean that we are much more likely to be successful as well as happy in that organization/position.

Even though the world is a competitive place and we may feel that it is vital to get the position anyhow rather than to truly find a match between it and our true selves, there are definitely places where we would be better matched and would not need to build and maintain a fake self. In our search for potential places where we could be successful and contented, we can surely be guided as much by the requirements as by our self-understanding. If we rate contentment as valuable, it will come from genuinely putting our energy into acquiring and polishing any areas of our personality or skills that we find need improvement rather than in presenting a false picture of ourselves at an interview. It is important to be true to ourselves when we present ourselves to others through any interaction. This is especially true of how we present ourselves at a selection interview, as the assessment made here may lead to determining our suitability for a particular organization and profile. A misrepresentation is sure to cause as much difficulty and discontentment to us, as to the employer.

Overall, an interview should be a pleasant experience if we approach it with due care to preparation and practice. Being comfortable and confident is easier when we have the right qualifications for the position and have conviction of our suitability. Being qualified for the position is not something we can acquire just for the interview; it is a sum of all that we are and have acquired in terms of learning through our track record up to that point and that is portable to other contexts or has potential for further enhancement in another role. Having that under our belt and having sufficient conviction as well as motivation are prerequisites for making a good impact at the interview. Our persuasiveness and our spoken communication are then to be used as effectively as possible to leave a strong, memorable, and positive impact on the interviewers. The more aware we are of the focus of the interviewers and what they would use for their assessment, the better we can ensure that we use every element of our presence and communication to add to the persuasiveness of our case.

Awareness alone is not enough and needs to be supported by thorough preparation. The more control we have over what we wish to communicate and the better equipped we are with sufficient understanding and information—about ourselves, technical matters, and general issues—the greater confidence we can project. The more practice we give ourselves of conversing and of the particular ways we would like to frame our responses to anticipated questions, the greater the likelihood of being unflustered and comfortable during the interview. With the richest medium of face-to-face communication, we have a very wide range of stimuli available to carry our messages to the receiver. However, this is also a challenge in terms of keeping them consistent and projecting ourselves in a suitable manner. For most of us, this is a daunting task and without sufficient care in terms of practice, it is difficult to feel confident or to ensure that we can effectively use the medium to its full potential and in the best possible manner.

CHAPTER 5

Extemporary Speaking

Most of us feel much more comfortable in speaking situations where we have had time to prepare, to practise, and probably to take along some supporting material/tools, than in situations where we are expected to speak off the cuff. However, many occasions need us to be prepared to contribute on the spot by speaking extemporaneously. It would reflect quite poorly on both our knowledge, and our confidence and conviction levels if we display reluctance to speak extemporaneously. Even if we preferred it, it would not be possible to speak only when we have had ample time for preparation and practice.

Although extemporary speaking seems challenging to many of us, we should look at it as an opportunity to make a big impact and we should do all we can to equip ourselves to handle it effectively. The potential to serve a number of objectives and to impress others means that we would be well advised to give it as much care and attention as we give to other speaking situations.

Extemporary speaking means a style of speaking that does not rely on extensive preparation and does not involve the use of a written script or detailed notes or visual aids such as OHP slides or a PowerPoint presentation. One common occasion for extemporary speaking—the meeting or discussion—was already covered in Chapter 3. Here we look at other formal occasions where we are required to speak extemporaneously before a number of people.

It is sad to see many brilliant, accomplished men and women unable to speak to a moderate- to large-sized audience with confidence and impact despite the undeniable depth of knowledge and experience they possess. Some shy away from extemporary speaking perhaps because of a few uncomfortable experiences in the past where they were not able to make the most of the opportunity to impact others, leading them to the unhappy conclusion that this is not their cup of tea. This perception and the consequent avoidance of such communication only go to further weaken their confidence in their ability and also make them neglect honing and refining it. However, if we can get over our negative self-perception in this regard and forsake this defeatist attitude, we can slowly build our comfort and confidence in such speaking contexts. The biggest fear underlying extemporary speaking is that of making a fool of ourselves in front of others and it derives from the perceived lack of control over our content and style in this mode. But this fear may be preventing us from making an impact through a very valuable mode of interaction. By avoiding occasions for extemporary speaking, we are limiting ourselves to only a few kind of situations. No doubt we may present ourselves very positively in these, but feeling more confident about extemporary speaking would add one more way to get our ideas and feelings to others. In fact, the impact made by extemporary speaking may be greater because it may be perceived as more spontaneous and therefore a better reflection of our true qualities—whether in terms of personality or technical expertise, or authority in our area.

Although lack of control seems to be the biggest challenge making extemporary speaking appear so daunting, there are many elements of such situations that are quite simple to be in control of. Firstly, barring some crisis situations, such speaking occasions are hardly ever completely out of the blue. Given our position and the occasion, the requirement (or opportunity) of speaking is seldom entirely unanticipated. We may generally be aware that given our role, a brief speech would be required from us or that it would be a good opportunity to address the group. In some occasions we may be explicitly informed of this expectation. We would categorize these as extemporaneous speaking because we would not be carrying notes or speak from a prepared script. Another element that is generally easy to determine is the capacity in which we would be required to speak as well as the constitution of the audience.

Regarding extemporary speaking as only about thinking on our feet and covering various aspects of the topic as they strike us is not the ideal way to maximize the effectiveness of our speech. It is also a recipe for acute discomfort and nervousness. Some preparation of what we should say and how we should do so helps to make our speech more memorable and impactful for our listeners than if we simply winged it. Understanding the context is of prime importance in giving us a sense of control and helping us to ensure that we serve the objective for the particular situation. Even in a situation requiring extemporary speaking, it is possible to give some thought to properly grasping the nature of the occasion, the setting, and the perspective and expectations of the audience. For example, as the head of the organizing committee for a seminar, we would expect that we would be required to speak in that capacity at the opening ceremony to give the background for the event or to introduce the Chief Guest or Keynote Speaker. As the leader of a team that has won a prestigious award, we would be expected to speak from that role when we accept the award on behalf of the team. As for the audience, again it is not difficult to know the composition in terms of background and interests. If it is a small set of internal people in the audience, we may even know the personal qualities, assumptions, and perspective of the listeners. In case of an external audience, the context would still allow us to make certain fair assumptions about their background, interest, and existing level of information and understanding on the topic. **The better we understand the context and use this understanding to guide what we speak and how we do so, the better we can ensure that we deliver value to our listeners. At the same time, this understanding**

helps us to be much more confident and comfortable.

Let us keep in mind a key fact—the audience expects its objective in listening to be served, regardless of how we prepared (or did not), of whether we had a choice of presenting with aids or without, and of how much effort and time in preparation we put in. What matters to the audience is that the ideas get conveyed with clarity and add value to them. Our choice of style of presenting our ideas should depend on the nature of the occasion. For example, it would be expected that a vote of thanks or words of welcome for a guest to an event are offered without the aid of a PPT or a prepared script. We would also not be expected to pull out a script to read when we wish to connect with people to inspire or congratulate them. The suitability of the speaking style has to do with how best it serves the objective and is in accordance with accepted norms. **The extemporary style of speaking has the advantage of allowing for a greater sense of spontaneity and strong connection with the audience, which may be very relevant to our purpose with certain audiences on certain occasions.** It is for us to make a careful choice in terms of occasions where we feel that we can add to the impact of our words by using our spontaneity to signal greater engagement with the audience and conveying perhaps a greater degree of conviction in what we say.

At the same time, the choice brings in its own challenges. Even though we speak without aids, we need to stay focused on a coherent central idea, and to flesh out our points with supporting examples and elaboration in a structured manner.

Without these, it is unlikely that the audience would be impressed with a sense of great value addition or carry a very positive assessment of the speaker. It is highly unlikely that these elements will all fall in place by magic. Clarity about our purpose, control over our content and structure are needed, as is the effective use of supporting non-verbal cues. All this cannot happen without effort.

The upshot is that although speaking extemporaneously may be a requirement at times and our preference at others, it is crucial to give prior thought to the topic and our focus in view of the audience and the objective, and to gather our thoughts and mentally plan for what to speak and how. By taking some steps to be in control of these before we reach the speaking stage, we can try to ensure that while we do use the impression of greater spontaneity to add to our connection with the audience, we do not struggle in articulating our ideas, in fleshing out our points, and in supporting these with examples and concrete details.

PREPARATION

'It usually takes more than three weeks to prepare a good impromptu speech,' said Mark Twain.

This paradoxical assertion surely deserves a closer look. Think about the occasion when you listened to someone whose brief, impromptu speech left an impression on you. You may recall that the content was focused and relevant, and the manner, fresh and engaging. You felt admiration and perhaps also a twinge of envy! 'I wish I could speak so effortlessly and engagingly on the spur of the moment!' But appearances can be really deceptive. In this case, you may bet on it that the spontaneity came from prior thought, planning, and preparation. I remember a mesmerizing talk where a distinguished visiting speaker very effectively engaged the audience in a fresh, conversational and spontaneous manner. Over a cup of coffee after the talk, he shared how around 7 am when the folks he was staying with, came to see if he was up, he had already been up for two hours, practising his extemporary talk in front of a mirror!

While spontaneity is expected and appreciated, it is important to keep in mind that for the listener in the workplace or business context, it is not about the speaker's apparent effortlessness or freshness but about their investment of time and attention. A speaker who does not provide this sense of value to the listener cannot hope to make an impact by mere spontaneity or witty turns of phrases. **As a speaker, we should be interested in appearing spontaneous not as an end in itself but as a way to connect with the listeners, and to get our message across most effectively. The bottom line is that the message remains the king.** The interest created in the listeners, the freshness of the presentation of ideas, the expression and style, are the tools we may use to get the ideas across with greatest impact. For certain kinds of occasions, the rapport with the listeners and the effect of spontaneity may be very important in serving to get the message across. In such cases, our choice of the extemporary mode of delivery is a deliberate and strategic one, and we should be guided by the opportunities provided by it to effectively convey our ideas.

The occasion for extemporary speaking may be a formal affair or a social event related to the work environment or one where we are required to speak to an external audience due to our position as an expert or as a person of some social standing. Even though we may not prepare a script or a presentation or carry notes, we need to collect our thoughts, and find a focus. Without this clarity, it is not possible to present our ideas in a coherent manner. It is especially important for a brief talk as we need to make an impact in a rather limited window of time. Although we may not prepare exactly what we shall say, there are certain ways we may try to help ourselves in presenting our ideas in a structured and focused manner rather than ending up rambling or missing out key points we wanted to make—in all, not being able to convey our ideas on the topic to the best of our ability.

The preparation we need for an extemporary speaking occasion is general rather than specific. It is not about preparing a script or visual aids to our speech. One kind of preparation that we need to make for such speaking occasions generally is that of ensuring that we are well-informed about our chosen topic. In addition, we should constantly keep updating our information base and understanding of the world around us. The wider and deeper our knowledge base, the more interesting people find our ideas and the more kinds of people we can relate to.

Merely trusting in our ability to dip into our pool of knowledge and experience at a given point in time, so as to draw out what is relevant for the occasion, is a rather ineffective and unreliable way of going about it. It may work out fine on a stray occasion or two, but it is not a trustworthy approach if one really wants to make an impact with one's speech. Rather, analysing our purpose, our audience, and the context, we should be updating our information and gaining as much insight as possible into the issue we wish to speak about. This not only works better in terms of how well we meet the objective in terms of audience's expectations and our purpose, it also gives us greater confidence. Our confidence and conviction come from true ownership of the ideas we want to get across and gaining depth of knowledge and examining our ideas deeply and critically is important for this.

There are also a few other kinds of general preparation that would help make our speech stronger and more impactful as well as reduce the natural anxiety we usually feel when faced with a formal speaking situation where we will not have the support of notes or a prepared script or a PowerPoint presentation.

AUDIENCE ANALYSIS

At all such occasions, the purpose and the audience are the key elements we must analyse in order to stay pertinent and to provide value to the audience. **The first step before thinking of any other component of our speech is to focus on the audience we shall be speaking to. It is essential to understand, as far as possible, who we shall be addressing.**

There is no one way of approaching a topic that works equally well for all audiences.

For every choice, whether it be of focus, references, examples, appeal, or humour, the most important basis is audience analysis. The greater the care we take to ensure that we understand our listeners' profile in terms of background and experience base, and the expectations they would probably bring to the talk, the better we would be able to take calls on appropriateness of our choices in these matters. The more appropriate these choices are, the greater the ease with which we will be able to relate to our listeners and to get them actively involved in sharing our ideas. If we neglect this crucial step, it is quite difficult to engage our listeners and to make our talk relevant, interesting, and useful to them. In terms of both content and delivery style, we can better engage with an audience who we understand rather than one that is merely an undifferentiated set of people for us.

DEFINING THE OBJECTIVE

As in all speaking contexts in the formal environment, we cannot afford to neglect gaining as much clarity as possible about our speaking objective. Are we speaking to inform or to persuade? To argue or to request? To explain or to motivate? If these questions remain a blur and not sorted out clearly in our mind, we may speak without impact. Although, if we speak distinctly enough and keep our expression lucid, our listeners may get the meaning of words and statements, but they are unlikely to go away with a clear idea of how these add up and the purpose they serve. Sometimes the purpose of our talk may be defined for us by others, as in the case of an invited talk on a particular topic, or may be clearly determined by the occasion and our role in a context such as thanksgiving or felicitation. In other situations, it is for us to decide on our objective. In the former situations, it is important to keep the desired or expected purpose in mind and be guided by it in every choice we make of what to cover and how best to serve that purpose for our audience. **Even when we are free to decide what to speak of, it is best to begin with clarity about our objective in the given context rather than approaching the speaking task with a vague sense of purpose or a simple idea of the topic or issue to be addressed.**

Naturally, our choice should also be guided by our own knowledge level or expertise so that we would be able to offer ideas with greater confidence as well as credibility. However, this is not enough. Unless we impose some filter, it is hard to pick out relevant bits from our storehouse of information, views, feelings, and insights on a particular issue. The particular objective, in combination with the particular audience, allows us to make appropriate choice of focus and treatment of the issue. Without consciously gaining this clarity and using this awareness to help us in shaping our choices in terms of focus, content, and delivery, we are unlikely to create a strong impact on our listeners and to serve our objective. For example, on the declaration of half-yearly results, we may decide to speak to our team to appreciate their performance and to motivate them to put in greater effort in meeting even more stiff targets for the next two quarters. We may have a hundred other things to speak to the same set of people and a clear focus on the particular issue is needed. Even focusing on the results at hand, there are various ways of dealing with the subject depending on whether our objective is sharing of the details or using the occasion to appreciate and motivate for still more effort. On the particular speaking occasion, we can create the required punch by keeping our objective for this particular interaction foremost in the mind and using it to decide every element of our approach—both in terms of content and of delivery. All our facts need to be picked out with a view to how well they will serve this objective for them. What details of the situation in terms of their morale, their emotions, their aspirations, and the like can we employ to help in serving the objective? What can we assume our listeners to be already aware of and what would we need to remind them of or highlight to bring home the need for unflinching hard work that we wish to motivate them for? If we neglect this we are in danger of diluting the effectiveness of our talk in serving the objective by bringing in elements that weaken the focus and coherence, preventing the listeners from taking away a sharp sense of the central idea.

DELIMITING THE TOPIC: ACHIEVING FOCUS

Whether we are given a topic to speak on or we decide on one, it is very important to try to achieve focus by delimiting the topic. **Formal extemporary speaking situations generally require a brief and sharply focused, rather than an elaborate,**

treatment of a topic. Rather than depending on our presence of mind on the actual speaking occasion to decide what to cover and what to omit, what to elaborate and what to leave aside, it is better to give thought to this before we speak. The actual speaking time is not the best moment to be making these decisions. If the choices of our objective and of our focus are clear to us, we are free to focus on the delivery aspect of our talk. Before we reach the speaking stage, we should decide upon our focus, taking into account our objective in speaking and the expectations, interest level, as well as the existing information level of our target audience. This clarity helps in narrowing our desired coverage and gives us the opportunity to gather the necessary material—in the form of concrete data, credible and complete information, or support for views and opinions—or in marshalling our thoughts and feelings on the issue. This would help us to make our talk more substantial and to provide value to our listeners. Without delimiting what we are speaking of, there is a danger that we go off in various directions triggered by the topic as they occur to us in a stream-of-consciousness style, or get carried away with a particular aspect, to the neglect of others. Without sufficiently narrowing down our coverage we may make disjointed or random and vague remarks and also be in danger of lacking support for some assertions as we would not have time to gather these if the points occur to us only during speaking.

If we have not delimited our topic and shared this with our audience, their expectations are likely to be much

212

wider and less likely to be served. **A speaker who neglects to delimit the topic is likely to do a far less satisfactory job because it is virtually impossible to adequately cover all aspects of the topic likely to be triggered in the minds of listeners.** It is impractical to attempt to speak on topics as wide and general as 'The Indian Economy', or 'Winds of Change in the Energy Sector', or 'Trends in Advertising'. Without hours at our disposal it would not be possible to present a satisfactory coverage of a topic that is not sharply defined. And even if it was possible to do so, we cannot assume that our audience would be able to, or willing to, give us that much time and attention. Think of how much better a job can be made in terms of treating our topic in a meaningful and useful manner if we were to delimit it by time, geography, aspect focused upon, perspective, or the like. The more sharply we are able to define our subject, the more deeply we can deal with that and the more value we can provide to our listeners by a lucid and coherent treatment. It is not sufficient to only decide on the depth and breadth of coverage for ourselves but it is also important to share these boundaries with our audience. This helps to control the countless possibilities suggested to individual minds on mention of the topic. It also helps us in deciding what to include and what to omit from amongst all the ideas or data available to us. If we are to achieve a clear and sharp focus, clarity on what we are *not* doing is as important as clarity on what we are. The effectiveness of our talk is greatly helped by clarity about our focus gained through taking into account the audience's interests and expectations, our own background and authority, and the time available.

PLANNING THE STRUCTURE

If we were to take our extemporary speaking opportunities as entirely impromptu occasions, it is likely that we would not only struggle to achieve a focus but also end up making points in a meandering fashion. This is definitely not the best way to serve our speaking objective. Structure is very important for a coherent and complete presentation of ideas or information. Even the most interesting ideas are likely to get lost in a jumbled presentation, resulting in lower impact on the listeners as they cannot carry away a clear sense of what they got from the speech. A structured way to present our ideas facilitates the listeners in following the chain of thought or of logic and to stay with us from the beginning to the end. Depending on our ability to organize material on the spur of the moment in a well-structured manner is risky. Not only is it a very unreliable approach, it is also likely to take away our focus from the delivery aspects during the actual talk. At that time our mind should be free, with our content and structure sorted out in advance, so that we may focus on maximizing the potential for connecting to our listeners and bringing our ideas alive by the way we get them across.

Although it is best to have sorted out the structure beforehand, it does not mean that we work out a detailed outline or plan out every transition or anecdote. But it is important to be clear on aspects of our structure such as how we will approach our beginning, how we could lead into the main body of our talk, how we elaborate our ideas, and how we conclude. It is a tall order to select relevant ideas from our mental store and put them together in the service of a particular objective for a particular set of listeners and to arrange the various parts in a manner that provides clarity and coherence to the listeners. **Rather than making these choices and decisions on the actual occasion of speaking, it would be far better to do so prior to it. Having given thought to this, we will be able to impose a structure on our ideas and weave them coherently together on the actual occasion, rather than stringing them along without any plan, as they occur to us.** The impact on the communication will only be enhanced by this preparatory step of giving thought to the structuring of our ideas. I am sure you would have listened to speakers who seem to be speaking at random, going backwards and forward, forgetting—and then returning to—related points. Such speakers make our task as listeners much harder and it becomes very easy for us to get distracted. The result is that there is often very little to show in terms of value of the time and effort expended by both parties. Using this experience as listeners, we should carefully plan how we may provide a more structured presentation of our ideas to take our listeners along.

The sequence in which we string together our ideas may be chosen according to the topic and focus. Some topics lend themselves to a chronological treatment, whereas others benefit from a sequence based on spatial relationship, while others still may be determined by an inherent pattern. For example, we may choose to arrange our ideas according to progression in time from past to present, and on to future, or begin from the present date and go back and forward in time to make our points. Or we may treat a process by beginning with the constituent steps and tracing the way in which these link up in a particular order or pattern. For other topics, perhaps obvious starting and closing points may be available for example, in terms of an organizational structure that has distinct parts or a hierarchical arrangement.

Having prepared to speak in this manner, with due thought to the occasion, the audience, and our objective, we can approach the speaking task with a greater sense of confidence and equanimity. This amounts to winning half the battle as our composure and pleasure in the interaction depend on how much in control we feel. Such confidence and equanimity allow us to derive the maximum advantage from this mode of spoken communication—the rapport and direct connection with the audience that is possible to create in presenting our ideas through extemporary speech.

PRESENTING

The very choice of this medium for our communication should be made with a view to its appropriateness for the desired impact on our listeners. We must select it as our preferred way of communicating with full awareness of the immense value of this very rich medium of communication so that we are able to harness it to serve our objective. **The spontaneity and the adaptability that come with extemporary face-to-face communication can be powerful ways to achieve rapport with our listeners and to connect with them.** This can be of crucial importance for serving certain objectives such as appreciating and thanking, inspiring and motivating, as well as for persuading and exhorting. For objectives that can only be served by detailed treatment of the issue and by the marshalling of a significant amount of data and logical analysis, such a medium would be quite inappropriate. Once we have made this choice of medium appropriately keeping in mind its potential for creating a connection between speaker and listeners we can attempt to maximize this potential. To do this, we would need to be in full control of our material whether it is concrete facts and information or a rational argument. This is not to say that we should have every sentence worked out, but we should not be in a position of searching for ideas or struggling to recall facts or carrying out impromptu analysis as we speak.

Being in control of the contents and having a clear idea of how we wish to structure these allows us to focus on really connecting with the listeners and articulating our ideas lucidly and in an engaging manner. The more we are in control of our material, the more we will be able to focus on this aspect of our talk. The more thought we have given to our focus in light of our purpose and our audience, the more confidently we can speak so as to create the effect of spontaneity deriving from ownership and conviction in the ideas. When the audience sees us speaking without effort and strain, assuredly providing an exposition, or presenting our argument, or explaining a process, or sharing pertinent and important information, they are able to share in our feelings of excitement, or optimism, or concern, as the case may be. We are also able to respond to feedback instantly without worrying about a rigidly set script or inflexible structure. Such feedback may come to us as explicit questions or as non-verbal cues indicating some confusion or disagreement. Our focus on the delivery, given the clarity and control over our message, allows us to be able to receive such feedback and to be able to respond to these by instant adaptation. Here lies one of the biggest strengths of face-to-face interactions, and especially so of extemporary speaking where the most direct communication with the combined force of verbal and non-verbal cues is possible. Used in perfect complementary roles, these can enhance the effectiveness of the communication manifold.

During the actual talk we need to take care of the following in order to maximize the impact:

Staying focused

While it is crucial to narrow down our subject to achieve a clear and sharp focus so as to prepare our material and approach accordingly, it is also crucial to share with our listeners the scope of our coverage of the topic. Doing so helps to keep their expectations within these limits and to focus their attention on our ideas and structure. Not only is the audience more likely to take away a clear sense of the message, we would also find it easier to stay on track and control the tendency to stray into tangential directions.

Linking and signposting—sharing structure to take audience along

Having decided on a structure to help shape our talk, it is also important to make this explicit to our listeners. Using devices such as 'to begin with', and 'in conclusion', as well as 'there are three possible explanations for this... Firstly, ... Secondly, ... Thirdly...' are good ways to take our listeners along with us. Linking devices such as 'consequently', 'further', 'on the contrary', 'similarly', 'on the one hand,' and 'on the other hand', are also very useful in indicating the relationships between parts and providing logical linkages between ideas as we move along. By indicating to our listeners a sense of our control over the structure of our talk, we can create a positive expectation of a structured presentation of ideas. In certain cases we may refer, right at the outset, to our objective and scope, indicating the number of parts we would break the topic into and clearly mention these as we come to them so as to help keep ourselves on track and to facilitate the listeners in following our ideas.

Engaging the listeners

The medium of face-to-face communication is potentially so powerful because of the ease with which the speaker can connect to the listeners and engage them in the communication. If we neglect this, it would amount to wasting a wonderful opportunity to reach out to the listeners for whose benefit we are speaking and to try to ensure that they get our message most effectively and respond in the manner we would like them to.

We may refer to our own responses as listeners to get into the shoes of our listeners and to try to avoid the kind of things that turn us off and prevent real engagement with the communication. None of us like to, or are really able to, take interest in someone who does not seem to care for us. This caring for us is not something for which concrete proof is needed but is simply assumed from what is evident through the speaker's focus and style. As listeners we get a sense of whether the speaker chose to focus distinctly on a subject and an aspect that is sharply defined and of potential use to us. Does the speaker attempt to relate their ideas to us, to present things from a perspective that would be possible for us to understand and use? Does the speaker use references and allusions that are easy for us to relate to, and examples that are from our experience base and can serve to bring clarity and sharpness to ideas? When a speaker does not seem to be focused on communicating with me as indicated by these steps, I am unlikely to respond with my full attention and involvement with the ideas.

Some speakers talk in a self-absorbed manner, from a lofty height, putting the onus on the audience for involving themselves in the ideas and deriving whatever they can from the communication. If we can keep in mind our own responses to such speakers as compared to those who seem to make an effort to connect to us through their manner as well as content, we would be conscious of the great importance of this element of our talk. The audience is there to connect to a real person who shows a focus on them, rather than feel that they are eavesdropping on a self-absorbed process of thinking aloud. **We can prevent our talk from turning into a soliloquy by treating it as a special kind of dialogue where the other party may not contribute through actual words but who is constantly to be kept in mind in terms of expectations and responses.** When every choice of content and style is made keeping the other party in mind and the delivery involves them by demonstrating the exclusive focus of the speaker on them, engaging the listeners becomes much more feasible. The best talk is one where every member of the audience goes away carrying the sense that they had been part of a dialogue with the speaker. This sense may be created by asking questions and actually involving the listeners to contribute and shape the communication. It may also be possible to create this sense by asking rhetorical questions that engage the listeners more actively in the act of listening and meaning making.

In addition to asking questions and using interesting anecdotes, examples, and allusions to shared experiences, we may use humour to bridge the gap between ourselves and our listeners. Unless the occasion is a very solemn one, requiring due restraint and decorum, some humour is in place and generally welcome. Humour is useful to break the ice and to reduce the distance that is set up between the two parties involved in the communication. It also allows for a lightness to be introduced—and this helps to break the tension for the speaker as much as for the listeners.

As with all humour, it is important that we take care to ensure that it does not become abrasive and caustic.

Generally speaking, we should aim at a light and gentle kind of humour that does not target a particular group in terms of race, ethnicity, religious and political beliefs. The better we can understand the constitution of the audience and ascertain its sensitivity, the better we can decide on the question of appropriateness of humour. It may also be a good idea to show one's lack of bias by equally targeting opposite parties—be it political groups, or lifestyles, or even competitors. When the affiliation or leanings of our audience are very clear, we may be more partisan in our humour and find a good response from our listeners who not only relate to our humour but also feel that the speaker understands them. Targeting oneself may also be a safe approach, unlikely to offend anyone. However, in all of these it is important to remember that one must use humour as a light seasoning rather than make it the dominant flavour, unless, of course, stand-up comedy is what we are aiming at! **If overdone, humour targeted at oneself may cost us our credibility.** It is sufficient to show ourselves as human or as fallible in some way, but we should be careful that we do not end up being so self-deprecating that we erode the very basis of authority and credibility from which we wish to provide value to our listeners.

Showing ownership of ideas

For our audience to give us their attention and to make the effort to listen to us and go along with our ideas, it is important that we display a strong sense of ownership of our ideas. It is very hard to create a sense of value in such listening if the speaker seems to be struggling with recalling their material or presenting it mechanically as if they were merely the mouthpiece for some anonymous author of a script. Listening is—as our experience of countless such occasions testifies—a difficult task, beset with many challenges and barriers. If the audience members feel that they can get the ideas through other sources more easily, they are unlikely to control the distractions and make the required effort to follow the speaker's words. This may, firstly, be in terms of the worth of the ideas and relevance to the context. That is, do the listeners feel that the ideas are of value to them and unlikely to be easily obtained with that particular focus and perspective, from other sources?

Secondly, and perhaps more importantly, even if the focus is appropriate given the audience and the occasion, do the listeners look up to the speaker in terms of being in complete control of the material they expect others to take interest in? A sense of ownership of information, views, interpretation, analysis, and whatever else we present before our listeners, is essential to create a greater credibility in the material as well as to make it easier to establish rapport between speaker and listeners. This leads to the listeners feeling that there is a value to the interaction that perhaps would not be possible through alternate forms of communication.

Presenting consistent messages through verbal and non-verbal cues

In a face-to-face situation, listeners are constantly, and almost unconsciously, checking the force of our conviction in our own ideas through the extent to which the verbal and non-verbal elements of our communication remain consistent. As long as these stay in tandem, they are almost imperceptible and do not draw attention to themselves as they seamlessly complement and reinforce the main idea. However, as soon as there is any inconsistency perceived between the verbal and non-verbal parts, it draws attention to itself and not only breaks the coherence of the communication but also throws our credibility into question. Most of us are quick to give greater credence to the message we receive from the non-verbal cues that are seen as more natural, rather than from the verbal ones that may be more artificial and constructed. Therefore, if we assert something in strong words, but our voice is weak or our eyes are shifty, it is likely that our words will be seen as less credible.

Similarly, if we are trying to get our listeners to accept a viewpoint as valid, while our manner of presenting it to them seems to not display conviction, it is unlikely to win us their acceptance however clear and strong our articulation may be. It would be a shame if despite our desire to get our ideas across to our listeners with all the force of our logic and feeling, and despite the strength of our ideas expressed in the verbal part of our communication, we compromise the impact of our communication by overlooking the importance of supporting and consistent non-verbal cues. Here, being in full control of our material is of great value. When our central message is clear to us and we also have a clear sense of the structure to follow, we are free to focus on ensuring that our posture, gestures, facial expressions, and voice elements remain consistent with our verbal message. When we are able to do so and provide a complete communication where all elements are consistent and in sync, we demonstrate that we are in control and we set up an expectation right from the beginning that we are to present a strong, coherent, and cogent message.

Projecting confidence through effective use of body language

The speaker's confidence is always one of the first things mentioned when you ask people about what sets a good speaker apart. However, we must remember that there is no way for an audience to really know if the speaker is confident or not. What we say about this matter is entirely made up of the assumptions based on what we can see and hear. Almost all of us have the tendency to make such assumptions based on what are generally perceived as indicators of confidence (or the opposite) beginning almost immediately from the point a person comes up to speak. And these assumptions, to a large extent, shape how much attention we give to speakers and the credibility we attach to the ideas presented by them.

Once again, we may use our own perception as listeners as a guide. Do we not have more positive expectations from a speaker and accord them greater credibility simply because we assume, from certain non-verbal cues, that they are self-assured and confident? And how do we arrive at this assumption? It would be largely based on the signs that we typically associate with confidence—an air of self-assurance evident from a firm gait as they come up to speak, a posture that is straight but not rigid, gestures that show control and naturalness, and facial expressions that not only suit the verbal part of the message but also reflect comfort and pleasure in the interaction. When a speaker displays such indicators of confidence we assume that they have something of value to share with us, that this must be credible enough to give them this assurance, and also that they are keen to get these ideas through to us.

When we come to speak to others, we must keep this common tendency of listeners in mind and make sure that right from the opening, through the entire duration of our talk, we exude a sense of self-assurance and confidence, as well as pleasure and comfort with the interaction, through every element of our presence.

Speaking clearly and distinctly

As in all speaking situations, it is very important to remember that all our effort and care with our material is dependent on the primary step of the message reaching the listeners clearly and distinctly. Our voice is the vehicle for our spoken messages and its role is even more critical in a speaking mode that is unsupported by any written or other visual cues. If our words do not reach our audience's ears as distinguishable elements and if our words so received do not easily and effortlessly cohere into units of meaning, there is no hope of our message reaching our listeners' minds.

This understanding should shape the care we give to both our speaking volume and our enunciation. **Our aim should be that our words should reach our listeners' ears without getting blurred due to clipping of the ends of sentences or the dropping of volume at the end of words, phrases, and sentences.** At the same time, we also need to take care over our speaking pace. If we speak too fast for our words to remain distinct from each other, it gets tiring for the listeners to make sense of our statements. It is always easier to pay attention to a speaker who speaks at a measured pace that is comfortable to follow. However, this does not mean that we should use a very slow pace as that may be taken to indicate low energy and a lack of involvement with the ideas and the communication.

Presenting with energy and conviction

The way we present our ideas can carry cues that make our listeners get a sense of our feelings towards our ideas, our listeners, and the interaction. Our enthusiasm and excitement or confidence and conviction may be expressed in words, but when we speak with force and belief, our voice itself carries these messages. Often, these subtler cues to our attitudes and feelings are more powerful in communicating than explicit avowal alone. Our style of presenting our ideas can subtly aid in creating the desired affect in our listeners. **When our audience sees us passionate about our ideas and about getting these across to them, they are more likely to respond sympathetically.**

Energy is almost palpable in a speech through the volume, the emphatic articulation, and the full involvement with getting our ideas across to our listeners. Think of an occasion when you may have listened to someone who spoke in a dispassionate, uninvolved manner, evident from the lack of energy in their voice, and the lack of eye contact or free gestures. Unless it was a particular situation calling for a deliberate control of emotion and a dry, dispassionate treatment, you may not recall it as very effective in impacting the listeners with the strength of the speaker's conviction in the ideas being presented. As this is hardly the impression we would like to leave on our listeners, it would be in our interest to ensure that we do not overlook the importance of presenting our ideas with energy and conviction.

With these common elements that we need to aim at for all extemporary speaking situations, let us now turn to certain particular kinds of situations where extemporary speaking may be called for.

SPEAKING ON A GIVEN TOPIC

One kind of extemporary speaking situation is that where we are required to speak on a certain topic or issue. We may have been invited to do so or it may be initiated by ourselves. In the former case it could be because of our position or because of the value of our perspective arising out of our position, experience, and expertise. For example, our views on the development in our field may be sought because we are recognized as an authority in the field or at least be known to have special interest in it, with a high level of knowledge and understanding of current developments as well as the background or history. We may also be expected to be able to speak extemporaneously about issues relating to our work profile, be it projects underway or further plans. Similarly, we ourselves may take the opportunity to talk to groups of people about an issue in order to inform about developments, to explain, to persuade and convince, or to encourage and motivate.

In all such cases, clarity about our objective is important as it allows us to stay focused. Without this we may be tempted to range across many issues surrounding the topic or issue triggered by what is on top of our mind rather than the suitability for who we are speaking to and the objective for that particular occasion. The result may be a jumbled set of somewhat disjointed ideas. A clear objective of the particular communication allows us to make appropriate choices about the direction we take and the details we bring in or omit. This allows us to strengthen our speech in terms of both coherence and effectiveness in serving that purpose for that set of receivers. For example, once we are clear that we are speaking to share the latest developments in a particular area that would be of great use to the listeners, we would make choices such as the details to include, how much to elaborate and how to do so, what examples to use and what parallels to draw, with an eye to how well these contribute to serving the objective. If we did not keep this objective in front of us, perhaps we would get side-tracked into other issues that may dilute the effectiveness of the particular objective. For brief, extemporary talks, focus is essential and for this, a sharply defined objective is essential.

While it is important to aim at a sharp focus on the topic in a manner that serves the objective while engaging the listeners and adding value to them, it is also important to establish credibility of material and force of ideas shared. When we speak on an issue, the onus lies on us to leave an impression on the listeners that we have something of value to provide—be it in terms of a balanced and objective treatment of various perspectives, or a unique stance based on our particular approach, or a logically rigorous argument informed by deep understanding and sufficient information. It is futile to expect the audience to look up to us as the speaker if we are unable to make our authority on the subject shine through. At the same time our desire to convey our ideas to them should also be reflected through our complete involvement with the communication.

Remember

The audience would look up to us only when our authority on the subject shines through as well as our desire to convey our ideas to them.

The onus lies on us as a speaker to show that we are providing value in terms in one of the following ways:
- balanced and objective treatment of various perspectives
- a unique stance based on our particular approach
- a logically rigourous argument
- information that is specially significant and not otherwise easily available

It is obvious that except for certain topics about which we are amply equipped to talk at a moment's s notice because of our deep familiarity and clearly defined perspective, and because these may be very close to our heart, acquiring the necessary authority over other topics may need some effort. And this authority and confidence in our own awareness level is necessary if we are to make an impact on our listeners. We would be doing ourselves a disservice if we were to tackle extemporary speaking opportunities without making an effort to equip ourselves with sufficiently deep understanding of our material as well as clarity about our focus in light of our objective and audience. **On the occasions when we are to speak on a topic about which we have wide and deep knowledge and clearly defined views that we could easily articulate, it is still advisable to give some thought to finding a focus as well as to structure our ideas.** We may also need to equip ourselves with credible data and facts to support our points. This would be necessary for almost all cases except those of topics over which we have complete mastery and such deep familiarity that all significant facts are always at our fingertips. Whether this involves quickly refreshing our memory, or updating our information so that it is current, or ensuring that we have not overlooked any relevant area, we owe it to ourselves and our listeners to make this effort. Neglecting to do this may result in a less substantial and impactful communication.

We should also make sure that except in cases where our authority on the subject is well known to our listeners or we are introduced in a manner that establishes it, we weave into our talk some way of indicating how we are equipped to speak on it with authority. This could be based on special interest, deep study, or long experience and first-hand familiarity. The listeners would be inclined to regard our views and information with more credibility and to expect more value addition if this was evident to them from early on in the talk. Many a time I have seen what perhaps you have too—a person in a senior position speaking to people lower in the hierarchy, with the breezy assumption that every opinion expressed, every bit of information shared, and every argument made by them will be received with appreciation and unquestioning agreement, while the audience listened only out of politeness. When we are in a position of seniority to our listeners we may fall into the trap of assuming that what we say has an inherent credibility. However, it is best to not take this as a given. People junior to us may be obliged to hear us out but they will give us their willing attention and involve themselves in our ideas only if our authority on that particular subject is somehow made evident to them.

OTHER COMMON OCCASIONS

- **Welcoming and introducing a guest to an assembly**

  We may be required to introduce a guest at an official function. Perhaps this seems simple enough as we feel we can pull out a profile of the guest and read it out to the audience. I am sure you have seen this done. But you may have doubted if the person introducing the guest knew the details or even if their words of delight and privilege in welcoming the guest were genuine. Naturally, if we do not want our listeners to similarly doubt both our familiarity with what we are saying and the sincerity of feeling, it may be better to treat this as an occasion where some preparation may be called for.

  When we introduce a guest to an audience, we should take care to familiarize ourselves with the necessary details of the event and of the guest. We need to be familiar with the nature of the occasion, the theme or topic (if any), and the agenda. This means both gathering the details as well as mentally charting out how we would structure and present these. Ideally, we should also be able to relate the occasion to the guest—establishing the appropriateness of the match between the occasion and the stature of the guest in terms of position, expertise, accomplishments, and the like. We should also be able to lead into the next part of the agenda with assurance. Unless we are able to speak about these with assurance and ownership of the details, it is unlikely that the listeners will feel that we are doing more than carrying out a formal duty.

The time available to us for this objective is generally very limited and rightly so as we do not want to stand between the guest and the audience. For this reason a control over the material from thorough familiarization and a sense of structure before we begin is important. Meandering aimlessly into irrelevant details or faltering and stuttering would not reflect us in a good light or serve the objective. The better we are in control of both the material and the structure, the more comfortable we can be and the better we can focus on sharing the ideas with warmth and enthusiasm.

Our objective being that of welcoming the guest, all elements of our demeanour and overall body language will be taken as signifying how we feel. Does our voice carry the excitement and warmth that would complement the words to this effect that we may be saying? Do our facial expressions and gestures match the meaning of our words of welcome? Does our appearance and posture communicate a positive attitude to this formal but happy occasion? Do our eyes make contact with the audience and the guest and create a connection with them? If we want to convey sincerity of feeling, the answer to all of these questions should be yes.

- **Vote of thanks**

  We may be required to speak at occasions where a vote of thanks has to be offered at the conclusion of an event. Here too, it is important to keep in mind the question of clarity of objective, and of complete control over the material and focus. Although it may be not entirely out of order to pull out a list of names of people to be thanked so as to avoid missing someone out, it would be best if we give sufficient thought to mentally assembling these details as well as to the structure. If we have gone sufficiently through these in our mind, we may carry a list but not need more than a glance at it while speaking. **The order of people to be mentioned may be determined by their positions or the magnitude of their contribution. However, when we come to the end of the list, we may use warm words rather than the unimaginative and clichéd 'last but not the least'.** If there is a protocol to be followed we should be familiar with it and the appropriate forms of address, and the correct names and designations of people.

  Our aim should be not to mechanically list the people who deserve thanks, but to exude a sense of warmth and genuineness of feeling. The more we appear to speak spontaneously, the more sincerity and genuineness is likely to be perceived in our words of gratitude. The more we have the content under control, the more attention we are able to give to ensuring that all elements of our body language complement our words and create the effect of genuine involvement with the ideas and with sharing these with the listeners.

- **Felicitating or conferring an award**

There may be times when we may be required to speak in order to felicitate or to confer an award on someone who has distinguished themselves. Although we may add a few words in our individual capacity, it is important to keep in mind that such felicitation is generally not by an individual and in the capacity of the speaker, we are generally only representing a larger group of people on whose behalf we speak.

There are some very formal felicitations and conferring of awards that require a citation to be read out. In most business contexts, it is unlikely that there would be such a requirement. However, it would be best to determine the tradition and expectations. Unless there is such a requirement, it would look very odd if we pulled out a script to read or fumbled with notes. It behoves us to be completely in control of our content—especially in terms of details of the awardee and the qualities or attributes to be mentioned in the felicitation—and to focus on presenting it with full involvement with the awardee and the audience. **Our words of congratulations and appreciation should ring true and this can happen when not only are the words well-chosen and the ideas**

well-structured but also when all our non-verbal cues combine to play a complementary role, enhancing the significance of the words. Trusting all this to fall into place is not a reliable approach and due care with framing our ideas and deciding a structure is advisable.

- **Receiving an award**

On the happy occasion when we are the recipient of an award or being felicitated for an achievement, we would be expected to speak before the assembly. A chess grandmaster once shared with me his extreme state of nervousness when he won a match and was asked to speak before the crowd. He said that the joy of winning was to a large extent clouded over because of the stress of impromptu speaking. I am sure many of us can understand his unease with such occasions of speaking without preparation. But are there ways in which we can handle these opportunities with equanimity?

To begin with, it may be reassuring to remember that the requirement of speaking is generally of a very short duration in such situations. We are not expected to launch into a lengthy exposition or airing of our pet theories of life and the universe. It would suffice to display a sense of gratitude for the award and the words of appreciation. A sense of humility is generally well appreciated. Although we don't need to be self-effacing or to belittle our achievement, it is good to be large-hearted, and to acknowledge the contribution of others who have helped us and strengthened our hands as we strove for the goal.

If we get some time, we should sort out our ideas mentally and decide our focus as well as a rough structure for presenting. Even if the moment is quite impromptu and we are taken by surprise, we should try to take a few moments to breathe deeply and to collect our ideas together. Spontaneity is expected and appreciated and if it is accompanied by coherent and smooth composition of our ideas, and presentation in an unflustered manner, it has a great impact.

At the same time, we need to be keenly aware that our words and demeanour together convey our message and control over both is needed so as to avoid sending out incongruous cues that dilute the impact of the total message. Thanks or words of appreciation mumbled in a manner indicating insincerity or mere formality reflect poorly on us. Some incoherence or searching for words may be taken as natural in the context, but anything in our manner indicating a formulaic approach or lack of feeling would do much damage to our credibility. Sufficient care over the non-verbal elements of our speech is necessary to counter this danger. It should not be that we overlook the importance of the non-verbal cues and do ourselves a disservice in not fairly presenting our true feelings of gratitude and humility.

- **Condolence**

  Another formal occasion when we may be required to speak extemporaneously is at a condolence gathering. It would be quite out of place to pull out notes to read on such an occasion even if we have had time to prepare notes. **The challenge of such speaking is that of presenting meaningful and relevant content in a structured rather than rambling manner.** At the same time, our feelings and emotions need to be mirrored in complete congruence between our verbal and non-verbal cues.

  Depending on closeness with the deceased, we may be emotionally shaken, and trusting ourselves to speak in a measured manner may sometimes be another challenge. Before we rise to speak, it is important to gather our thoughts and to decide on a few things we would like to recall about our association with the deceased person. Structure is largely up to us, but having a sense of how we would like to proceed would allow us to appear more coherent and to let the audience follow us more easily. Some mention of the circumstances of the demise may be in order and of course our feelings of sorrow and pain. Prayers for the departed soul and support for the bereaved family are also appropriate. At the same time, it is important to ensure that our speech does not end up appearing formulaic and predictable in content, thus negating all effect of genuineness of feeling.

  In terms of delivery, an appropriate demeanour for

the sombre occasion is called for. We need to ensure that in terms of appearance, posture, gestures, and tonal inflections, we convey due respect for the deceased and match the care, warmth, and sense of loss that our words signify.

In conclusion, it would be good to reiterate that occasions of extemporary speaking provide great opportunities for us to reach out with our ideas and connect to people. Some of us shy away from such opportunities because it appears like a daunting task to speak without preparation and yet be able to add value to our listeners. However, as we have discussed above, it is important to see these as valuable opportunities to connect with others and to impress them with our ideas in a persuasive manner that benefits from the spontaneity and richness of the medium.

Extemporary speaking has many potential advantages through the role of complementary non-verbal cues in supporting our verbal message, establishing rapport with listeners, and the availability of constant feedback that allows for immediate adaptation of the message. It would be to our advantage to make the effort to take up the challenge of speaking extemporaneously rather than shying away from it. By practising and refining our performance in it we can hope to significantly increase our comfort and confidence in this mode of speaking. Doing so will give us ample dividends in terms of reaching out to others through a powerful medium that can effectively serve a number of important objectives such as persuasion, motivation, appreciation, quick exposition, or updating information. It also serves to impress others with a stronger sense of our ownership of ideas as well as of conviction and self-assurance in communicating our ideas compared to other kinds of communication where much more preparation is evident. If we look around us we may find only a few people who excel at this kind of communication. Whether we are leaders, aspiring leaders, or team members, honing our skill in handling it will definitely help to get us noticed and to create a favourable impression on others while helping us connect to people and serve many important objectives.

CHAPTER 6

Presentations

All of us have sat through mind-numbing presentations, stifling yawns, and doodling on note pads while someone drones on about things that seem to make sense only to them, reading bullet points off a slide that we are quite capable of reading ourselves, if only we cared. Of course, it is a different story when we are the presenters—we have spent sleepless nights dreading the moment, days putting together the ideas and making the slides and other visual aids, and are trying to deliver the ideas to people who seem to not care except when it comes to question time, when they wake up to grill and embarrass us.

It doesn't have to be like this—for either set of people involved. And I am sure we have occasionally sat through presentations that clearly stood out from the average and left an impact both in terms of the ease with which the ideas were understood and the memorable impact made by the speaker's personality. Is there a secret formula or are such unique individuals just blessed with a gift the rest of us may admire but not hope to emulate? No doubt, an outgoing personality and experience of delivering talks and presentations helps, but there are many things any of us may do so as to reach closer to the level of ease and impact that these speakers display with such panache. Let us look closely at how to go about improving our effectiveness in making formal presentations and what care we need to take in order to meet our objectives.

WHY AM I MAKING THE PRESENTATION?

The starting point is clarity about why the presentation is being made. Presenting cannot be an end in itself. Our target should be to ensure that the audience's time and effort of attending and listening are worth it in terms of the value they gained. Whether the presentation had value or not cannot be judged without clarity about its objective. Regardless of the topic, the starting point of a presentation for the speaker has to be clarity about the objective that it is meant to serve, and for the audience it is targeting. We can help focus on our objective by asking ourselves: Are we trying to inform about developments or findings, or persuade about a theory or approach, or argue about the suitability of an approach or idea? Clarity about this will greatly help when it comes to making choices about where the focus should lie, what to include and what to avoid, what to emphasize and what to downplay. It will also help in deciding the tone and appeal to use.

Another crucial aspect of the why question is that of the mode itself. Why are we making the presentation rather than submitting a report or using any other written form or even a pictorial or graphic medium? Are we choosing the spoken mode appropriately in view of the advantages it provides? Are we going on to make optimal use of these potential benefits to aid us in meeting our purpose?

While choosing the mode, we should not overlook the advantages to writing and disadvantages to speaking. When the choice between speaking and writing is made by default rather than with a careful view to what better serves the needs of the objective, we are already making a basic error in our communication effort. When we choose to speak after due consideration of its advantages, despite the disadvantages, we are ready to make the most of the former and know that the latter are not too relevant for the particular context. Some questions arising from this consideration are given in the box below.

When choosing to make a face-to-face presentation we must ask ourselves the following questions:

- Is our objective likely to be better served by our being able to build a rapport with the listeners and relate to them and by our making our presence add value to what we are saying?
- Is our objective likely to be better served by our being able to respond continuously to the way we perceive our ideas being received?
- Is our objective not going to be negatively affected by the fact that listeners may get distracted, and may not be able to retain much of the concrete details?

> • Are we gaining so much more through our choice of speaking that it is worth the investment of time and effort that our listeners are making?

A presentation relies on active listening which is a demanding activity even though it has the appearance of passivity. It requires both speaker and audience to set their other commitments aside and to match their schedules to play their roles in the presentation. The cost in terms of work time as well as money is much more substantial as compared to written communication and to be worth these costs, it should yield a sufficiently high value. We need to think if the listeners will be served so much more efficiently through the advantages that these negatives will be canceled out.

Once again, if we have chosen our communication mode carefully we are likely to be much more aware of the need to maximize the unique advantages and minimize the disadvantages that we get through the choice. For example, we would try to engage the audience in such a manner that they are less likely to be distracted; we would keep our focus clear, and make every effort to take the listeners along, with devices such as roadmaps, signposting, recapping, and summarizing. At the same time, we would bring a personal touch to the ideas and the weight of our personality in order to make a better impact. In my discussions with a number of presenters from the corporate, financial, academic, and scientific world, a persistent perception that has been highlighted is that formal presentations, especially those on 'technical matters' are not expected to be engaging and light. In other words, they are expected to be dull and plodding. There is a kind of safety for the presenter in such perceptions. Moreover, these are reinforced by the numerous dull 'technical' presentations we face on a regular basis, thus giving a comforting message that it is fine. Let us stop and think. If we do not engage our audience, is there any point in a face-to-face presentation? A disengaged audience really amounts to a futile presentation. After all, we are not speaking for ourselves but for the audience.

A common mistake in identifying the objective is often encountered in 'technical' presentations. It is often erroneously assumed that there is no difference between say a technical report and a presentation on it. Although both may concern the same matter, and in fact, the presentation may be based on the report, the difference in the mode of communication should imply quite different foci and objectives of communication. A written report or paper would have the objective of providing a complete treatment of the subject—thorough, detailed, referenced, and supported. When the same reporting is to be done orally, the objective should change to providing the overall idea and the salient points about the experiment, analysis, project, or study as the case may be, by the person or team responsible for it, along with the possibility of instant clarification. Many of us may recall having watched novice presenters being stopped in the middle of a plodding presentation that is too detailed and being asked to highlight key problems, challenges, or results. Although in many cases, the audience is not in a position to stop us, such questions about focus and relevance to them are topmost in the minds of all listeners. We must always keep in mind that as a presenter we can command the attention of the audience only by providing a clear focus that is in keeping with their expectations and in line with their objective as listeners.

WHO IS THE AUDIENCE? WHAT IS MY RELATIONSHIP WITH THEM?

Allied questions to consider are:

• What is their interest in our presentation?
• How much do they already know about the subject?
• What would be relevant and useful to them?

One of the essential starting points for any presentation is an analysis of the audience. We need to be as clear as possible about who they are in whatever terms are relevant. For example, personal details such as age, gender, and ethnicity may be relevant in some cases. It would help to know their professional/technical background, special interests, and level in the hierarchy. Further details such as their level of existing information on a given topic or views on the issue under consideration would be very handy. We need to know whether the listeners have strong views on the subject. How are they likely to be affected by a proposal or development that we wish to talk about? What is their likely response to the ideas we wish to present? The correctness with which we can determine these or the fairness of the assumptions we can make about our listeners would go a long way in helping us to meet our objectives.

At the same time, it is also important to consider who we are. Firstly, we need to answer this question in terms of the subject. For example, am I presenting on the strength of my deep knowledge of the subject or because of first-hand information that I have generated, or primary research or analysis that I have conducted? Secondly, we need to answer this question in terms of my position with regard to the listeners. Am I presenting in my individual capacity or as a spokesperson of a larger group? What is my relationship with the listeners? Are they internal constituents, and if so, are they senior or junior to me? Are they external people, and if so, where do we stand in relation to them? Am I in the position of a supplicant, a seller (of ideas or a proposal), an expert, or an analyst?

Our clear understanding of these points is essential groundwork for our presentation. The more clarity we have on this, the better equipped we are to make important decisions about our approach to the presentation, our style, and our material. For example, whether I adopt an easy and free manner or a more formal manner will depend on my recognition of the audience's constitution in terms of people well-known or new to me, people very senior to me or my own level, people from my professional/technical area or other fields. Again, without conscious deliberation over my audience's constitution, I would perhaps miss out on understanding their interest in the presentation and their perspective on the topic or issue. Choices such as the level of technical jargon to be used, the kinds of examples or analogies that would help to make ideas more clear and vivid, and the nature of supporting evidence for arguments would depend on a clear understanding of the audience.

A mistake commonly made by many speakers is to pull out the same set of material regardless of audience, if the topic remains the same. However, much to their disappointment, and perhaps, puzzlement, they find that what worked beautifully with one set of listeners fell flat for another. When using material used in an earlier presentation, it is best to refine its focus in line with the needs, expectations, and background of the new audience. This is likely to necessitate a shift in focus. Deciding the objectives of the listeners as well as our objective specific to this set of listeners helps us in choosing an appropriate focus. Without being set on what we want to present, we need to examine our material for what the particular set of audience would find relevant, useful, and interesting. Our choices in terms of many elements of our presentation will depend on how well we understand the audience. Why are they listening? What would make their effort worthwhile for them? Because after all, we must keep in mind that the listeners are expected to make considerable effort to follow us, to understand messages from all our cues, to make literal as well as contextual sense, to engage with the ideas, to reciprocate in our efforts to reach out to them, to listen critically and take our ideas further. Without them our presentation is meaningless, and without their active involvement, it is a damp squib. The more we keep the particulars of the listeners before us when planning and delivering our presentation, the better we can make them engage in their role, and match our enthusiasm for the communication.

WHAT WE SAY: THE CONTENT

Gathering material

If we are lucky, we get to speak about issues that we have at our fingertips. The challenge here may be that of narrowing to an appropriate focus for the context and the purpose. There are other topics and issues about which we have information and views at the back of our minds and brainstorming would bring them to the surface. However, we cannot always limit ourselves to such topics as we already have all relevant information on. When we need to speak on something it is our responsibility to equip ourselves with sufficient understanding of the subject. This means more than what our listeners already possess or can acquire quite easily. If what we speak has to have value for our listeners, and if they are to listen with interest, we must take care of the depth of our knowledge of our material. Without this, our credibility may be severely compromised and people may only sit through the presentation out of politeness.

250

Without a sense of authority over the subject we speak of, it is hardly possible for us to evoke credibility in our listeners. This authority comes from the breadth and depth of our preparation, whether it is a subject already known to us or a fresh one. **Research and brainstorming may often be necessary to get the facts and data we require on a subject new to us.** When facts and information are already known, our value addition may be through interpretation or analysis. This too becomes an essential part of our preparation of material for our presentation. It is easy to assume that it is a cakewalk in case of material we already know well. However, choosing a focus that is in line with the specific objective and with the needs and expectations of the specific audience is very important. With a focus on the objective and the audience we may find that even familiar material requires some additional work in terms of details or analysis or examples, and the like. With a new subject, sometimes we need to do groundwork in order to equip ourselves with sufficient depth of understanding and to decide a focus. Once we have done so, we require more effort for specific things such as support for an argument, understanding of the existing nature of ideas, views, theories, or experience on the issue or material that would help to elucidate or exemplify our points. No amount of charisma and flair in delivery can compensate for solid material whether in terms of self-generated ideas and analyses or of well-researched data. Both of these need sufficient investment of time in preparation.

Structure: introduction, body, conclusion

Many presentations end up being rather like a rambling on the topic or issue, with the listeners facing trouble in following the speaker in a coherent manner. The lack of a strong structure is a serious flaw in a presentation. It signals a lack of clarity about the central focus and how the parts cohere around it to make a meaningful whole.

A useful formula for structuring a presentation in way that we take our audience along is:

- tell them what you are going to tell them
- tell them
- tell them what you told them

By using the formula given in the box above, we display a sense of control, purpose, and design. We clearly signal what the listeners should expect by setting up a promise, going on to elaborate on it and substantiate it, and then wrapping it up in a manner that ties up all the parts into one whole.

Effective introduction

An oral presentation is not suitable for an elaborate thesis or for complex, extended arguments. Paring our mass of ideas into something with a clear and sharp focus is essential to make the best impact through an oral presentation. Both our focus and objective need to be brought before the audience as soon as we begin so that we bring their attention to focus on these. When our objective and focus are in line with the audience's needs and expectations we can be confident about taking the audience along with our message. The introduction, therefore, has a very special importance in serving several objectives. This is the place where we grab the audience's attention to:

- strike a rapport
- relate to them by bringing in awareness of their needs and benefits
- establish our own credentials and of our material
- provide a sense of direction for the presentation through sharing our structure, agenda, or plan.

To grab the audience's attention, we may begin with a startling fact, a brief and relevant anecdote, or a humourous icebreaker. Having done that and ensured that we have their attention, we must provide them a clear promise of what they may expect ahead and why they should be listening to us. This is where our clarity of purpose, focus, and structure needs to be communicated to the audience so that they may—right from the beginning—feel that their time and effort are worth it.

The audience would also be more willing to give us their attention and credence to our ideas if we can establish credibility. Credibility may come to be naturally associated with us when we have acknowledged expertise or authority on a topic or when our track record for that area is beyond compare. However, in most cases, we need to touch upon the credible bases for what we are going to present. These bases may be our first-hand or long association with the issue, our deep study of the subject and relevant references, or our unique personal experiences related to it.

The audience also needs to feel that you are talking to them and not to an undifferentiated mass. It means, therefore, that you need to give them a sense of your understanding of their familiarity with the issue, their particular needs, and their expectations from the presentation. Striking a rapport may be done by inclusive language such as 'as we all know', 'as you have no doubt experienced', 'I can relate well to your situation'. It may be done by demonstrating our understanding of their uniqueness by including examples, or making references that they can instantly relate to.

It is also desirable to show your sense of control on the message by sharing your design and structure in the introduction. By doing so you indirectly promise the audience that you are not planning to ramble on without a plan or a sense of purpose. Only in the case of some unwelcome news or an idea to which we expect resistance or a negative response do we need to deviate from this and perhaps not clearly state our intention till we have had time to contextualise the issue and to provide a background that leads up to our core message in a logically coherent manner.

With a good introduction, we can achieve a lot. Without an effective one, we may lose our audience before we get to the main part of the presentation.

Effective middle

Our aim in the middle or the main body of the presentation should be to flesh out the promise of the introduction and to develop the ideas in a coherent manner around the clear focus announced there. Rather than dumping data, facts, or unsupported assertions, we need to be careful to provide focused data and facts and logically supported assertions. Our understanding of our audience is crucial here to decide what we may include and what support we may provide. What the audience already knows may be useful to keep in mind to serve as a base and to remind us to add value to that rather than to provide information redundant to them. Examples and allusions should be from the experience base of the particular audience so that they serve to exemplify the point rather than further confuse.

It is necessary to ensure that we avoid disjointed ideas that do not get built upon. When we do so, we make unnecessary demands on the audience for connecting these bits. Our attempt should be to provide a smooth flow so that ideas build on each other and serve to take the listeners along to the conclusion we have in mind. We must also avoid repetition unless it is deliberately for dramatic effect. We need to make sure that we say a point completely and powerfully once, and move on. However, in a long presentation, it is advisable to recap crucial points at the end of a section, so that these may not be in danger of being lost when we move on to build upon them in the subsequent section.

Effective conclusion

The conclusion is where the promise of the introduction in sharing useful information, or making a recommendation, or arguing in favour of a position gets crystallized. The strong opening and equally strong conclusion provide a satisfying sense of a promise delivered. Here is the opportunity to recap our main points and summarize our discussion to underline our central idea. We must ensure that we end with a strong, memorable closing statement. Our foremost concern should be: What do I want the audience to remember and take away? Do I want the audience to do something based on what I just presented? Do I want them to go away in agreement with a stance? Do I want them to take away conviction in my analysis and recommendations? Do I want them to apply new information that I shared with them, in their own specific work areas?

Sometimes I have found presenters worrying about the conclusion becoming repetitive. Keep in mind that without recourse to turning the pages and reminding ourselves of the salient points that we have as readers of written material, we appreciate such repetition in the summation when we are listeners. From the speaker's perspective, it allows us to emphasize the key points that we have covered, to connect these to our central point and purpose and to close with the final message we wish to leave with the audience.

Transitions

As we move from one part of the presentation to another, we need to provide connecting tissue so that while we go into details and supporting points, the main thread running through it all is visible to our audience. Merely moving from one point to another, or one section to another with 'let's turn to . . .', or 'moving on' is not enough. It is best if we show our listeners why we are moving on to the next point, and how it is connected to the earlier one. It may be a relationship of mutually dependent parts, or cause and effect, or a similarity or contrast. And if we cannot find such relationships to serve as the logic for transitions, it may caution us about the need for more care in terms of relevance and coherence. By taking such care we demonstrate to the listeners our clarity about the task, which, in turn, gives them confidence in the value of what they are spending their time over.

As important as it is to have a strong structure for the content of our presentation, it is also important to share this structure with the audience rather than leaving them to figure it out for themselves. **It is part of our responsibility to help the listeners by showing them where we are taking them. We may use our slides to help keep the audience on track with where we have been, where we are, and where we are headed.** Some amount of repetition is necessary in presentations as compared to a written document. This is because a listener does not have the luxury enjoyed by a reader, of going backwards and refreshing their recollection and understanding of a point. The periodic recapitulation of key ideas covered till that point facilitates the coherence with which the listeners are able to connect material which they are largely receiving through the medium of sound. We may also take the aid of some visual representation of our framework or roadmap for this purpose. Listeners find it much easier to make sense of the presentation's parts as well as of it as a whole when they can see the path ahead, when they are periodically reminded of what they have covered, when they are shown the connections between ideas rather than jerkily taken from one to another, and when transitions are made explicit to them. And that is what we as presenters are aiming at—getting our ideas through to our listeners with the most ease, clarity, and coherence for them.

When we move from one point to another, the logic should be made clear to the listeners so that they can follow with ease. Many presenters simply follow the disjointed headings on their slides as the transitions. The audience can read the heading too. What may not be apparent to them is why you are moving to this point. Is it because it is another aspect of the situation you were describing, a different perspective on it, an inference drawn from the earlier point? 'However', 'nonetheless', 'moreover', 'in addition', 'at the same time', 'as a result', 'consequently', are some transitional words that allow the listeners to see that there is a connection between the preceding point and what you come to next. Similarly, transitions between parts are also useful. 'Having looked at the challenges, let us turn to what can be done to address these', or 'With these political issues in mind, it would be useful to turn to the economics of the proposed change' are better than simply moving on and leaving the listeners to figure out the logic and structure for themselves.

Very often we find that poor introductions and conclusions mar what could have been a good presentation. These parts of the presentation allow us to do a number of essential things, and neglecting them can be a serious flaw. A presentation with a strong introduction and conclusion is more likely to serve its objective by providing clarity at two crucial points when the attention of the listeners may be taken to be highest. We may use the introduction to state our objective, and to define or limit our subject. That is, we may set up clear expectations by stating our subject and specifying what our focus is, or negatively, by specifying what we are not covering. It should also be our job in the introduction to provide an overview of the entire presentation. Such an introduction effectively serves to provide coherence to the presentation, preventing it from lapsing into a collection of stray thoughts or ideas and facts/ figures loosely connected with a hazy focus. A central theme introduced here becomes the thread that runs through our presentation providing it with coherence. As we go through the main body of our presentation, this central idea and the objective need to be constantly kept before the audience through repeated reference and through tying up the various parts and points subtly to our objective.

Too many presentations end with a slide saying 'The End' or 'Any questions?' This is more in the league of 'That's all, folks!' in a Looney Tunes episode—an ending alright, but not a conclusion. The conclusion has an important role to play in providing a summation of the entire presentation or a Q.E.D. [from the Greek *quod erat demonstrandum*, meaning 'that which had to be demonstrated'] that shows the promise of the introduction to have been met. The various parts of the presentation are held together and the centrality of the main body of the presentation is effectively highlighted by the device of introduction and conclusion. Like a piece of candy is kept in place by the twisted ends of the wrapper, the core of the content needs to be tightly held in place by an effective introduction and an equally effective conclusion. It is this that gives coherence to the distinct points and keeps it unified and focused.

Visual Aids

Speakers have always benefited from visual aids such as whiteboards, flip charts, graphics, and overhead projectors for facilitating our communication through presentations. Technology has today placed a ubiquitous tool in our hands, namely PowerPoint. It allows us to combine the powerful channel of connecting with our listeners through our voice and personality, and the strong communicative power of visual representation.

However, many of us, in our role as listeners, may have very often found this tool being used as a replacement for direct communication with the audience. We watch a visual show and read points on slides but miss out on connecting with the presenter. The result is that we gain not much more than what we could have gained through perusing the material in printed form. As a presenter one may feel a sense of control in having everything one wishes to present, safely down on a slide. We may feel that this reduces our anxiety about speaking in front of an audience. But we must remember that the impulse to put everything on the slides results in cluttered visuals and this, in fact, reduces our control rather than increases it. Moreover, a serious error is that by doing so we convert what should be communication through speaking and listening into one that is through writing and reading.

Going back to our choice of the spoken mode to communicate, it may be good to recall the bases for the choice. We must remember that writing is better suited when the matter to be communicated is very detailed, complex, and substantial. Speaking is to be preferred where a more general overall picture needs to be presented, with key broad points rather than a lot of detail, and where the overall logic or feeling behind ideas is to be communicated rather than complex logical processes or large amounts of pure data. If we make an appropriate choice of medium based on these relative advantages of written and spoken communication, there can be no real justification for cluttered and complex visuals that hamper the very advantages for which we made our choice. **In a presentation done to utilize the true benefits of the spoken medium, the visuals should not be cluttered or too detailed.** Their function lies in making things more vivid and easily comprehensible, thus saving both time and effort of the speaker and listener while contributing to the overall objective. As presenters with technology at our side, it would be pointless to use words for what could be more easily presented, and even more importantly, more easily grasped by the listener, through visuals. However, use of visuals needs to be based on its utility in the service of the objective rather than as an end in itself. Some presenters get quite carried away by the design and content of the visual material on their PowerPoint presentation but overlook this important condition. Unnecessary and indiscriminate conversion of every point into a visual changes the nature of the communication from spoken to written, from aural to visual, and also takes away the central role of the speaker, replacing him or her with the visuals.

When deciding whether to use a visual to convey or support something, stop and ask yourself:
- Will it convey the information more quickly and with less effort for the audience?
- Will it enhance the impact by reinforcing the message?
- Will it make the message more memorable?

Design of visuals

We come, next, to the design for a presentation. While doing so, it is important to keep the following in mind:

- While we can effectively present substantial amounts of information through pie charts, tables, diagrams and other pictorial representations, we must keep in mind the fact that in most cases some verbal content is necessary to make proper sense of these. For example, without the legend and labelling on a map, the heading and labelling on a diagram, and proper labelling on a graph, the audience cannot make much sense of these. We must ensure that such written text on the visual is sufficient, clear, and unambiguous. Titles on textual slides as well as headings on pictorial representations need to be descriptive rather than general and meaningless ones. For example, instead of a slide titled 'Sales', it would be better to describe what about sales is it depicting, e.g. 'Sales performance since 2010' or 'Sales across geographies'.

- While we generally think of PowerPoint slides as visuals, there is often significant amount of verbal content on them. The care that goes into the preparation is wasted if the audience cannot read the content. We must ensure that we use a font size that is easily legible given the size of the room. In any circumstance, a font size of 30 or higher for headings, and of 20 or higher for main text should be used. Not only does this help with legibility, it also forces us to pare down our verbal content to key words and absolutely essential content. By keeping less content on our slide, we are able to keep the attention of the listeners on our words and body language rather than on the material on the slides.

- Although some presenters think that using all capitals on their slides, especially for headings, makes them more clear and legible, it is not so. In fact, this may appear to be the equivalent of shouting and is also generally perceived to be childish. Headings are best presented in title case that involves capitalizing the first letter of every word, except for articles.

- We must remember the importance of ensuring correctness in language use on slides. Grammar in terms of sentence structure may not be very relevant here, as we should minimize our use of full sentences and large blocks of text on slides. However, spelling is very important. Errors show up big and embarrassing on screen and whether they cause confusion in meaning or make people laugh at our sloppiness or even suspect our language ability, their impact is only negative. In order to prevent these avoidable errors, proofreading is of crucial importance. We may make inadvertent typing errors that we miss on casual reading because we really don't read the word letter by letter, as we already know what we meant to write. However, to a reader, it is immediately apparent. We need to go through the textual context of our slides carefully looking at every word distinctly in order to spot errors we may have made. Here are a few steps we should take:

- We need to check that we have transcribed names, dates, and numbers correctly from our sources/notes. It may cause miscommunication if the audience does not note the mistake and takes it as correct. In case the audience knows the correct form, then our meticulousness (and in worst case, our credibility) may become suspect.

- We need to be particularly careful with similar words such as affect/effect, four/for, there/their, cite/site. Another common error is of missing or transposed letters as in incmplete, howver, teh, ecomonic.

- Punctuation also needs care, especially the appropriate use of capital letters, commas, colons, quotation marks, and apostrophe. Although it may be ages since we left the dreary grammar lessons of school behind, it may be a good idea to brush up on these important punctuations and their correct usage to give us clarity and confidence in our understanding. There are a number of authoritative websites where one may quickly find credible information on these points and this would prove to be very useful to us wherever we deal with written English, whether in a long document or small piece of text on our slides for a presentation.

- **For both verbal and graphic representations on a PowerPoint presentation, we must remember to be careful in providing good colour contrast to aid in legibility and clarity.** Many times, presenters overlook this one element in their design, but with the sad result that their efforts in making the slide are wasted due to poor legibility caused by the colour contrast. It is good to use a solid background with a lighter colour for the text. White text on blue is soothing to the eyes while very sharp in contrast. Of course, white on black is also good and may be seen as more formal. Black text on white often does not come out on a big projector screen with the kind of clarity one sees on a smaller screen. One may experiment with other colour schemes as long as the legibility and sharpness of clarity is not compromised. The colour scheme must also look professional and sober, therefore, avoiding excessive use of colours and garish shades is best.

- Animation, again, is best kept to a minimum so as to avoid giving a childish appearance to our presentation. At the same time, some subtle animation may be useful in terms of providing some dynamism to the visual content. It is also a good idea to animate our bullet points, if all of them are not necessary to be taken together (at least to begin with). By animating these to come up only at the click of a mouse, we control when the point comes up. This way we only reveal a bullet point when we are ready to talk of it. If this is not done, and all points are presented together, the audience may go ahead of us, with the consequence that they may read points before we have been able to build to them, as well as they are distracted from our spoken words about a particular point because they are reading ahead.

- Bringing some variety in the layout of our slides adds to the attractiveness. We may use double columns for comparative data or a list of bullet points with parallel structure, or incorporate AutoShapes feature with the text. Complex and cluttered visuals, however creative, do not serve the purpose if the audience cannot make sense of them quickly and easily. We should resist the temptation to put a number of graphs or charts on the same slide. The size of each reduces automatically, and although it may appear perfectly fine on our computer screen, it may not be sharply clear when projected on to a large screen. We should be cautious and not get carried away by extreme effects that may make it appear childish and distract from the clarity of the intended meaning.

- It is a good idea to test out the entire presentation in Slide Show mode for ourselves because we may spot some errors or layout problems in that mode and be able to fix it rather than being taken by surprise when these show up in magnification on a large screen.

HOW WE SAY IT

Having looked at what to say and the accompanying visuals, we come to the delivery—the actual presentation of our ideas to the audience. Here too, we have a choice to make.

The style

Reading

One option of presenting our material is to read from a prepared script. For certain occasions such as a formal official statement, this is preferred so as to avoid any variations from the carefully crafted communication. It is also a preferred method for certain fields such as academic disciplines in the humanities and for formal occasions such as keynote addresses, commencement speeches, or announcement of government policies, or political speeches. This may be because for such contexts, the complexity of the ideas as well as the very precise expression in a coherent manner is considered essential. Any deviation in the form of extempore elaborations, except during Q&A time, may be seen as casual and may lack in nuanced expression which may be regarded as essential. For such a mode to be effective, the writing needs to be really strong. Of course, in the case of some of the examples given above, skilled professional writers may actually work behind the scenes to produce the impeccably worded text.

Thus, when this is the accepted norm in a given context, it would be fine to read from a printed script. While doing so, certain care should be taken.

- Complete ownership of the ideas as well as the expression is essential. In case the text is written by others, not only do we need to be in perfect sync with them for adequately representing the ideas, if we have any say in the matter we must try to ensure that the expressions are such that we will be able to carry them off in a natural manner. If this does not happen, we may find ourselves stumbling over words that we have not encountered before or struggling with sentence constructions that may be awkward or unfamiliar to us.

- It is best to hold the pages of our script loosely together with a binder or pincer-clip that we take out before we begin. As we finish a page, we should slide it aside rather than turn it over, so as to cause least noise and distraction.

- Facial expression, tonal inflections, pace and volume of speaking need to be used well to bring expression into what we read. Infusing feeling and additional meaning through our facial expression and voice should ideally make listening to the material much more meaningful for the listeners than if they were to read it for themselves.

- Eye contact is one of the best ways to establish rapport with our listeners and that is one of the most important reasons for a face-to-face presentation of our ideas rather than a written one. Therefore, although reading means that our eyes are busy with our script for most of the time, we must try our best to know the material very well through practice, so that we may be able to look up at the audience more often. Completely depending on the script so as to not raise our eyes from the pages, gives the idea that we do not perhaps own the material fully and that dents the credibility that we wish to project. It also removes any opportunity for us to establish a connection with the listeners or to get a sense of the response of the listeners as we speak.

It is best to avoid reading as a presentation style, except where such norms or expectations exist. Its major pitfall is that it eliminates the possibility of establishing rapport through connecting with the audience through many elements of body language. We need to stand or sit in a particular place and cannot vary the physical distance between our listeners and us, through the course of our presentation. Our gestures are limited due to our hands being busy with the sheets of paper before us and also not visible if we are using a lectern to speak from, which is often the case in such contexts. Our eye contact generally gets quite limited, the more we have to read, and in a completely read out script, it may result in complete absorption in the text, leaving no eye contact for the listeners. Although listeners in certain contexts may be used to this, this lack of eye contact may seriously compromise our success in connecting with our listeners in other contexts. Reading may also give an impression of extreme nervousness as the choice may indicate the lack of confidence in remembering our material and in speaking extempore. Although by choosing to read, we may make it easier for ourselves in terms of ensuring that we do not make a fool of ourselves by going blank or collapsing, this is quite apparent to the listeners too. This affects the impact we can create of ownership of the ideas, our desire to share these with our listeners, and real keenness to reach out to them with excitement and other feelings as the case may be.

Putting our script on slides and reading from there to our audience is another ineffective alternative. By doing so we lose the advantages of written communication from the perspective of the receiver, because the listener—unlike the reader—cannot enjoy the greater flexibility in choosing a suitable time for receiving, the luxury of going backward and forward for gaining greater clarity and coherence, the ability to file for future reference that the written mode normally provides. At the same time we lose the chief advantages of spoken communication—the spontaneity and naturalness, and the potential of connecting with our audience through body language. We also give an impression that we are not confident of facing the audience or in complete control of our material. At the same time, by reading aloud to our audience we may be seen as subtly insulting their ability to comprehend it on their own.

Memorizing

This is one step better than plain reading aloud to our audience. **It is better in terms of not showing our complete dependence on written material and thus our lack of ownership of it. It also leaves us free from a focus on our script or slides, so as to freely use our body language to augment our verbal content.** Writing out a script and then memorizing it seems to be a safe bet for those worried about panicking and forgetting their material, or not being able to articulate them well.

However, the real pitfalls of this approach are the danger of memorized scripts vanishing from the mind in the event of panic setting in on facing the audience, and the consequent wooden expression and tone that often accompanies memorized material that is simply regurgitated. Complete reliance on memory means that one is quite incapacitated if the memory blanks out. Of course, with sufficient practice, we may be able to get a good hold of it in our memory and also to be able to bring in body language elements such as voice modulation and gestures. However, it is quite hard to bring naturalness to delivery of memorized material without being a proficient actor. And unless we test it out on many occasions, taking the risk in stride, we will not know whether we will blank out or recall all that we memorized. In my experience, people who follow this approach often report that they actually skipped quite a lot of their material or lost the structure, because of difficulty in recalling correctly. In fact, even worse is the experience of those who, once they stumble on one part, get so overwhelmed by panic that they cannot continue and have to call it quits.

Extempore

Once we have prepared and practised well, the best way to present is extempore. This means that we have a good sense of what we are going to say and how we are going to say it, we have a structure worked out, as well as concrete details, supporting ideas, examples and illustrations, but we leave the actual articulation into words to the very moment of speaking. This is immensely superior in effect to reading or memorizing because it really serves the objectives of direct communication. Our extemporary articulation of ideas may be a little less polished, and a little less well-phrased, but it is more than made up by the sense of spontaneity and freshness that it brings in. The audience gets the feeling that we are having a conversation with them rather than delivering a set piece. The advantage offered by face-to-face spoken communication of being able to modify our content as we go along on the basis of the constant feedback that we get from our listeners, is best utilized in this style of speaking. Only when we are free from a set script that we read out or that we have rehearsed till we are perfect at it, can we really utilize this potential advantage of spoken communication. If we waste this we are sacrificing one of the very significant reasons for choosing to present our ideas through face-to-face speaking in the first place. Another very important reason behind this choice, if made appropriately, would have been the opportunity that it provides to connect with the listeners and to establish a rapport. Again, this is best served when we give the impression of having a conversation with our listeners where although we may have the major speaking part, the listeners play a very significant role through their involvement.

Speaking extemporaneously does not mean that we speak in a stream-of-consciousness manner that may end up in a rambling that does not serve the purpose. It does not mean that we speak on points that just occur to us at the moment or that we come to the occasion unprepared with what we need to say. It involves all the preparation of sound material and a logical structure, in-depth understanding and belief in ideas we present, and sufficient practice with the material to know it inside out and to establish ownership. It then boils down to giving words to the ideas extemporaneously on the actual occasion of speaking. This brings in a freshness to our articulation of ideas that cannot be matched by the best delivery of memorized material. As one searches for words to articulate our ideas as one goes along, the listeners feels that they are interacting with the person rather than with words alone.

Many of us don't trust ourselves to speak extemporaneously in the fear of being unable to recall all that we mean to say and in a structured manner. However, speaking extemporaneously does not mean that one can have no aid to one's memory about the points to be covered or about the structure. We can certainly carry a palm card or chits with our points and even an outline to keep us on track. We may note down key facts, a few words to remind us of an example that we might give, and concrete details such as names or figures that need to be rendered exactly. In certain kinds of speaking occasions, we may also use a PowerPoint presentation to provide us with a structure so as to keep us on track as well as key words that jog our memory and help us recall much more. Being able to do this without making our PowerPoint presentation carry an entire script, require so much familiarity through practice that a mere glance at it brings back the entire idea that we wish to share and can go on to articulate on the spot.

Presenting with visual aids

Today formal presentations have become almost completely synonymous with PowerPoint and other similar tools that provide us an excellent opportunity to add visual content to our presentations. As an aid to spoken communication it has excellent potential for supporting us in our objective of clearly conveying our ideas to the listeners. However, more often than not, this tool is used not so much as an aid but as an alternative to directly communicating through the spoken word. For presenters it provides a way to make something challenging and daunting manageable for themselves. With it in one's armoury, one feels that there is less need to worry about one's mind blanking out, the need for presence of mind and thinking on one's feet, or the self-consciousness and anxiety associated with having to face an audience directly.

I am sure each one of us has sat through presentations where the speaker seemed to be more engaged with the slides on her PowerPoint presentation than with us in the audience. On such occasions, our attention is constantly drawn to the material on the slides which we are given to understand constitute the focal point. This centrality of the visuals in indicated right from the beginning through the presenter appearing more focused on arrangements for the visuals than on connecting to the audience. In many cases, the opening as well as the concluding thanks and invitation of questions is also done through slides. During most of the presentation, the speaker's posture and gestures seem to be directing our attention towards the screen while she herself, constantly keeps her attention on the slides. Such disproportionate importance to the visuals makes them change from an aid to the presentation itself, and consequently, the communication as one of reading and watching rather than of listening.

In fact, we have become so used to such presentations that we go for one expecting a visual rather than an aural experience. It is hardly likely that we think much of the presenter whose role seems to be limited to showing us the slides in a certain order, reading out text or briefly elaborating on points on the slides or commenting on visual information. Presenters may actually show that they are unable to proceed in a coherent manner unless the visual prompt is there. It is hard to carry away an impression of ownership of the material or conviction in the ideas from such a presentation. If these are actually present, one does oneself a great disservice by presenting in a manner that gives quite the contrary impression. Although we may commend them on the design and structure of the PowerPoint presentation, even that is unlikely to be completely in their favour as we may in fact attribute it to others working behind the screen. We are unlikely to go away with a sense of having connected with an individual's mind and having really benefited from the communication in a way that makes the time and effort spent worthwhile.

When this happens it implies that the presenter is not optimally using the unique advantages available to them through the rich medium of direct, face-to-face communication. In comparison to a written document, perhaps all that the presentation is ensuring is the simultaneous delivery to the intended receivers. The advantages of connecting with the audience to establish a rapport, of being tuned in as to how they are going along with our ideas, of constantly gathering feedback and being ready to respond to it through modifications in the style and content, and of adding additional supporting messages through non-verbal cues, are all sacrificed or severely compromised by such an approach to presentation. At the same time, the advantages of written communication for receivers are also compromised because they do not have the luxury to pore over it at length at a time of their convenience and at their own pace, to refer back and forth within the material, or to file it for future reference. Therefore, we see that using PowerPoint or any other visuals as the focal feature of the communication rather than as support, leads to the loss of many advantages of spoken communication and indicates a poor choice of medium.

When it comes to our turn as presenters, we should learn from this common experience of PowerPoint presentations we have often had as listeners. While we may certainly use this tool, we must remember to use it as an aid rather than as a replacement of direct communication with an audience chiefly through the spoken word. This applies as much to its design and content as discussed in the earlier section, as to the delivery. In order to make the best use of the potential advantages of a face-to-face presentation, we must ensure that we as the presenter and our spoken words remain central to the communication and we turn to the visual support for representation of parts that would be more effective through this means. In order to achieve this effect we may try some of the steps suggested in the box below.

- Take all steps such as setting up the projector, loading the PowerPoint presentation, arranging for a pointer before you come up to speak.
- When you come up to present, stand in front of the audience facing them squarely with your feet pointed in front rather than sideways.
- Make your opening remarks without the use of a visual. It is a good idea to break the ice and to share the objective of the presentation without turning to the PowerPoint. One may use an anecdote or a startling fact or pose a question or even opt for a direct announcement of the purpose. But one must do it in a direct communication with the listeners, using all elements of body language to show one's keen desire to convey the message and to connect with the listeners.
- When you turn to a slide, do so with a clear indication that you are doing so for a particular purpose, not merely for your own comfort or as a jog to your memory. You may explicitly say, 'here is the agenda,' or 'let us look at these figures,' or 'I draw your attention to this flowchart where we can see . . .'
- For brief textual content on a slide it is better to assume that the audience has read it almost as soon as it came up so there is no need to read it aloud. Reading aloud to the audience is a waste of time because it takes much longer than it does for the audience to take it in through their eyes. At the same time, reading aloud is insulting to the audience's intelligence as it certainly indicates our

doubts about their ability to read it properly.

- If you do not want the audience to read ahead, it is a good idea to animate your slides in a manner that each point comes up only when you want to.

- We must also remember that simply turning some data into a visual does not make it self-explanatory. In addition to explanation, sometimes, the audience needs more time to actually grasp all that is represented in a big flow chart, a table with many rows and columns, or a slide with a number of graphs on it. For such material, it is important to allow time for the audience to take it in. If the size of some visuals is too big, resulting in problems with legibility for the audience, it is a good idea to break up the figure into simpler representations. It is useful to visually highlight relevant parts on a diagram, graph, or table by circling it or colouring it differently and by pointing to it during the presentation. We may also give handouts of complex data or figures that do not fit well on to a slide and become small and less legible on the screen.

- While it may also be a good idea to provide handouts of complex visuals or detailed data so that the audience may be able to read and follow it better, there is a caution to be taken in terms of the timing of handing out the print copies. I have seen presenters distribute handouts before starting their presentation, only to find the audience distracted with reading these rather than listening. As we cannot prevent the audience from reading the handouts once they are given to them, it is advisable to control the timing of the distribution itself. Try giving out the supporting print material when you come to the point where it needs to be referred to. You will find that the purpose is much better served and without causing distraction. Handouts that are supplementary material may be given after the presentation is over.

- It is absolutely important to know our presentations so well that a mere glance is sufficient for us to keep on track with the visuals and to avoid the problem of turning our face away to read it. We must remember that every time we do so we give the message of the centrality of the visual rather than our spoken communication, we break eye contact and thus the rapport with the listeners, and by doing so we lose the opportunity of registering the feedback from the audience. Further, each time our face turns away while speaking, our voice does not carry to the audience.

- It is not essential that if you are using a PowerPoint presentation you need to have a slide for every minute of your presentation. You may introduce blank slides when you want to focus attention on what you are saying and in interacting with the audience and where the visual representation is not relevant.

- In all, through our delivery style we need to ensure that the visuals—whether text, or charts, or diagrams—are clearly used as aids to help in the clarity and impact of what we are communicating rather than as the actual presentation.

Body language

Think of all the impressive presentations you have attended. I am sure you have noticed how an effective speaker's impact begins even before they begin to speak. The spring in their step, the smile on the face, the look in the eyes, the energy, and the composed appearance, as they come up to speak, whether in a large conference hall or a small meeting room already gives a positive impression of their capability. These first impressions may, of course, be modified as the interaction proceeds, but it is important to keep in mind how much we gain by using our body language to convey favourable impressions right from the word go in a face-to-face situation. **As listeners we are more willing to listen favourably to a person who radiates comfort, confidence, conviction, and eagerness to communicate with us as compared to one who seems shaky, fidgety, lacking in composure, and apathetic.** Research shows that perception of a speaker's persuasiveness is affected by non-verbal cues such as eye contact, gestures, posture, head nodding, distance from listeners, touch, facial expressions, and vocal elements of fluency, variations in tone, pace, and pitch.

In order to make the best impact with our combined verbal and non-verbal cues, it is important to be guided right through our presentation, as in all our interactions with others, by the understanding that it is not our words alone that are doing the communicating. Because we are there in person, all elements of our presence will carry messages for the receiver, whether intended or not. This applies to virtual presence too as in video-conferencing. The more aware we are of this fact, the more we can try to ensure that all the messages convey the same, or complementary/supportive, messages. If we do not ensure this, it is likely that what we communicate through our words is contradicted by what others may find being conveyed through other cues. For example, we may be vouching for the reliability of our proposed system or product, but the lack of enthusiasm and energy, our lack of eye contact, and nervousness as seen from our odd posture or gestures or fidgeting with our loose change and keys in our pocket, may indicate the contrary to our listeners.

This multiplicity of messages through body language may be a liability for a speaker who does not handle it well, but for an effective speaker it is actually one of the biggest advantages of spoken communication. If the choice of spoken communication has been made appropriately, it means that in our judgement the interaction would gain from our personality coming into the equation. One of the important reasons for such a considered choice would have been the possibility it allows as the richest medium to impact the receivers through multiple sensory messages and the potential of better serving the objective of the communication through these. If we were to go on to not employ these additional messages to their fullest potential, we are wasting a huge advantage uniquely offered by this communication mode. Remember, your physical presence and personality should not be regarded as problems or as bothersome baggage—these are *you*! Use them to add to the impact you make. Stamp your presentation with your personality, make it unique. No one else, even given the same material and slides, can ever present it quite like you. Use this knowledge to its full potential. Once you have prepared the presentation to the best of your ability and practised it enough, be confident, and project your delight and comfort in sharing your ideas, thoughts, or findings with the listeners.

It is through your positive body signals that listeners will conclude whether you believe what you are saying, whether you and your material are trustworthy and credible, whether you are nervous or relaxed, and many things to boot. Where do they get these inputs from? The answer is: from everything about you—your walk, your posture, your use of your hands, shoulders, the fleeting expressions on your face, the way you look, your use of the space available to you, the expression in your eyes, your gaze, the speed of speaking, the volume and the energy displayed. As is human tendency, the best of people cannot resist judging others in the first few minutes based not on what is being said verbally but on what is perceived through the non-verbal cues. At the same time, throughout the communication, people are prone to fall for any distraction offered by these non-verbal cues. In case the verbal and non-verbal messages clash, which will be trusted? No surprises here—it will be the non-verbal! We've got to be on top of this game. Everything about us has to be within our control and to be used consciously for effect—even if the effect we are aiming at is unaffected spontaneity! Ask any person who you judge from their style as spontaneous and natural and you will find, if they are being truthful, that the spontaneity and naturalness is achieved though considerable conscious choice, planning and practise. Other than this, some degree of the spontaneity and naturalness comes from being relaxed and treating the occasion as an opportunity to connect and establish a dialogue that gets the listeners involved and responsive, even if their response may be largely non-verbal.

Why should a listener be interested in, excited by, or convinced of what you are saying, if you don't seem so yourself? And how does one seem so? It is through the manner of our speaking, our tone of voice, the expression on our face, and every component of our body language as we speak. In fact, as the speaker, we need to show a shade higher of excitement and conviction so as to convey these to the listeners. If we want to infect others with our ideas and our belief in them, we need to show this conviction and eagerness to communicate. And this is best done by our body language rather than through words. As our own experience tells us, we are not likely to believe someone simply because they ask for it from us or tell us how much they believe in it. Even if they do, we need these messages to be corroborated by the body language of the person which we feel is a more reliable indicator.

Posture: walking, standing

Whether we sit or stand, the posture of our body will allow people to make judgements about our level of energy and commitment. We should be conscious of this so that we make sure that all our efforts in terms of preparing excellent content are not nullified by inadvertently allowing our posture to reveal lack of interest or of commitment.

As we walk up to take our place in the front of the room to make our presentation or speech, we must remember to walk briskly and purposefully so as to convey our eagerness to present our ideas and confidence in ourselves. It is not essential that we really feel so. We are talking of the message to be conveyed by keeping our posture straight and our strides strong and firm. As the audience sees us display signs that are taken as conveying confidence, they begin to have positive expectations from us, and this means we are off to a good start.

It is a good idea to have a remote slide changer and pointer so that we are not forced to stay in a certain spot. Alternatively, we may use the help of another person to change the slides. However, practice would be needed to ensure that you are in sync with each other. Having freed oneself from the necessity to stay near a computer, one may move so as to appear more natural, relaxed, and confident. However, this movement should ideally be purposeful, in the sense that one moves up to the front or laterally to the sides of the room or occasionally, as during Q&A time, even a little into the audience. This movement should be controlled and quiet—no squeaky shoes or dragging of feet! Also to be avoided are two other kinds of walking about: the vigorous marching or stamping that gives an appearance of aggression; and a set of rhythmic movements that suggest that the speaker is responding to a regular musical beat, indicating nervousness to the point of lacking awareness of how they are moving. Many a times I have pointed this out to presenters during feedback only to be met with an incredulous response. When shown video evidence of it, they admit that they were not even aware of it due to their nervousness. As for all elements of body language in general, the more in control we are and the more we can ensure that the message being conveyed by the particular non-verbal cue is positive and in tandem with our verbal content, the better it will enhance the effectiveness of our communication as a whole. It is quite natural that audience interprets such congruence of all parts of the communication as confidence. In fact, when it is done well, the non-verbal elements blend in so well with the verbal message, so as to become quite invisible. It is in incongruence that they draw attention to themselves and pose a dilemma for the receivers as to which message to trust.

When we stand before an audience we must remember that our very stance can convey positive messages such as confidence and energy or negative messages such as nervousness and apathy. We must begin with standing so as to face the audience squarely, with our weight on both feet and this is the posture we must aim at for most of our presentation. During a long presentation, it is fine to move one's weight naturally from one foot to the other, as not doing so may begin to indicate a stiffness that implies nervousness. When we need to draw attention to a flipchart or a visual on the screen we should turn slightly towards these and make sure that we are not blocking the audience's view. However, a posture constantly angled towards the visual aids gives these a centrality and converts the presentation into a slideshow. We must also remember that we must not give an impression of having grown roots into a particular spot. With a large audience, we may move from one side to the other through turning our body or by taking a few steps on either side of the centre. Experience of many presentations shows that most of us seem to have a natural tendency to keep our bodies slightly inclined towards one side of a room. This does not help in establishing rapport with the entire audience and in keeping eye contact with them to establish a connection as well as to receive feedback from them. We need to be alert for this and consciously ensure that we do not miss out on engaging the entire audience simply because our posture prevented us from connecting with them.

In cases where we speak from a lectern, and movement away from it is not possible, we need to take in to account the fact that we do not have one of the ways of conveying certain positive impressions. Therefore, we must compensate by using our posture effectively. We must stand straight with square shoulders and turn ourselves slightly as we speak, to face all parts of the room.

Gestures

For a nervous presenter, the hands seem like awkward and inconvenient appendages as he struggles with the question of what to do with them. One may clasp them in front or behind the back, put them away in pockets, or use them to smoothen neckties or hair or some other such fidgeting actions. Doing these only makes the nervousness apparent to the audience. Since nervousness makes our hands shake we may feel it best to lock them tight or to keep them out of sight. However, that is exactly the meaning that is given to such devices by the observers, thus defeating the purpose. **Since most people normally use their hands in a natural manner when speaking in informal and relaxed contexts, not using our hands at all while speaking is interpreted as artificial and uncomfortable.** On the other hand, excessive or obsessive and repetitive gestures may also be taken as indicating nervousness. It is true that when we are nervous we are not quite aware of the repetitive patterns of hand movements we may be making. While we must not be wooden and not make any gestures, at the same time we must not overdo them. The challenge is to reach a level of hand movements that appears natural and comfortable and goes to reinforcing the verbal content without drawing attention to itself. Unless our purpose is to provide amusement and entertainment, we must avoid giving any cause for these by providing distractions through our inappropriate or excessive gestures. Listeners may grab any opportunity for distraction—whether it is a repetitive gesture or uncontrolled jittery movement or constant fiddling. Effectively used, gestures may indicate size, expanse, and shapes, or be used to indicate numbers, or to underline and emphasize our words. While doing so, it is best to not appear stuck with a particular gesture which, by its overuse, begins to jar on the receivers.

Like all parts of the speaking task, this too needs practice to make it work most effectively in adding value to the communication. By practice we can increase our repertoire of gestures so as to avoid overuse of any one in particular. Taking feedback—either from a mirror or from friends—helps us in identifying any tendency to either extreme of using gestures. We may then consciously work out how we will use our hands during the presentation, not as a liability or as unnecessary appendages, but as useful tools for conveying positive meanings about our confidence and comfort level and to add to the meaning of our words.

Appearance

Even before he or she begins to speak, the speaker's attire and grooming make an impression upon the audience. People may rush to make assumptions based on these elements and these assumptions may colour the interpretation of the content and overall responses to the presentation. A neat and tidy appearance and attention to grooming and attire give an indirect message that the speaker takes the occasion seriously. A dishevelled and unkempt appearance may be taken as indicating a casual approach to the situation or extreme nervousness. Both these interpretations are unlikely to work in the favour of the speaker's impact or in serving the objective of the presentation.

When we put in considerable effort over all parts of the preparation, why compromise it all by neglecting our own appearance? Why not take care to show our understanding of the requirement in terms of the level of formality of the occasion by dressing appropriately? The precise definition of 'appropriate' is obviously dependent on context. **As far as possible, we must try to understand the context and the expectations in terms of dress and appearance while preparing for a presentation.** For an in-house presentation it is easy for us to know the norm and to dress accordingly. In the case of other contexts, if we cannot find out the precise expectation, it is advisable to err on the conservative side. It is best to wear something simple and elegant rather than messy and complicated. It is also best to avoid fiddly accessories and ornaments that not only give an appearance of casualness but may also prove distracting. When we give attention to our clothes, we must also take care of our footwear and accessories. They should be as per expectations so as to not be distracting.

The overall purpose of such a dressing style in accordance with expected norms is to avoid drawing attention to the appearance. Once it registers on the audience that the appearance is fine according to the norms for the occasion, it stops mattering and focus shifts to the actual communication. On the other hand, anything extreme or not in accordance with the norms becomes a constant source of distraction for the audience. As for all elements of body language and non-verbals, the less our dressing and appearance draw attention to themselves by being as per expectations, the better they allow the focus to remain on the ideas and sentiments being communicated.

Voice

It should be obvious that our voice is of paramount importance in spoken communication; it is the primary vehicle of the message. Our voice allows us to convey energy, enthusiasm, and feelings, and if we have chosen spoken communication for the advantages it brings us over other modes, we should be really concerned about making the most of these. However, it is surprising how often we listen to people who speak without caring about this element of their communication. Voice includes clarity of enunciation, tonal inflections, and variation in pitch, speaking pace, and volume. When these are not taken care of, the audience struggles with audibility, words that are not clearly recognizable, sentences that go on for too long, and fragments that make not much sense, and soon they begin to lose interest in the talk. This is regrettable because there is so much a presenter can do with their voice to not only make sure that the verbal content reaches the listeners clearly and completely but also to add additional meanings through good use of variations in tone, pace, and volume.

Inability to control our pitch and volume and delivering our presentation in a flat monotone give to the audience a sense of our being ill at ease and nervous. Demonstrating control over these elements of voice not only brings additional shades of meaning and effects to our words but also adds to the impression of confidence and control that we wish to create.

Clear enunciation is an essential component of spoken communication. **Unless we clearly and distinctly enunciate complete words in a manner recognizable to our listeners, the spoken communication is doomed.** It is important to breathe deeply before speaking and in the natural pauses, so that we do not run out of breath at odd places and consequently swallow some of the syllables in words, or even entire words in a sentence. Instead of letting our listeners guess whether we mean 'forty' or 'fourteen', 'many' or 'any', 'go' or 'grow', we must make sure to say words clearly and to the last syllable. Listening is hard work and unless we make it easy for the listeners they might yield to the temptation of mentally wandering off.

One of the ways in which we turn off our listeners and lose the connection we may have built is through making it hard for them to get our words. When we mumble instead of speaking distinctly, we give the audience an excuse to tune out. If the topic is very interesting to them or what you say is of great value to them, they may try hard to focus on the words and fill the gaps but in the face of mumbling may just give up and start doodling or daydreaming, planning to catch up on the content later from someone who was able to hear, or through handouts. Listeners may find habitual mumbling, chewing off of final sounds of words, and trailing off at the end of sentences, annoying and taxing as it forces them to work harder to fill in missing bits. When we choose to speak in order to get our ideas across to people, the basic responsibility that comes with it is that of speaking clearly and distinctly so as to get our words through to our listeners without undue strain and confusion.

It is also very important to remember that we should be facing the listeners while speaking so that words are not lost to them. If we have the tendency to look at our slides on a projector screen while we speak, many of our words would not reach our audience clearly because of the movement of our head in the opposite direction. With a fixed microphone, the effect can be very bad. Even with a collar microphone clipped to the tie or the shirt front, any extreme movement of the head, causes the same effect. It is best to move the entire torso rather than the head by itself.

Pronunciation, again, is important in allowing spoken words to be recognized and understood by the listener. However, it is a little trickier as there are some words for which there may be alternate pronunciations. When communicating in English, it would be advisable to try to figure out as far as possible, whether a particular set of listeners would be more comfortable with the American or British pronunciation of a word or whether there are other local variations in its pronunciation. It may also be a good idea to slow down over words that are less common and to take extra care over their pronunciation and distinct articulation while watching the response of the audience for checking if it has been understood in congruence with the context or if it has caused any confusion. However, for most words, there *is* a correct pronunciation that can easily be checked by referring to a dictionary or some other authoritative source. The problem with mispronunciation is not only that there is a certain snob value attached to speaking the language correctly, but more importantly, the fact that it can lead to miscommunication. Such miscommunication may be sometimes prevented by an alert listener making sense from the context, but the onus really lies on the speaker to facilitate correct decoding of the words by using the generally accepted pronunciations.

Pace of speaking can contribute significantly to the meaning conveyed. We must aim at speaking at a good pace without use of fillers such as 'umm', 'ah', 'er'. These are best kept to a minimum although ruling them out altogether is not possible when speaking in a natural manner. Avoiding excessive sprinkling of such fillers helps in giving the impression that the speaker is comfortable with the speaking role and is in control of the material. This, in turn, puts the listeners in a receptive state of mind. This is not to say that one must speak at breakneck speed. In fact, it is advisable to use a slightly slower pace of speaking compared to one-on-one conversations so as to help give clarity to the articulation by not jumbling up the sounds. Some moments of reflective speaking, or an occasional 'er' or 'umm' as you search for the precise expression for the shade of meaning, or an occasional pause for effect are of course perfectly acceptable and may give a positive impression of naturalness and spontaneity.

In Sir Ralph Richardson's words, 'The most precious things in speech are the pauses'. A good speaker knows how to use pauses to good effect and make them add to the impact of the points. It is a fallacy that one must speak without pause so as to give a good impression to the audience of the fluency of our ideas and articulation. In normal circumstances, no one speaks without breaks. In fact, when we speak in this manner, we give away our nervousness that has made us speed up unnaturally. We also give a sense of discomfort with being the centre of attention and our wish to minimise the time spent in this position by hastening the end of our speaking role. At the primary level, therefore, pauses provide a more natural speaking style and subtly show our comfort with the speaking role. This is no small matter; it is very important for the speaker to be seen as comfortable and keen to speak to the audience rather than struggling or going through an onerous duty. An appearance of comfort in the role also indicates confidence in one's ideas and material.

We must also keep in mind that, to begin with, pauses are necessary for a very basic but essential function. In the absence of punctuation marks that serve to aid the receiver of written communication in getting the correct sense of sentences, pauses help the listener in this purpose. If we speak without perceptible pauses to indicate dashes, commas, and full stops, we may produce a garbled mess of words which the listener struggles to make sense of. But, there are also more subtle ways in which well-timed pauses can add to the impact of our points.

Pauses may be used for:

- **Effect**
  Do we not wish our carefully worked out points to be distinctly received by our listeners? Then why would we

bury them indistinguishably among the ordinary verbal mass such as articles, connective tissue, and transitory phrases? Try taking a little pause before you utter the key words, the riveting phrase, the beautiful image, the clinching data, or the answer to the problem posed. Coming in the middle of continuous, even-paced sounds, a pause focuses attention by its novelty. By pausing, we bring back the attention of the listeners that may have wandered, so that they do not miss the next utterance, and consequently, the effect we are trying to build on it.

Pauses help to build an expectation, and prepare the receiver for our words. They have to, therefore be used judiciously. If there are too many pauses, it is no longer a novelty, but establishes the norm for that speaker, and the listeners settle to that pace. In this scene, no expectation builds up because the pauses are soon perceived to be not signalling any significance. In fact, they may begin to be interpreted as lack of preparation or nervousness.

Pauses can also be used when we want to create a sense of urgency or of excitement. We choose a brisk style, where the speed of our delivery matches and builds the mood. We may then pause for dramatic effect so as to build suspense before we reveal the solution or the discovery or result or an announcement. A sense of drama helps to break the scourge of speaking that is monotony and dullness. Without variation in pace and tone, we create a soporific effect on our listeners. And unless singing a lullaby, this is definitely not the effect we are aiming at!

- **Reflection**

  As we speak, one of our purposes may be to get our listeners to examine what we are saying and to go along with us as we build our reasoning or provide our well-structured ideas. We must keep in mind that listeners are doing a challenging task and that too without the luxury of time available to a receiver of written material. Listeners need to relate the sounds received by their ears to the literal and contextual meanings. At the same time, they may wish to evaluate the logical rigour behind inferences, the authenticity and correctness of information, and validity of findings. Generally, they bring existing information and views on the topic, and wish to correlate what they receive from the presenter with their own ideas. **If we keep hurrying on from point to point, or from assertion to assertion, or keep heaping fact upon fact without pause, we may build up a processing backlog that may become so big that the listener may give up trying to deal with it.** Therefore, with taking the audience along with us being of utmost importance, it is essential that we allow time for the listeners to process what they hear and to reflect on key points. We do this through well-spaced pauses at the right places. The right place being: after utterances that would require some moments to sink in and to be reflected upon in the light of the context, the preceding points, or the listener's own perceptions.

- **Emphasis**

By well-timed pauses you can emphasize your ideas in a way that would help them to be received in the intended sense. A pause draws your listeners' attention to certain parts of what you are saying and makes these parts stand out. Once you make a certain point or present information that you would like to register as significant, it is again a good idea to provide a pause. **Providing a little break in the pace of speaking serves the purpose of an underlined or bold text in writing.** If, on the other hand, you were to continue without a pause, there would be no special emphasis on the particular part as it would all be in the same stride. Similarly, when you want to sum up your argument or your position memorably or you come to the culmination of the points you have been making, and are aiming at an impressive climax, don't go on in an unvaried pace, with the risk that the climax may go unnoticed. Pause to signal its significance, letting listeners get alerted to the moment, and building expectation. Coming after the pause, the conclusion or climax will have a much greater impact.

Volume can also be used effectively to add meaning to our words. While, of course, we must use at least the minimum level of voice to be audible, we may introduce variations for effect within the comfortably audible range. As with all other vocal elements, after a norm has been established, any variation tends to draw the attention of the listeners. This is thus an effective way to bring the audience to focus on the significant parts of the presentation and to bring in particular emotional shades to what we are saying. For example, slightly but noticeably lowering our volume generally makes listeners focus more keenly on what comes next and this may be effectively used to highlight certain significant points. Lowering of volume may also be effectively used to bring an element of seriousness or somberness to certain words or sentences. A variation on the other side, that is, by slightly raising the volume, may also work to signal excitement, importance, or urgency. However, one must remember that the effectiveness of these variations lies on their sparing use. It subtly draws attention to particular parts because of the change from the established pattern and this would be lost if it was over-used.

Facial expressions

People in the audience make judgements about the sincerity and feelings of the presenter from the facial expressions. We have all heard presenters who speak with no expression on their faces. Our perception of such persons is that they are too nervous or don't care very much about the subject. This may or may not be true but as observers we have no way of knowing the truth in this matter. It is for the speaker to be aware that their facial expressions are also carrying messages and if they are not aware enough to ensure that these match what they wish to convey, there may be a clash with their intended messages and those received by the audience. As in the case of all elements of body language, any incongruence leads to a choice on the part of the listener about which message to give precedence to. While we may be overlooking the non-verbal message, the audience may, in fact, trust it more than our carefully constructed verbal message.

Our face is taken to reflect our feelings about our subject, the speaking situation, and our audience. If our face does not reflect positive feelings about these, we are in grave danger of disenchanting our audience. It is very unrealistic to expect the audience to be enthused with a subject about which the speaker does not appear enthusiastic in the first place, judged from the facial expression and voice. Moreover, our words gain additional meaning by being reinforced through our facial expressions, thus giving more clarity to the ideas. A frozen or deadpan expression is likely to be taken to indicate extreme nervousness. Whatever we speak should be presented with expressions that indicate the emotional undertone whether it be of gravity or lightness, happiness or worry, excitement, or concern.

It is advisable to smile at the beginning and to have an expression on the face that indicates our eagerness to convey our thoughts to the listeners, respect for the occasion, and an appropriate demeanour. The expression should be dynamic and should reflect and be congruent with what we are saying. **Although smiling is a positive signal, it may not be appropriate for all parts of our presentation and a fixed smile may, in fact, indicate nervousness.** As we go along into the main part of our presentation, we should allow ourselves to behave in our natural way, reflecting on our face the feelings evoked by the ideas we are speaking of. Just as we do not speak in normal life with a single expression on the face, we should strive to speak in as natural a manner as we can if we want to indicate a natural and comfortable and confident state of mind.

Eye contact

The success of a speaker really boils down to one word—rapport. The key to rapport lies not so much in storytelling and humour or in asking questions as in eye contact that makes each member of the audience feel connected to the speaker and feel that the speaker cares about his or her presence and their receiving of the message. The speaker who looks at the floor or at the ceiling or out of the window is likely to be perceived as nervous or uninterested. It is not enough to look ahead, over the heads of the audience members. People in the audience are able to feel whether you are looking at them or above their heads. Unless you are speaking to over fifty people it is quite possible to ensure that you are able to look at every single person and hold their gaze for a few seconds in the course of a 20 to 30 minute talk or presentation. The sense of the presenter speaking directly to them is gratifying to the listeners and is irreplaceable in its role as a binding agent between speaker and audience. If listeners get the sense that the presenter seems to be conversing more with their shoes or the ceiling or the slides or notes, they don't feel particularly inclined to make the effort to pay attention.

Our feeling for the value of the topic and our keenness to share our ideas with the audience are best reflected in our eyes. Our receptivity to the audience's reaction is also reflected through our eye contact with them. Rapport and our responsiveness to the audience's feedback in terms of adaptability of our material and our approach are the key advantages of spoken communication. And this depends on our maintaining eye contact with them rather than with all other alternate places where we are tempted to gaze. **Another crucial importance of eye contact that cannot be over-emphasized is that it indicates a confidence and comfort level of the speaker that, in turn, leads to positive expectations in the audience.**

There is no final, guaranteed-to-win, universally successful and replicable body language formula. The rule of thumb is: whatever is perceived as natural to the speaker and blends seamlessly into the material without drawing attention to itself is fine. Speakers can have vastly different styles in terms of body language, and each of these may be highly effective. As critical observers and listeners we can watch a really good presenter and try to replicate some of his or her mannerisms. We may be able to pull off some while others appear unnatural for us. However, there's no need to worry. Each one of us is a unique individual and like our signature, our style can never be exactly the same as another's. That is not to say one should not try to learn from others. One should do so, but with the knowledge that if one style does not work for us there are literally endless other combinations that we can attempt till we construct a repertoire that is effective while appearing most natural and unstrained for us.

For a presentation to be effective it needs to address both the question of 'Why?' (in conjunction with 'For whom?') and of 'How?' Without equal effort and planning of both, it is unlikely that the presentation will be impressive and memorable. Excellent content is that which has been worked out with a clear understanding of the objective and the audience. Even on the same topic, the material needs to be re-selected in terms of breadth and depth, when the objective of the presentation or the set of audience (or both) change. But even if a presenter has the best material worked out, they may botch up the delivery through a style that is not impressive and memorable. If that happens, all the effort on the appropriate content comes to naught as it does not even register on the intended receivers. At the same time, all the style in the world cannot fill in the blanks where solid ideas should have been. Given time and resources, it is easy enough to work on ideas and to gather information but the 'How?' is something one has to handle 'live,' on-the-spot. And it is for this reason that it is used to separate the good from the ordinary, and the best from the merely good.

If you ask people what sets apart an impressive and memorable speaker from an ordinary and dull one, the first thing they are likely to say is 'confidence level'. But if we look closely we realize that audiences cannot really see and hear the confidence level, for the simple reason that it is not something that can be seen or heard! But that does not stop them from judging it based on a number of visible and audible cues associated in their minds with confidence. **Generally speaking, a speaker seems confident to an audience when he or she appears at ease, has a relaxed posture, seems to be in control of gestures, eye contact, movement, and uses voice and facial expressions to support the verbal content and to show full involvement and conviction.**

The audience really has no way of knowing what is going on inside your mind. If they cannot see or hear signs of your nervousness, it does not register. So, what should a beginner speaker (or even an experienced one with a new audience) do at the beginning of a talk? Simple: Fake it till you feel it! And you will feel it very soon! As you project confidence through your controlled and supportive gestures, posture, head movements, facial expression and voice elements, you tide over the hardest part, that is, the beginning. After that, once you have established a rapport and credibility and got the audience engaged, the need to fake it disappears like water evaporating from washing hung out in the crisp summer sun.

When audiences decide that the speaker was effective and memorable they reach that conclusion based on little bits of input about confidence, comfort, energy and enthusiasm, sincerity and commitment. All of these are assessed on the basis of nothing other than body language. Despite a wide range of delivery styles, the one single common element shared by all effective and memorable speakers is the total control over all parts of their non-verbal communication. It is not so much a question of how much, as of blending into the verbal part; supporting it without distracting from it; and displaying the control of the speaker, and indirectly the ease and confidence with not only the subject and the audience, but with all elements of the speaking situation.

Connecting with the audience

This is of vital importance to any situation of speaking to a group of people. If we cannot keep the focus on the listeners and keep them involved, all our efforts are in vain. Only when the listeners feel involved will they be willing to give us their attention and to make the effort to put meaning into the sounds they hear. We often forget what an important role the listener performs and get carried away by all that we as speakers are doing. Yet, the listener is the key player. Take away this piece and our speaking loses all meaning—instead of being effective or impressive it becomes a mad act! More seriously, the listeners have a difficult job—listening to the sounds of a human voice and putting together the inputs received from many sensory sources, to make connections and allow their minds to be guided along a particular line of reasoning that is not their own, to control other stimuli from the environment around them as well as distractions from their own minds. All of this adds up to a tremendous deal to ask of someone. And yet, most speakers forget both the challenging role that the listeners are playing and the fact that the presentation is meant for them, and treat them as furniture or worse, as enemies.

Customizing to audience's needs, interests, and background

Whatever ground-breaking information and argument one brings to a presentation, it is all wasted if we are not able to make a connection with the listeners and involve them in the communication. Of course, the material must be authentic and credible, but the over-riding question should be whether it is of interest or use to that particular audience. To involve the audience in our message we need to couch it in terms that reflect the focus on them and their needs, interests, or benefit. **The value of your information is not absolute; it should relate to the audience and their 'What's in it for me?' outlook.**

Choosing our focus and making the right selection out of the available material is part of the tailor-making that is required. When we decide what we are going to speak, this choice cannot be determined on the basis of our own interest or knowledge alone. What is of primary importance is the audience—what do they already know, what do they want from listening to you, what will they do with what they get from you? **How we elaborate our subject, what examples and allusions or references we make, how technical we make our terminology, everything should be shaped by the audience's level, needs and expectations.** This is how we customize what we have to say to our audience and connect with them by indicating that it is meant specifically for them, and not for just any audience. Having ensured such customization of content, during the delivery again, we have to keep the focus on the receivers, connecting with whom is of paramount importance.

It is their presence and active listening that will make or mar the presentation. To ensure the active listening of the audience is also part of the challenge of the speaker. It is easy to dismiss the audience as uninterested, bored, blasé, uninformed, and the like. Yet, it is amazing to see the same audience that sat listlessly through an average speaker's talk, spring to life when another takes the podium. The differentiator is the speaker's complete focus on the audience or lack of it—whether in terms of content or the way of presenting.

Share the structure and provide signposts

In order to connect with the audience it is important to keep in mind that you are speaking for the benefit of the listeners. Not only should your material be selected and organized in a manner to be of interest, use, and benefit to them, the way you speak should show that you care to take them along, that you want to involve them, and that you are speaking for them. **Share your plan unless there is some exceptional reason to keep the suspense.** Before you begin, listeners generally only have your title or a broad topic for your talk. Don't assume that the focus and the way you are choosing to proceed follows naturally from these. In many presentations, the speakers plod along in a way they think is natural and logical, but by the time they approach the key points or the important findings or analysis, they have already turned off the audience who may have built some other expectations and kept measuring it against that, in the absence of any declared plan from the presenter.

Asking questions

Many speakers are under the impression that asking open-ended questions is the way to get audience involvement. But remember, this is only one of the ways to do so and not the most effective one at that. Such questions pass the control to the audience and with an audience that is uninterested or antagonistic, this can bring the talk to an awkward point where the speaker stands helplessly waiting for an answer so that she can proceed. Sometimes, the answer is deliberately meant to throw the speaker off track and can create awkwardness. **Rhetorical questions are a good device, and used with personal pronouns that build on common ground between the speaker and listeners, can bind these two units of the presentation.**

Understanding the audience is the key to deciding how to involve them. The better one can know the audience the better one can use that understanding to build a common ground between the two parties. Involvement stems from seeking out such common ground, building a bridge on that base, using examples and references that appeal and make sense to them. At the same time, we need to adopt a delivery style that shows keen desire to reach out to the listeners, full involvement of the speaker as evident through body language, and keenness to seek and respond to constant feedback. Such a style cements the bond that builds between the speaker and listeners. The importance of an animated, conversational tone and eye contact with all audience members to achieve involvement of the audience cannot be over-emphasized. During the actual presentation these serve as the invisible thread that connects the two equally important pillars of the talk.

Storytelling

We can also build interest in our material by using narrative techniques rather than heavy-handed theorizing. By telling a story we can tap into the human instinct for storytelling—the oldest of the oral communication traditions. People would much rather hear something that answers 'what happened?' than a theoretical exposition. Although the latter may be essential in certain situations, our effort should be to bring in the 'story' element wherever we can. Can we create characters and use names of people and places to make a problem appear more real and fully-fleshed? Can we paint a scenario in details so it may be easily visualized by our listeners? Moreover, when doing so, do we have our finger on the pulse of the audience in terms of their interests, likes, and attitudes? The better we can do this, the greater the likelihood of our story touching a sympathetic chord in the minds and hearts of the listeners.

Humour

The use of humour is an effective way to build rapport and break the ice as well as provide relief to the receivers from the tedium of listening. If we can infuse humour into our storytelling it, so much better. Except on the rare occasion that we are speaking at a funeral or a condolence meeting, or presenting a formal statement on a somber occasion, there is no need to appear and sound dead serious. **Most audiences** relate better to speakers who don't take themselves too seriously. Humour has been used in literary and dramatic arts to make criticism palatable or to approach difficult subjects such as social reform. George Bernard Shaw, the great iconoclast, used humour to get people to absorb radical ideas without noticing them. Humour lowers defences and makes people more susceptible to ideas. However, humour too needs to be in tune with the audience's profile. Being especially culture-specific, humour may not be perceived in the same way by different sets of people. We need to take care that we understand really well what is perceived as appropriate and inappropriate in a given context. Generally speaking, it is better to avoid humour targeted at specific sets of people according to race, gender, or physical characteristics. Aiming at mildness and gentleness rather than a scathing or abrasive approach is best. It is also a good idea to make oneself the subject of some of our humour so as to show oneself as not too self-important and uptight. However, this should be done in moderation so as to not dent our credibility.

A lot of us find it hard to get jokes right and are afraid of launching into one only to forget the punch line or to mess up the comic timing. Although we can try to gain comfort in this through practice and through memorizing appropriate jokes, a safer and more effective approach would be to ditch jokes for wit. Wit and a clever, fresh turn of expression create a memorable impact and is a higher level of creating humour appropriate for verbally skilled people. It binds the speaker and audience in a special connectedness of 'getting it.'

Other than connecting with the audience and bringing in some lightness, the use of humour also serves to demonstrate our comfort and ease with the speaking situation. This can work wonders in conveying our confidence. Some speakers work under the illusion that adopting an impersonal approach makes them and their material appear more 'serious' and 'professional'. However, the use of passive voice and third person phrasing of ideas and a dead serious demeanour and style of presenting our ideas only de-personalizes our message and makes it sound dry and bookish and makes our communication appear as an assigned task we are completing rather than something we care about or enjoy. It is very hard for listeners to warm up to our message if we seem to be not enjoying the interaction. And demonstrating our ability to bring in some wit and humour into our communication serves to convey our genuine relishing of the interaction and, in turn, makes the audience respond more favourably.

DON'T LET ANXIETY DERAIL YOUR PRESENTATIONS

Do you get sweaty palms, a dry throat, trembling hands, palpitating heart, and shaking legs when it comes to facing an audience? Do you fear your mind may go blank and people may lower their opinion of you? Or that you may not be able to get words out of your mouth or that your trembling may incapacitate you or that people would find your talk dull and drab? You are not alone. We all feel worried to think we are being judged. We all dread being a laughing stock and inadvertently making a fool of ourselves. The more unfamiliar the audience or the place, and the more challenging the task, the more nervousness we experience. Well, don't worry. It is absolutely normal. Don't take my word for it? Well how about Mark Twain's? He said, 'There are only two kinds of speakers: the nervous and the liars.' A speaker who claims to never feel any nervousness is either lying or jaded beyond the point of caring. So take heart from the comforting knowledge that everyone is nervous about speaking before others and that some nervousness is actually beneficial to our performance. In fact, the most experienced of presenters knows that this slightly heightened emotional state gives us the extra energy that is called for in presenting our ideas before others. Getting completely rid of this advantage, therefore, is not really desirable.

However, nervousness that almost paralyses us and hijacks our composure and memory, is surely a liability. The advantages of the spoken medium can only be realized when we retain our ability to be in control of our prepared material, to stay focused, to think on our feet and to be receptive and responsive to ongoing feedback from the listeners. We also need our composure to indicate a sense of comfort and confidence that is essential for the listener to feel inclined to go along with our thinking.

When anxiety and nervousness are so common, how do we overcome these and feel the necessary confidence and composure? The answer lies in preparation, practice, and positive self-talk.

- The better prepared you are, the easier it is to feel calm and in control. In terms of your topic or the issue at hand, it is best to prepare more than you will need. Although your treatment in the actual presentation should be sharply focused according to the needs of the occasion defined with a view to the purpose and the audience, don't limit yourself to gaining understanding of only what will be needed within the limits of the talk as defined by this focus. The greater the time and effort invested in gaining complete ownership of the ideas and information, the more you will feel in command. The mastery over the material to a much larger extent than what will be minimally required is the best inoculation against anxiety.

- As we have all experienced, anxiety is at its highest before we begin and in the initial moments of our presentation or talk. Once we get into the flow of our ideas and when we begin to get appropriate responses from our listeners, we are in a much better place. At the same time, the indications of nervousness in the initial moments may fluster us so much that we may not reach a point where the ideas begin to flow effortlessly. Seeing this, the audience is also unlikely to warm up to us and respond positively. In sum, if nervousness (or at least, the indicators of it) is not controlled at the beginning, it may cause serious problems to the overall effectiveness of the interaction. It is a good idea to have one's opening lines worked out. Knowing that we have the most nerve-racking bit covered, we can counter our anxiety when it's likely to be at its highest and when we find that that goes well, we have a great sense of relief and can relax for the remaining part of the interaction.

- Another point in our presentation that should not be left at risk of derailment by nervousness is the conclusion. This is the crucial part that needs to be presented effectively so as to clinch the objective. We need to provide an elegant and effective conclusion to wrap up our ideas and serve the objective. But if nerves were to attack us at that point, it may undo the entire exercise. Therefore, it is best to not leave this very important part to inspiration and on-the-feet thinking that require more composure than we may be feeling at that point. It is best to prepare a strong conclusion and to practise it, perhaps to even memorize it, so that there is no danger of it getting compromised or missed out through an attack of nerves at that point.

- The importance of practice in giving us confidence, of course, cannot be overstated. Strong preparation gives us all our material but only practice can help translate that into effective communication. We do not want to stand before our listeners fumbling for details or forgetting key points, if we want our words to carry credibility and impact. We need firstly, practice of speaking out in general. We do ourselves a great favour when we try to face the challenge head on and grab all opportunities to engage with people—presenting our ideas, opinions, information, or analysis to others through speaking.

When we do so we not only try out the soundness of the content and gauge its reception by others, we also try out the various small components that combine to add to an effective oral presentation of the ideas.

- Despite all the planning we may have done, it is quite another thing to try and convert it all into actual spoken delivery. **During practice we may try out different body language components, visuals, or content elements such as humour, examples, and anecdotes. By trying these out we may get a sense of what we can carry off and what supports our objective better.** Practising by oneself can be done in front of a mirror to give some feedback to ourselves on how we are presenting our ideas. Another useful way is to try to get together a mock audience who can give a better feel of the real situation by simulating the reception of the ideas and by giving more objective feedback. Using the learning from such practice and the feedback—both subjective and objective—we have the opportunity to refine both our content and delivery style. Such effort is well rewarded by a huge gain in confidence. In comparison to someone who merely trusts presence of mind and aplomb to see them through, someone who has taken the trouble to practise will always be able to carry it off with greater suaveness and effectiveness. William Cronon, President of the American Historical Association in 2012 recalls how he happened to drop into the office of Professor Richard N. Ringler, just half an hour before he was to teach a class only to find him 'actually delivering the lecture that we were about to hear. His performances in class had always seemed so extemporaneous, so stream-of-consciousness, so thinking-out-loud in their brilliance, that it had never occurred to me how much they might be scripted; indeed, how much he might have polished and rehearsed them to produce the rhetorical and interpretive effects—maybe even some of those famous and beloved digressions—that he seemed to generate so effortlessly in the magical space of his classroom'.[1]

- If a brilliant professor who lectures day in and day out, can care about improving the delivery by thorough practice, it would do all of us good to emulate him. It would have no impact on the impression of spontaneity on the audience as is evident from the fact that but for this accidental discovery, Cronon would have continued to assume that that perfect falling together of all elements of Ringler's talks was perfectly spontaneous. As presenters, we must do all we can to ensure this effect on our listeners and that means as much preparation and practice as we can out into it. This effort not only reduces our anxiety and increases our confidence, it shows that we care enough about the communication and about making the most of the direct, face-to-face nature of spoken presentation, to practise till it appears absolutely spontaneous, however paradoxical that may sound!

---

[1] Cronon, William. 'Storytelling.' *The American Historical Review* (2013) 118 (1): 1-19.

- Positive self-talk and visualizing our success in meeting our objectives is a good way to snap out of the doomsday scenarios we are likely to paint for ourselves due to our fear. Even when we have prepared well and have taken our objective and audience into account while working out our material and practised our delivery, it is still likely that we feel nervous when it comes to actually facing the listeners. This is the time for positive self-talk and banishing all ideas of fear and doubt. We can practise a little cognitive therapy on ourselves, examining our fears under the cold light of logic and reason, till they pale and wither away. This works on the understanding that our thinking affects our emotions and that anxiety, fear, and depression result from illogical thinking. The negative emotions can be countered by actually examining the thinking rather than fighting the emotion. If we are afraid that we will fall down or that we will blank out or that the audience will boo us, we will need to look at these fears realistically and remind ourselves that although we have felt like this before, it has actually not really happened. We can also remind ourselves of how we have hardly ever seen it happen to anyone. It is a good idea to focus on the positives from any earlier experience, and to remember the good feeling we got and the response from our listeners and to tell ourselves that it will be even better this time! We need to remind ourselves of all that we have done right, that we have everything under control, that we know what we are going to say. We must regard the audience as friendly and open-minded and interested in the success of the interaction. We must keep in mind that listeners do not go to a presentation hoping for it to fail or for the presenter to make a fool of themselves. They are interested in their time being well-spent. From this we must go on to visualize our presentation or talk succeeding, the audience responding and appreciating, and our overall objective getting served.

HANDLING Q&A TIME WITHOUT ANXIETY

Question and answer time seems to be one of the foremost reasons why most of us dread making presentations. While the actual presentation does fill us with anxiety, we feel we can be in control through thorough preparation and having visual aids such as PowerPoint slides or notes with us. By practising, we may boost our confidence. But when it comes to Q&A time, we feel less in control and consequently, more fearful. The safety provided by our prepared material and structured ideas cannot be relied on at this point and we stand in fear of being exposed through any oddball attack on what we presented or questions about aspects of the issue on which we are inadequately prepared. Such anxiety often translates into behavior that reflects a defensive attitude during this part of the presentation. Presenters may keep maximum distance between themselves and the listeners or move away from them or hide behind the safety of the podium. Other tell-tale signs are the crossing of arms across the chest, the wringing of hands, increased fidgetiness, or a tense expression on the face. Much of this happens without our awareness. So how do we get over this fear and its manifestation in behavior?

Firstly, it is important to remember that we may be able to choose when we take questions. With certain kinds of material and for certain communication objectives, you may feel it would be better to take questions as you go along, so as to ensure that points are well understood before building on them further. However, in other cases, it may be more important to get uninterrupted time to build your entire case, or to present the full picture before people begin to ask questions. One kind of approach would be quite counter-productive for the other kind of situation and you as the presenter are the best judge of this and need to make this clear to the audience or the organizers/moderator. Having the timing of the questions according to our preference is one way of getting control over our anxiety about questions popping up too early or too late and throwing our structure out of joint and causing anxiety for us.

However, the most primary change required to get a grip over our anxiety is one of attitude and perception. Why do we regard the audience as opponents or enemies who are waiting to pounce on us? Let us step back into the occasions when we were in the receivers' role. Were we really hostile and belligerent? Were we itching to attack the presenter? I think the answer would be a resounding, No! Then why do we think our listeners will be less civil that that? On the other hand, have we seen presenters lose their impact through anxiety and nervousness during the question time? The answer is probably, yes. When the presenter shows signs of being defensive or afraid, it may draw out more adversarial responses from the audience. **If the presenter was to be positive and welcoming of questions, the audience would feel that he or she is confident about their ideas and facts, and would approach the questioning as more of a clarification than a challenge.** Thus, as presenters, not only would a change in our attitude towards questioners make us more relaxed, it would also make for an environment of pleasantness rather than sparring and cutting rejoinders.

In order to regard one's audience more positively, another important fact that we should keep in mind is that those who ask questions are paying us a compliment—they found our words worth listening to, and they did not simply receive our ideas passively, but found them interesting enough to want to know more, or to examine them from their own perspective and to seek elaboration or clarification. Moreover, they also do us a service; through their questions we get an insight into the responses of perhaps many in the audience who may have similar responses but cannot be bothered to ask questions. The questioner, rather than being our foe, is actually an ally who is handing us an invitation to speak more, to reinforce our ideas through elaboration, through clarification, through examining from other perspectives, and the like. No doubt, there will be the odd questioner who may speak, not so much to pose a question, as to air his/her own ideas or theory. Or worse, there could sometimes be someone mean and malevolent. However, the latter is an exception, and we should not paint all questioners with that brush. As for the long-winded respondent who clearly has got tired of listening, or is not used to this role, and wants to grab speaking time, there are ways to handle them.

Once we have a positive attitude towards our questioners, the Q&A time loses much of the fear associated with it. Of course, it is difficult, if not altogether foolish, to trust that the attitude alone will see us through if we don't have sufficiently deep knowledge and ideas to handle the questions. As discussed earlier, good preparation for a presentation is actually over-presentation. If we limit ourselves to just enough understanding of our subject to suffice for the presentation, we will be in trouble during Q&A time, and necessarily nervous. By how much must one over-prepare, you ask? There is no concrete limit. While we may be very focused in our presentation, our preparation should have been more wide ranging. There is no better antidote to anxiety than control over our subject, to a level and degree beyond the strict requirements of the structured presentation.

Another kind of preparation that can go a long way in making us less fearful of questions is that of anticipating likely questions from the listeners. Given the context of the presentation, the constitution of the audience, and our own position, it is possible to come with many questions that may pop up in the minds of the listeners. The more thought we give to the point we make in our presentation, the more clearly we can anticipate the kinds of questions that we may face. Going through our presentation, during our preparation, specifically looking for such openings for further elaboration or development of points is a good way to anticipate questions. The more we can anticipate these and have responses thought out, the less anxious we feel.

One further step in preparing to handle questions with greater equanimity is through practice of our presentation before a mock audience and taking questions from them. Of course, it would be best to have a mock audience of the professional and technical background of the intended audience, but even a reasonably similar profile would give us quite a good sense of how our ideas are getting across, and what kinds of questions are being thrown up. Preparing for these gives us more confidence, and the more questions we can anticipate and reflect over, the more stress we mitigate by reducing the unexpectedness of the line of questioning.

If we recall, one of the biggest benefits of spoken communication is the ability to receive, and respond to, immediate feedback. Feedback in terms of overall sense of engaging with the listeners, and reception of the ideas may be visible to us from the body language of the listeners and we get a sense of it by maintaining eye contact with the listeners and observing their non-verbal responses. It is, in verbal feedback, during question time that we get a clear idea of the audience's response, and an immediate opportunity to get our ideas through more effectively. If we let this opportunity go, we are losing a huge advantage for which we chose to speak in the first place.

Another way in which we reduce our anxiety about the

Q&A time is to prepare a strategy for handling the three kinds of questioners: the genuine ones who want a point clarified or wish for elaboration or wish to know our response to their perspective/experience; the ones who grab the opportunity for some airtime due to a desire to be in the central role of speaker rather than listener, and speak for a long time with hardly a hint of a question you may answer; and the heckler or trouble-stirring questioner.

The first kind of questioners are the ones we need to engage with and treat cordially and respond to in a forthright manner. Welcoming the questions both with positive words as well as through positive body language is essential to demonstrate one's comfort with the questioning and one's confidence in the thorough understanding of the issues. It does not mean that we are obliged to have complete and validated answers to every question. But the tone is set by how we welcome the questions and how well we can field most (not all) of them. For the odd one that we cannot answer, it is quite acceptable to say we do not have a reply and leave it at that. Or, in certain contexts, it may be appropriate, to say that we would get back to the person after checking it out. While answering one person it is essential that we include all others in the audience so as to not give the appearance of a private clarification. **If a question has been asked in the public setting rather than over coffee in the break or even later, it is understood that the response must be addressed to the entire audience.** The question itself may be repeated by the presenter in a paraphrased form or simply by asking the questioner to repeat it for the benefit of all. While answering the question it is useful to try to relate it to one's central idea and to keep a sharp focus. By not getting diverted into side issues we give a better sense of having addressed the question, and we can also be succinct and allow time for others who may have questions.

For the second category of respondents, it is important to recognize that there is no need to answer what is not a question. If the person simply wishes to propound their idea or speak of their experience, without posing a question, it is good to leave it with, 'that's an interesting observation', or 'thank you for sharing that'. If necessary, we may reframe their observation as a question and use it to elaborate on something relevant. However, often, such a person is not satisfied without getting the last word and may want to keep returning to their own thesis or observations and it would be best to leave it at that and not giving them too much time at the cost of others who may have genuine questions. At the same time, it is necessary to remain civil and not snub the person as it does not show us in a positive light and may end up turning off genuine questioners.

For the third category of questioners—the most feared ones—it is important to retain one's cool and not pay them in the same coin. **The contrast between the person's heckling and your grace and suaveness, impresses the rest of the audience even as the heckler gets frustrated in their attempt to provoke you.** You may attempt to underline your central idea and perspective, and close by pleasantly saying something such as 'I guess we will have to agree to disagree on that', and move on to the next person with a question. If you, rather than a moderator, have the choice about whose question to take, you may ignore the heckler for the rest of the time, as you have shown fairness by giving them time, and now you may fairly give time to others. Their negative and hostile attitude becomes evident to the rest of the audience and your moving on to others makes sense.

PUTTING IT ALL TOGETHER

Preparation: There is no magic to a good presentation. If you go beyond the surface, you will find in each and every case of a good presentation, that a great deal of preparation has gone into what appears to be effortless and controlled. In certain cases, such as impromptu speaking, the preparation amounts to continuous upgrading of information and an ongoing strengthening of one's analytical capabilities. In other situations, such as long talks or presentations, it is a range of preparatory activities on which the style element can be applied as icing on a delicious cake. The preparation may include:

- gathering material
- structure
- writing, revising, proofreading (handouts/slides)
- visual aids
- anticipating questions

How do we distinguish a good speaker from an ordinary or ineffective one? With your experience of various kinds of speakers in various situations, would you agree that effective speakers who leave an impact share the following characteristics?

- They appear sincere, enthusiastic
- The material is well-structured and focused
- The speaker seems confident, as evident from their:
  - relaxed posture
  - sense of being at ease
  - voice, facial expressions and gestures under control
  - speaking without fumbling for ideas/words, seemed to know the material well
  - establishing a rapport with the listeners
  - establishing credibility of their material

WHAT NOT TO DO IN A PRESENTATION

Even those of us who have not had much experience (yet) of formal speaking can use our considerable experience as listeners of such speaking to be able to generate a checklist of what to avoid in a speech or presentation. Have you not sat through presentations bored to death, faking attention and wishing you were somewhere far from the droning voice and the unending PowerPoint slides? Can you put your finger on what was going on that turned you off? Let me try reading your mind:

- the speaker's voice was monotonous, pitchy, inaudible or too loud
- the speaker seemed to be going through an imposed duty

- the speaker seemed to want to get it over with and return to his/her normal work
- the speaker did not seem very enthused or convinced by his/her own words
- judged by his/her gestures, posture and movement, the speaker seemed ill-at-ease
- the speaker depended completely on the slides
- the speaker's purpose seemed to only be that of presenting the material on the slides
- the speaker seemed to be there to help the audience to understand the slides
- the speaker seemed more focused on the visual aids than on the listeners
- the speaker seemed to be there to help the audience to *read* the slides.

In order to avoid repeating these mistakes and having a similar impact on our listeners, I propose a few tests!

Test 1

Remember this simple test of a PowerPoint presentation: think (or actually try it out) of what would be lost if you were to print or email the presentation to the receivers rather than gathering them together to listen to you. If there would not be much of a loss then you have already ensured that you are peripheral to your own presentation.

If you decide that presenting it in person is essential for your purpose then it is crucial that you make your presence the central point and do everything that the written words alone would never have done. Avoid making your own presence redundant and a nuisance in the audience's focus on the slides. It is up to us as the speaker to indicate whether the visual material is the central focus or we are. When we constantly keep our eyes on the slides rather than make eye contact with the listeners, when we position ourselves right from the opening to one side and keep the screen in the centre, it is only natural that the audience focuses on it and the occasion becomes one of visual communication rather than aural, about reading and seeing rather than a conversation. As we mentioned earlier, there are strengths of written communication too, but if we get people to listen to us face-to-face, we must use the special benefits unique to speaking. The problems that occur with focusing on our visuals are given in the box below.

When we keep our focus on the visual material, the following problems may occur:

- If you keep speaking while the audience is trying to read a good deal of information from the slides, you are taking away the focus from yourself, in fact, becoming an irritant in their effort to read and understand the material. Either they will listen to you and ignore the slides, thus making all your effort a waste, or they will read the slides and ignore your speaking.
- Worse: If you explain what is already there on the slides you are insulting their intelligence!
- Worst: if you read it to them you seem to indicate that they cannot even read!

Test 2

Ask yourself the following key questions:
- Can I put the central idea and objective of the presentation or talk into one sentence?
- Have I tailored my focus, language, examples, supporting material and other decisions regarding the content for the particular audience I am addressing?
- Have I timed the whole presentation?
- Have I given thought to the need for audio-visuals?
- Have I designed visual aids keeping in mind their visibility and lucidity?
- Have I packed too much material onto each slide?
- For most of the given time is my speaking the focus of audience attention or the visuals?

Test 3

After listening to the presentation can people in the audience put the central idea and objective of the talk into one sentence?

Test 4

Even in a one-to-many speaking situation, every member of the audience must go away with the feeling that they had a one-to-one interaction. Have I ensured this?

Test 5

'Will every member of the audience get the sense that I believe in what I presented and took genuine pleasure in sharing it with them?

Having prepared our presentations with a clear understanding of our objective and the audience, having practised to give us a level of comfort and confidence, having anticipated the likely questions that our ideas may evoke, and having tested our material and style on the above criteria, we may rest assured that we have done our best to derive the most out of such opportunities. After that, it is for us to enjoy our interactions and to be constantly open to feedback so as to keep polishing our ability in this crucial area. Happy presenting!

CHAPTER 7

Conclusion: Talk Your Way to Success

Lee Iacocca said, 'You can have brilliant ideas, but if you can't get them across, your ideas won't get you anywhere.' Communicating our ideas is at least as important, if not more, than having the ideas. And the spoken word is a very important mode of communicating our ideas. **Our ability to impact others with our ideas is so powerfully tied to our ability to articulate our thoughts and ideas that it is difficult to imagine achieving this effect without the help of language and especially of speaking.** Whether it is problem solving, consensus building, motivation, persuasion, or argumentation, the value of the outcome often depends on the quality of spoken communication in its service.

Similarly, it is hard to think of rapport building and strong interpersonal relationships being built and nurtured without spoken communication. How well we are able to get information across, or impress others with our understanding and insight into issues, as well as with the depth of our emotions and feelings, very largely depends on how effectively we are able to use spoken communication for these purposes. It is hardly likely that others will magically be able to gauge our potential if we keep our achievements, our treasure box of information and our fund of accumulated wisdom, our original ideas and sharp critical faculties, locked up in our mind. These need to become available to others either as actions and artefacts or translated into written or spoken words. There is no question of getting ahead without hard work in acquiring knowledge and skills and in putting in sustained effort to achieve our true potential. No amount of polishing of verbal skills alone can create a positive impact if the fundamentals are weak. At the same time we must acknowledge that our depth of knowledge, understanding, and insights are often evident to others through our actions and achievements. But when complemented with a strong ability to express these in words, the impact is even more powerful. We do ourselves a great disservice if we neglect to polish our ability to convey our ideas to others in a powerful and effective manner.

Verbal communication is a wonderful tool available to all of us but not all of us use it with the same élan and to the same effect. Specifically looking at spoken communication, we find that among the people we have come in contact with, there are varying levels of ability and effectiveness displayed. We may have realized that how well one uses this tool may make the difference between how one is regarded by others. This, in turn, has consequences on our interpersonal relationships in personal life and at the workplace, as well as on our career growth. With so much of our personal impact tied to our ability to interact with others through the spoken word, it would not be fair to ourselves if we stayed resigned to our current level of awareness and ability or were complacent about it. The former attitude results when seeing those who are more successful in impressing others with their abilities and their potential and enjoying the benefits of stronger interpersonal relationships and various forms of appreciation, validation, and rewards, we attribute their success to inborn qualities. We may see them as lucky and blessed rather than as people who have benefited from favourable circumstances and from conscious, sustained effort to polish their verbal skills. The latter attitude of complacency often results from a lack of critical approach and of the attempt to realistically measure ourselves against others in this attribute. Both these attitudes are recipes for lack of growth. We will be motivated to put in constant effort to polish our own ability only when we accept that it is something acquired rather than inborn and when we can counter complacency by accepting that there is scope for us to further polish our ability to use speaking opportunities more effectively.

When we take a critical look at others and ourselves, we may find that there are some who display a level of polish and confidence that makes them stand out and that helps to serve their objectives and enhance their impact in many subtle ways. Once we accept this and can measure ourselves against the best models that we may have encountered, we can take control of honing our own ability to impact others through speaking opportunities. It is good to remind ourselves that each of us picks up the ability to communicate through speech way back in our early childhood almost without conscious effort. Those who display it to a more polished and accomplished level have probably had an advantage in terms of circumstances that facilitated its practice and refinement. When we can look at others and see the differences in effectiveness of spoken communication, as well as recognize the fact that it is something in our hands, we have already taken a significant step towards improving our own effectiveness and benefitting from it. Looking around us we may also come across those who use their glib speaking skills to impress others but whose behavior and performance expose their insincerity and even lack of real merit. Such people may evoke admiration for their verbal ability for some time but are soon seen as manipulative and insincere, based on the contradiction between their actions and their words. It is, of course, important to aim at integrity in terms of standing firmly behind our avowed positions and practising what we preach. Without this approach, our successes through clever use of speaking skills may be limited to a short time and to those who do not know us well. Soon enough, duplicity and pretence are exposed and irreparable damage is done to one's credibility. The polishing of speaking skills that we are focusing on here is based on the premise that given merit and ability, knowledge and useful ideas, and sincerity of feelings, it would be a disservice to ourselves if we did not try our best to get these across to others in the most impactful manner.

Speaking is only one mode of communication, but a very powerful one. Its power derives from certain great advantages it offers. As we have discussed in this book, the biggest of these advantages are the possibility of directly engaging with the listener and using the constant feedback to modify and refine our communication, the combining of many supporting non-verbal cues, and the complementing of ideas with the force of personal qualities through building a rapport with the listeners. At the same time, there are some inherent disadvantages to the spoken medium in terms of a lack of record, the difficulty of achieving precision and clarity that comes from careful review, and the low attention span due to mental distractions and fatigue. If care is not taken to match our objective with what the medium offers us, the very choice of medium may go wrong. This may happen when we choose to speak in a context where the advantages may not contribute to the objective or where the disadvantages may outweigh the advantages. Not even the best of speakers can make an impact if they neglect to choose whether to speak or write, on the basis of their objective and the target audience. Spoken communication—especially face-to-face spoken communication—is the richest medium, allowing for multiple sensory cues to be concurrently used, with the potential to greatly enhance the effectiveness of the communication. Understanding this is important because we may have seen speakers who cancel out the impact of their words by overlooking the accompanying non-verbal cues. We must remember that for listeners, the meaning communicated is the sum of all messages received by their senses and therefore, if care is not taken with all parts of our communication, we may find that we are not as effective as we had hoped to be. In fact, when these cues convey conflicting meanings, much damage is done to our credibility. When we do take care to ensure that all verbal and non-verbal cues combine to support and supplement the message to be communicated, the richness of the medium really helps to enhance the effectiveness. Only when this choice has been made with clarity, are we on the path to making the most of the advantages offered and to not let the inherent disadvantages create a barrier.

The preceding chapters have looked closely at various common objectives that may very effectively be served by spoken communication and various kinds of situations of communicating through the spoken word, with the underlying belief that the ability to speak effectively is an acquired one and we may try to improve our effectiveness through awareness of what we need to achieve and through a critical approach to constant learning and refining. Awareness of the great value of this ability in serving these various objectives is a good impetus to take a look at where we are currently situated on this dimension of our personal repertoire of skills and a concurrent look at some models in those around us who leave a great impact on others through their verbal interactions in various situations. From these initial steps our journey of self-help towards growth can begin. This book has tried to show the path forward through practical suggestions for various kinds of speaking contexts.

The key to our growth is to be constantly on the search for more effective ways to translate our thoughts into messages that may convey our intended meaning to our listeners with the kind of affect we aim at. To a large extent, becoming a good speaker is related to becoming a good listener. Not only does being a critical listener allow us to distinguish between effective and ineffective models and to aim higher and still higher in terms of polishing this skill, it allows for a crucial insight into the kind of response evoked in the listener by various strategies used by a speaker to serve their objective. Getting into our listeners' shoes is easier when we have been critical listeners ourselves, breaking down the way the speaker's choices have affected our response. When we speak for serving certain objectives for particular listeners, it is they who are our chief priority. The better we can relate to their needs and the better we are able to anticipate their responses, the more effective we can make our choices of strategy and approach as well as of focus, details, support, examples, references, and the like. How well we can reach our listeners to serve the objective depends on how much care we have taken to be clear about our purpose in speaking to them, and how well we have attempted to relate to their perspective and expectations. Our experience would tell us that it is very hard for listeners to engage intellectually or emotionally with a speaker who does not display this focus through their content as well as through their delivery. A speaker mumbling the best of ideas in a self-focused manner, not bothering to engage the listeners is hardly likely to impress them. On the other hand, content that lacks clarity, credibility, focus, and structure fails to impress even when presented in an engaging manner.

Of course, there is no magic pill for change and it will not happen overnight. It takes patience and will power, but it WILL happen! In Stephen Covey's words, 'Be patient with yourself. Self-growth is tender; it's holy ground. There's no greater investment.' **So, invest in your growth, and stay the course.** Constantly review your own level and seek feedback from others. Set yourself concrete goals in terms of addressing areas where you realize you need to improve. Stay positive and take satisfaction in every improvement that you or others around you notice. Constantly strive to keep your goals in front of you and remind yourself how the effort to impact others with your verbal ability is allied to these goals! Take joy in equipping yourself with necessary information and knowledge, and in applying all your abilities in the best possible manner to bring you closer to your goals in your career and life. None of us is an island nor can function as if we were alone in this world. Others are important in this journey —how they regard you as a person, how they value your achievements, what assessment they make of your potential. Whether it is to work amiably and effectively with others, to get agreement and willing cooperation, or to be recognized and rewarded by being given challenging assignments and opportunities to grow and rise higher, impacting others is of crucial importance. With spoken communication occupying a very important role in our personal impact, none of us can afford to neglect it or to be content with where we are. It is an area in which there is always room to grow further and to constantly refine and hone our skills with the only limit being where we set our sights.

All the best to you as you take a more critical look at spoken communication and take up the challenge of sharpening your ability to impact others through every speaking opportunity. May speaking become a powerful ally as you reach for your goals!

Acknowledgements

I would like to express my sincere thanks to the people whose support has been invaluable in writing this book.

First of all, I owe a debt of gratitude to Professor Samir Barua who invited me to contribute to the IIMA Business Books series and put me in touch with Random House. The idea of this book had been simmering for some time, and I needed someone to push me to get down to writing it. The confidence displayed by Professor Barua was a big motivator for me.

My thanks go to Milee Ashwarya and Radhika Marwah from Random House, for their positive response right from the word go. Milee's constant encouragement and enthusiasm kept up my spirits through the writing process. My thanks also go to Trisha Bora for her critical reading and meticulous editing.

Behind all that I am, lie the shaping influence and blessings of my parents. Their pride and joy in every big

Acknowledgements

and small achievement of mine crowns all the effort that I put in it. I am grateful to the Almighty for my good fortune in having had this influence and blessing.

No words of appreciation and thanks would suffice for Shishir, Ruchir, and Ananya who have been with me every step, supporting me in countless ways, cheering me up when I got exhausted, and encouraging me when I worried about missing deadlines. I couldn't have done it without you!

A note on IIMA Business Books

The IIM Ahmedabad Business Books series brings key issues in management and business to a general audience. With a wealth of information and illustrations from contemporary Indian business, these non-academic and user-friendly books from the faculty of IIM Ahmedabad are essential corporate reading.

www.iimabooks.com

OTHER BOOKS IN THIS SERIES

IIM
AHMEDABAD
BUSINESS BOOKS

**STRATEGIES
FOR GROWTH**

Help Your Business Move Up the Ladder

ATANU GHOSH

IIM
AHMEDABAD
BUSINESS BOOKS

**BUSINESS LAW
FOR MANAGERS**

Kaleidoscopic Tales

ANURAG K. AGARWAL

IIM
AHMEDABAD
BUSINESS BOOKS

**DAY TO DAY
ECONOMICS**

SATISH Y. DEODHAR

IIM
AHMEDABAD
BUSINESS BOOKS

**CONTRACT
TERMS ARE
COMMON SENSE**

AKHILESHWAR PATHAK